THE PRACTICAL ENCYCLOPEDIA OF

GARDEN PLANNING DESIGN & DECORATION

THE PRACTICAL ENCYCLOPEDIA OF GARDEN PLANNING DESIGN & DECORATION

PETER MCHOY AND TESSA EVELEGH

HERMES HOUSE

This edition is published by Hermes House

Hermes House is an imprint of Anness Publishing Ltd
Hermes House, 88–89 Blackfriars Road, London SE1 8HA
tel. 020 7401 2077; fax 020 7633 9499; info@anness.com

A CIP catalogue record for this book is available from the British Library

Publisher Joanna Lorenz
Senior Editor Caroline Davison
Assistant Editor Emma Hardy
Designer Ian Sandom
Jacket Designer Michael Morey
Production Controller Ben Worley

Printed and bound in Singapore

1 3 5 7 9 10 8 6 4 2
Previously published as two separate volumes, *The Ultimate Garden Planner and Decorating Your Garden.*

■ ABOVE: This elegant stone urn would make a decorative contribution to any garden.
■ PAGE ONE: Blue and white flowers are a classic planting combination.
■ PAGE TWO: An attractive winding pathway adds definition to this garden.
■ PAGE THREE: This climber, *Mina lobata*, has been underplanted with marigolds.
■ OPPOSITE TOP: *Convolvulus sabaticus* tumbles prettily from a terracotta pot.
■ OPPOSITE BOTTOM: In summer, a well-planted container can brighten up the corner of any patio.

Contents

INTRODUCTION

Every garden benefits from careful planning, design and decorative details, and whatever your needs, this book will enable you to gain maximum impact and enjoyment from your garden. The emphasis of the first section is on planning and designing the garden, showing how finding the right overall style should be the first step in creating your ideal garden. Remember, however, that while tastes in gardening styles vary, the test of a good garden is whether it appeals to you.

Practical, step-by-step photographs guide you through drawing your first plans to planting and simple garden construction, while hundreds of inspirational pictures show what other enthusiastic gardeners have done as well as ways of making the most of unpromising plots.

As your garden is very much a part of your home, there is no reason why you shouldn't decorate it in much the same way as you might decorate the inside of your house. Once the basic planning and design have been completed, decorative details can be introduced that bring the style of your own home into the garden. Packed with imaginative and practical ideas, from innovative treatments for outside floors to beautiful details such as containers, the second part of the book focuses less on the structural elements and plants in the garden, and more on the details that will make your garden a reflection of your personal tastes.

The original ideas in this book will give visual impact to your garden, helping you to create an exquisite, personalized outdoor room of your own, guaranteed to last a lifetime.

■ ABOVE:
A stone mouse peeping out of the undergrowth brings a sense of fun to the garden.

■ OPPOSITE:
The abundance of bright colours belies the thought behind this careful planting.

Planning Your Garden

■ ABOVE:
The pathways and box hedging give strong definition to the beds in this formal herb garden.

■ OPPOSITE:
Clipped box balls and climber-clad arches give a clear structure and shape to this elegant garden.

INTRODUCTION

Few of us are totally content with our gardens. Despite the immense pleasure we derive from them, there's always something that could be better. Most of us long for a larger garden, a few for something smaller and more manageable, but the vast majority of us have to make the best of our existing plot. Improving it, coaxing the maximum impact from it, is an enjoyable challenge that most of us would rise to – if only we knew how.

Gardening is about growing plants, but the setting in which we place them is probably the element that makes a garden appealing or otherwise. Tastes in gardening styles vary as much as in other aspects of living, and what appeals to one person may not appeal to another, but the test of a good garden design is whether it appeals to *you*. This book sets out to help you create a garden that reflects your taste, your personality.

It also lifts the lid on the magic box of imagination and inspiration. It shows you what other enthusiastic gardeners have done, and how others have made the most of sometimes unpromising plots. This is an eminently practical book, too, and it will guide you through drawing your first plans to planting and simple garden construction.

■ ABOVE
A garden that looks lived in will be used.

■ OPPOSITE
Paths and walls form a backdrop for plants.

GARDEN PLANNING MADE EASY

You can have your garden designed and constructed by professionals, but it will cost a great deal of money, and the chances are that it won't give you as much satisfaction as having created a garden by your own efforts.

This chapter explains the basic techniques for simple garden design, but it's up to you as to how you interpret them and what you create with the tools provided. The remaining chapters are packed with inspirational ideas, but only you can decide what's right for your garden. Tastes in gardens vary as much as in interior decor and preferences in music or art. The acid test of whether your new design has worked is whether it pleases you.

Use the techniques suggested to experiment on paper – you will soon develop skills that will enable you to design your garden with confidence.

■ ABOVE
A striking garden, which uses water and paving in a highly structured design.

■ OPPOSITE
An informal, country-style garden, with colourful borders overflowing with flowers and shrubs, yet with a clear sense of design.

Taking Stock

If you're planning and planting a new garden from a virgin plot of land, then your starting point is a wish list of features to incorporate. But if you are redesigning an existing garden, it's also important to decide whether there are features that you would like to retain.

Never let an existing feature dictate your new garden, unless you have no alternative but to work around it. For instance, you may be limited by what you can do with a large tree or unsightly garage. While you may not want the disruption of digging up the drive and moving the garage, don't be dictated to by the presence of ordinary garden paths. They may be tiring to lift, but a straight path down the centre of a narrow garden will limit your ability to be creative with your new design.

Make lists of what has to stay and what you want to work around and improve.

THE WISH LIST

Make your wish list before you attempt your design. It is unlikely to be fulfilled completely, but setting down those things that are a priority to you should ensure that the most important features are included.

Everyone has different preferences, so decide which features you regard as essential (it may be something as mundane as a clothes drier or as stimulating as a water feature), those that are important but less essential for your ideal garden, and those elements that you regard simply as desirable.

While designing your garden, keep in mind those features listed as essential. Try to incorporate as many of them as possible, but don't cram in so many that a strong sense of design is sacrificed.

It will immediately become apparent if the list of the most desirable features is not feasible within the limited space available, but you will probably be able to introduce some of the more important ones. However, attempt to include only those features ticked (checked) simply as desirable if you have space.

GARDEN PRIORITIES

	Essential	*Important*	*Desirable*
Flowerbeds	[ ]	[ ]	[ ]
Herbaceous border	[ ]	[ ]	[ ]
Shrub border	[ ]	[ ]	[ ]
Trees	[ ]	[ ]	[ ]
Lawn	[ ]	[ ]	[ ]
Gravelled area	[ ]	[ ]	[ ]
Paved area/patio	[ ]	[ ]	[ ]
Built-in barbecue	[ ]	[ ]	[ ]
Garden seats/furniture	[ ]	[ ]	[ ]
Rock garden	[ ]	[ ]	[ ]
Pond	[ ]	[ ]	[ ]
Other water feature	[ ]	[ ]	[ ]
Wildlife area	[ ]	[ ]	[ ]
Greenhouse/conservatory	[ ]	[ ]	[ ]
Summerhouse	[ ]	[ ]	[ ]
Tool shed	[ ]	[ ]	[ ]
Fruit garden	[ ]	[ ]	[ ]
Herb garden	[ ]	[ ]	[ ]
Vegetable garden	[ ]	[ ]	[ ]
Trellis/pergola/arch	[ ]	[ ]	[ ]
Sandpit/play area	[ ]	[ ]	[ ]
Clothes drier/line	[ ]	[ ]	[ ]
Dustbin (trash can)	[ ]	[ ]	[ ]
Compost heap	[ ]	[ ]	[ ]
....	[ ]	[ ]	[ ]
....	[ ]	[ ]	[ ]
....	[ ]	[ ]	[ ]
....	[ ]	[ ]	[ ]
....	[ ]	[ ]	[ ]
....	[ ]	[ ]	[ ]
....	[ ]	[ ]	[ ]
....	[ ]	[ ]	[ ]

■ OPPOSITE
The initial sketch can be simple and need contain only the basic dimensions. Do not bother with anything that you do not intend to include in the new garden.

Surveying and Measuring

It is much better – and less expensive – to make your mistakes on paper first, rather than in the garden itself. Start by making a sketch of the garden as it is, and then work up your ideas.

If your garden is large, divide it into sections that can be pieced together later, but for a small garden the whole area will go on to a single sheet of paper. Leave space around the edge for measurements.

Write down the measurements of all the main features such as a tree, path or garage. Do not include anything that you are already sure you will not retain. Small rectangular gardens are very easy to measure. Sometimes the boundary can be calculated simply by counting fence panels and multiplying up the length of a fence panel and post. Most other features can be fixed by measuring at right angles from the boundary.

If the shape of the garden is more complicated, it is usually possible to determine a position by laying a piece of string at right angles from the known straight edge, then measuring at right angles from this line.

WHAT YOU WILL NEED

- A 30m (100ft) tape measure – preferably plasticized fabric as this is easy to work with but does not stretch.
- A 1.8m (6ft) steel rule for short measurements.
- Pegs to mark out positions, and to hold one end of the tape in position (meat skewers can be used to hold the end of the tape).
- Pencils, sharpener and eraser.
- Clipboard with graph paper.

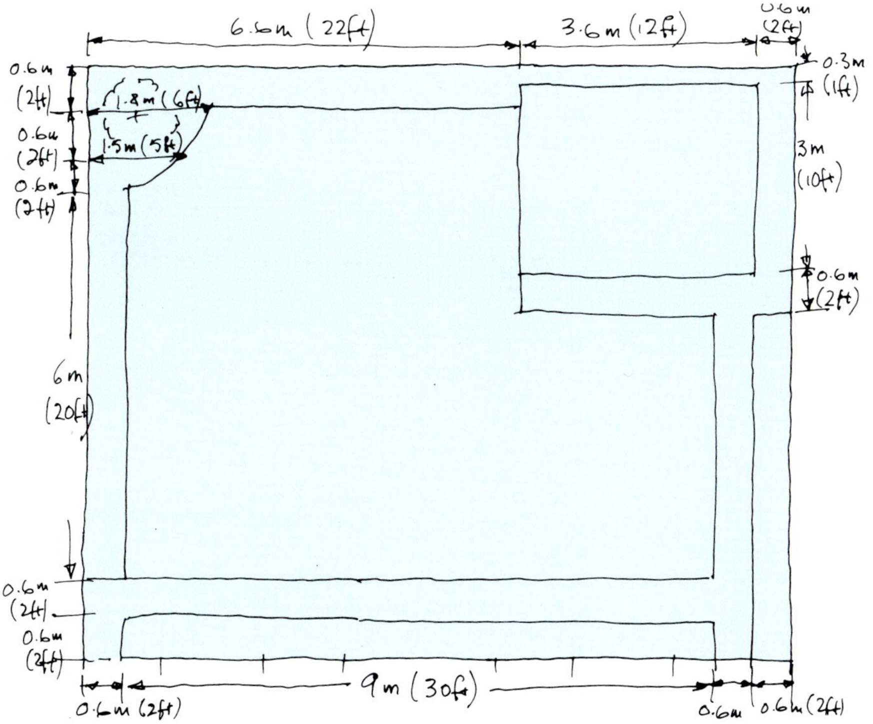

Putting the Plan on Paper

The exciting part of redesigning a garden comes when the basic structure is on the drawing board and you can start to work magical transformations as you try to test your ideas. Drawing to scale is the next step to reach this goal.

With the rough sketch from the garden drawn accurately to scale, the stimulating part of garden planning can begin. It is when dreams can start to be translated into reality. Making an accurate scale drawing of your existing garden is an essential starting point if you want to simplify the design work that follows.

The rough sketch must be transferred to a scale drawing before any detailed plans can be sketched out. Drawing it to scale will help you to calculate the amount of any paving required, and also enable you to tailor beds, borders and lawns to sizes that will involve the least amount of cutting of hard materials such as paving slabs or bricks.

Use graph paper for your scale drawing. Pads are adequate for a small garden or a section of a larger one, but if your garden is big, buy a large sheet (available from art and stationers' shops).

Use a scale that enables you to fit the plan on to your sheet of graph paper (or several taped together). For most small gardens, a scale of 1:50 (2cm to 1m or ¼in to 1ft) is about right; for a large garden, however, 1:100 (1cm to 1m or ⅛in to 1ft) might be better.

Draw the basic outline of the garden and the position of the house first, including the position of any doors and windows if relevant. Then add all the major features that you are likely to retain. You should have all the necessary measurements on the freehand sketch that you made in the garden.

Omit any features that you are sure will be eliminated from the new design, to keep it as uncluttered as possible. In this example, the summerhouse has been drawn in because it was considered to be in a good position and would be difficult to move. Although the corner tree was removed in the final design, it was included at this stage as a different design might have made use of it.

QUICK ON THE DRAW

Try these tips if you are not used to drawing garden plans:

- Draw the outline of the garden first, together with the position of the house and any other major features, and make sure you have the correct measurements for these before filling in any of the other elements.
- Next, draw in those elements that are easy to position, such as rectangular flowerbeds, a circular pond or the garden shed, if you are reasonably certain of their position and know they will remain in your new design.
- Ink in those elements of the garden that are fixed and will not change, such as boundaries and paths that you know you will not move. Draw the more movable garden features in pencil first, as it is quite likely that you may have to make slight adjustments before the plan is complete. Ink them in when you know everything is in its correct place.
- Use a pair of compasses to draw curves and circles if possible. Not all curves are suitable for this treatment, but you can buy flexible rules that can be bent into any reasonable curve.

USING YOUR PLAN

1 Even expert designers make a number of rough sketches of possible designs before finalizing the chosen one, so devise a way of using your master outline again and again without having to keep redrawing it. One way is to make a number of photocopies or use tracing paper.

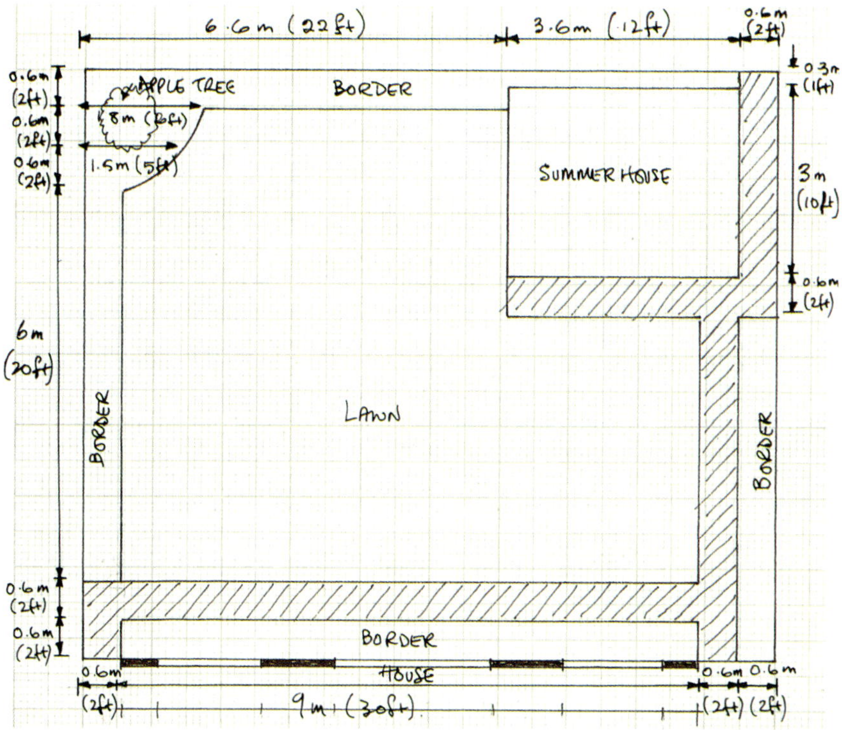

■ **LEFT**
Using the information included on the freehand sketch made in the garden, draw a scale version that you can use during the design process. You may find it helpful to use graph paper.

2 If you have a drawing board, simply use tracing paper overlays for your roughs while experimenting with ideas. If you do not have a drawing board and your garden is small, you may be able to use a clipboard to hold the tracing paper firmly in position.

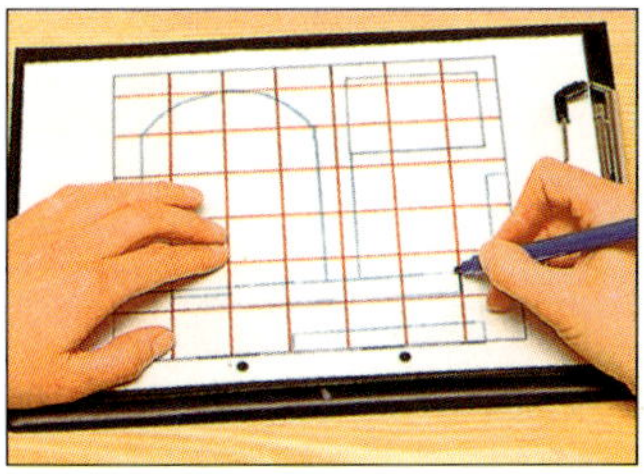

3 Film and pens of the type used for overhead projection sheets are effective if you prefer to use colours that can easily be wiped off for correction.

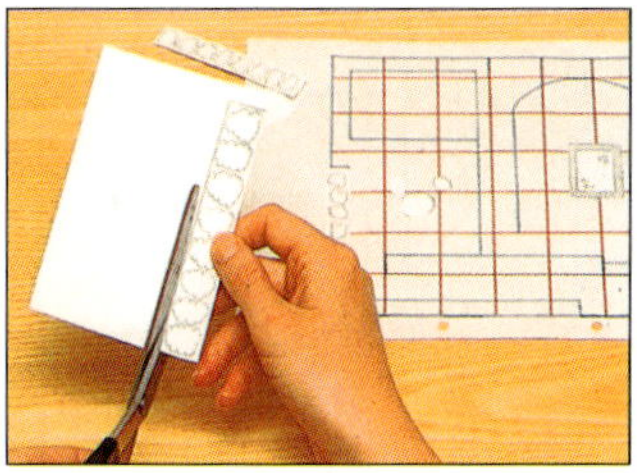

4 Try drawing and cutting out scale features that you want to include in your finished design, such as a raised pond, patio furniture or raised beds. These can be moved around until they look right, but they should be used as aids only once the overall design has been formulated in your mind. If you try to design your garden around the few key symbols that you have placed, it will almost certainly lack coherence.

Creating Your Design

The difficult part of redesigning or improving your garden is making a start. Once you start drawing, the ideas are sure to flow, especially if you have other gardens in mind that you like and can use as inspiration and a starting point. Don't attempt to copy someone else's plan in detail – it probably won't fit the size or style of your property, or your requirements – but such plans are excellent to refer to for inspiration when developing your own design.

If you decide on a garden with strong lines, rather than irregular flowering borders, it is worth deciding on whether you are going to plan a rectangular or diagonal or circular design. Any of these can be adapted to suit the size of your garden, and in the case of the circular pattern you might want to include overlapping circles. Where circles join, try to make any transitional curves gradual rather than abrupt. Whichever you choose, draw a grid on top of your plan to aid design (see opposite page). In a small garden surrounded by fencing, it can be useful to base the rectangular and diagonal grids on the spacing of fence posts – usually about 1.8m (6ft) apart.

A rectangular grid has been used in the example opposite, but as part of the trial-and-error phase it is worth trying different grids. A diagonal grid is often effective where the house is set in a large garden with plenty of space at the sides. The patio can be positioned at a 45-degree angle at the corner of the house, for example.

The size and shape of the garden will usually dictate the best grid, but if in doubt, try the other possibilities to see which one is most appropriate.

Bear in mind that many excellent, prize-winning gardens are created without such a grid, and sometimes these have, to some extent, evolved in a more flowing manner, developing feature by feature. Grids may help you, but do not hesitate to adopt a more freestyle approach if this comes more naturally.

LOOKING FOR INSPIRATION

Don't despair if inspiration does not come easily, or initial attempts seem disappointing. If you try these tips, you will almost certainly produce workable plans that you will be pleased with:

- Look through books and magazines to decide which style of garden you like: formal or informal; the emphasis on plants or on hard landscaping; mainly foliage, texture and ground cover or lots of colourful flowers; straight edges or curved and flowing lines.
- With the style decided, look at as many garden pictures as possible and for design ideas that appeal. Do not be influenced by individual plants; these can be changed.
- Choose a grid, if applicable, and draw this on to your plan. This will help you think ideas through on logical lines.
- Start sketching lots of designs but do not attempt to perfect them at this stage. Just explore ideas.
- Do not concern yourself with planning planting schemes at this stage – concentrate on patterns and lines.
- Do not spend time drawing in paving patterns or choosing materials yet.
- Make a short list of those overall outlines that you like best. Then forget them for a day. It pays to take a fresh look at things after a short break.
- If you still like one of your original roughs, begin work on that, filling in details like paving, surface textures such as gravel, and the position of focal point plants, etc. Don't include any planting plans at this stage.
- If your original roughs lack appeal when you look at them again, repeat the process with another batch of ideas. You will probably see ways of improving some of your earlier efforts, so things will be easier this time around.
- If you find it difficult to visualize sizes, peg the design out at full size on the ground with string, then modify the layout and your plan if necessary.

BEGIN THE DESIGN

1 Draw in any existing features to be retained (in this example the summerhouse), and the chosen grid (unless you want an informal style where a grid may be inappropriate). Use a different colour for the grid lines, to prevent the plan becoming cluttered and confused.

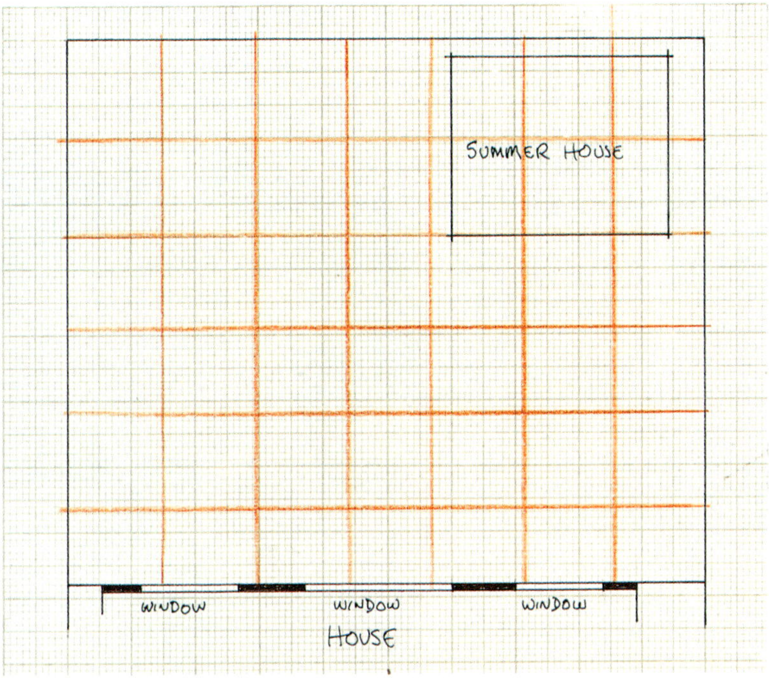

2 Use overlays (or photocopies) to experiment with a range of designs. Even if the first attempt looks satisfactory, try a number of variations. You can always come back to your first idea if it turns out to be the best one.

At this stage, do not include details such as patio furniture or individual plants (except for key focal-point plants and important trees or shrubs). When you have a design that you like, pencil in things like patio furniture (or use scale cut-out features if you prefer).

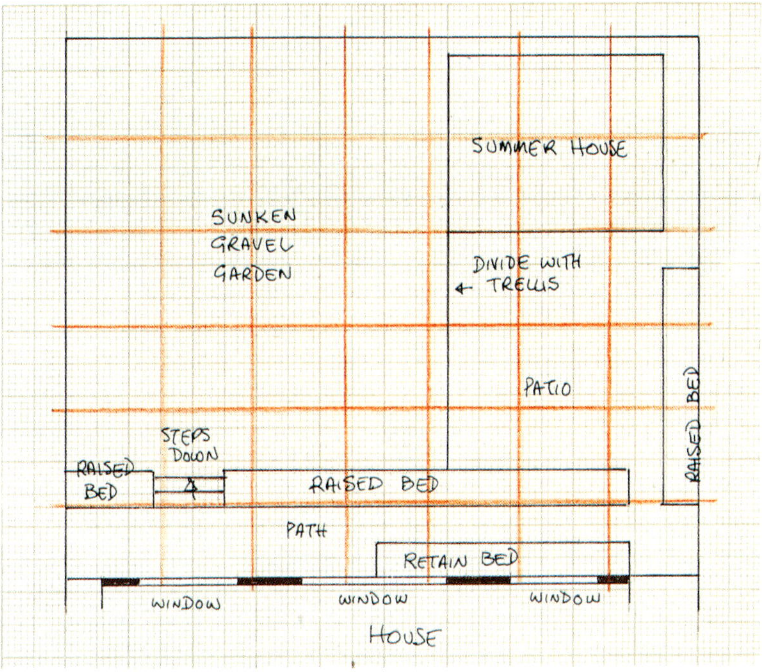

BASIC PATTERNS

Having decided on the style of garden that you want, and the features that you need to incorporate, it's time to tackle the much more difficult task of applying the theory to your own garden.

STARTING POINTS

The chances are that your garden will be the wrong size or shape, or the situation or outlook inappropriate to the style of garden that you have admired. The way around this impasse is to keep in mind a style without attempting to recreate it closely.

If you can't visualize the whole of your back or front garden as, say, a stone or Japanese garden, it may be possible to include the feature as an element within a more general design.

If you analyse successful formal garden designs, most fall into one of the three basic patterns described here, though clever planting and variations on the themes almost always result in individual designs.

■ RIGHT

CIRCULAR THEMES These are effective at disguising the predictable shape of a rectangular garden. Circular lawns, patios and beds are all options, and you only need to overlap and interlock a few circles to create a stylish garden. Plants fill the gaps between curved areas and straight edges.

Using a pair of compasses, try various combinations of circles to see whether you can create an attractive pattern. Be prepared to vary the radii and to overlap the circles if necessary.

■ OPPOSITE LEFT

DIAGONAL THEMES This device creates a sense of space by taking the eye along and across the garden. Start by drawing grid lines at 45 degrees to the house or main fence. Then draw in the design, using the grid as a guide.

■ OPPOSITE RIGHT

RECTANGULAR THEMES This is a popular choice, and many garden plans end up with a rectangular theme – even though there may have been no conscious effort to do so. The device is effective if you want to create a formal look, or wish to divide up a long, narrow garden into smaller sections.

Formal and Informal

If you like straight lines and everything neat and clearly done to a plan, a formal garden should please, but for some gardeners an informal, more casual style that looks more like a simple setting for plants is likely to have more appeal. Informal gardens are also more adaptable to family use, with the lawn providing opportunities for play as well as relaxation for adults.

It's important to decide at an early stage whether the formal designs represented by some of the grids described earlier are right for your style of gardening, or even whether they fit your lifestyle – a growing family may prefer a more casual style of garden. Those who are interested in flowers and foliage rather than hard landscaping are more likely to feel at home among sweeping borders, hidden paths, and seats tucked into arbours or overlooking a wildlife pond.

Anyone who loves the informality of cottage gardens, which may be little more than a couple of borders either side of a path or lawn, may find a very structured garden unappealing. With informal gardens, it is the positioning of plants that gives it gardener appeal. Even the style of planting may be less planned, with self-sown seedlings coming up between other plants in the border, or among the paving.

If this is your kind of garden, follow your instinct, but remember that focal points and flowing curves are still important. Arbours, pergolas and ornaments, well-positioned garden seats, and a sense of overall planning and good planting sense are just as relevant in this kind of garden as in a more structured one.

■ **RIGHT AND OPPOSITE** These two designs show how different a garden of the same size can look depending on whether a formal or informal style is used. Deciding on the degree of formality in the design comes early in the planning stage.

KEY TO PLAN

1 Ornament (on plinth)
2 Herb garden
3 Shed
4 Trellis
5 Climbers (e.g. ivy, parthenocissus and clematis) against trellis
6 Sundial or birdbath
7 Mixed border
8 Large pot with shrubs/shaped clipped box
9 Garden bench
10 Pool with fountain
11 Arch
12 Group of large shrubs
13 Screen-block wall
14 Patio furniture
15 Vegetable garden
16 Trellis arch
17 Path
18 House

FORMALITY

INFORMALITY

■ BELOW
The planting here gives the impression of informality, but the symmetry of the design is formal.

KEY TO PLAN

1 Garden bench
2 Lawn
3 Herbaceous plants and bulbs
4 Shrubs
5 Thymes and other aromatic herbs planted between crazy paving
6 White metal garden bench
7 Pond
8 Bog garden
9 Red-stemmed dogwood
10 Dwarf conifers and heathers
11 Birdbath or sundial, with plants around base
12 Tree
13 House

Unusual Shapes

It may be possible to turn a problem shape to your advantage by using its unusual outline to create a garden that stands out from others in the street. Because of its originality, what was once a difficult area to plant will soon become the object of other gardeners' envy. The seven designs shown here illustrate how difficult sites can, with imagination and some careful planning, produce promising gardens.

■ ABOVE LEFT AND ABOVE CENTRE

LONG AND NARROW The plan on the left shows a design based on a circular theme. The paved area near the house can be used as a patio, and the one at the far end for drying the washing, largely out of sight from the house. Alternatively, if the end of the garden receives more sun, reverse the roles of the paved areas. Taking the connecting path across the garden at an angle, and using small trees or large shrubs to prevent the eye travelling straight along the sides, creates the impression of a garden to be explored. The plan on the right shows the use of diagonals to achieve a similar effect.

■ ABOVE

LONG AND TAPERING If the garden is long and pointed, try screening off the main area, leaving a gateway or arch to create the impression of more garden beyond while not revealing the actual shape. The tapering end of the garden could be used as an orchard, as here, or a vegetable garden.

Staggering the three paved areas, with small changes of level, adds interest and prevents the garden looking too long. At the same time, a long view has been retained to give the impression of size.

■ ABOVE

ANGULAR CORNER SITE Corner sites are often larger than other plots in the same road, and offer scope for some interesting designs. This one has been planned to make the most of the extra space at the side of the house, which has become the main feature of the garden instead of the more usual back or front areas.

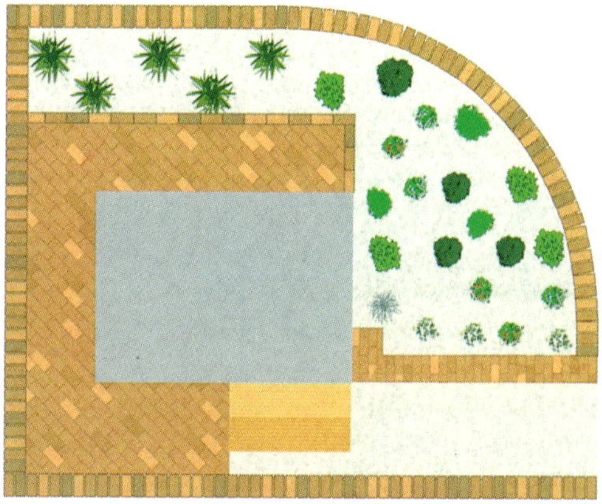

■ ABOVE

CURVED CORNER SITE Curved corner gardens are more difficult to design effectively. In this plan the house is surrounded by a patio on the left-hand side, and a low wall partitions the patio from the rest of the garden, making it more private. For additional interest, a path separates the drive from the gravel garden. Gravel and boulders, punctuated by striking plants such as phormiums and yuccas, effectively marry the straight edges with the bold curve created by the corner site.

■ ABOVE

SQUARE AND SQUAT A small square site like this offers little scope for elaborate design, so keep to a few simple elements. To give the impression of greater space the viewpoint has been angled diagonally across the garden. For additional interest, the timber decking is slightly raised, creating a change of level. A small lawn can be difficult to cut in a tiny garden, but you could try an alternative to grass, such as chamomile, which needs trimming only infrequently.

The diagonal theme helps to counter the basic rectangular shape of the garden and makes the most of available space.

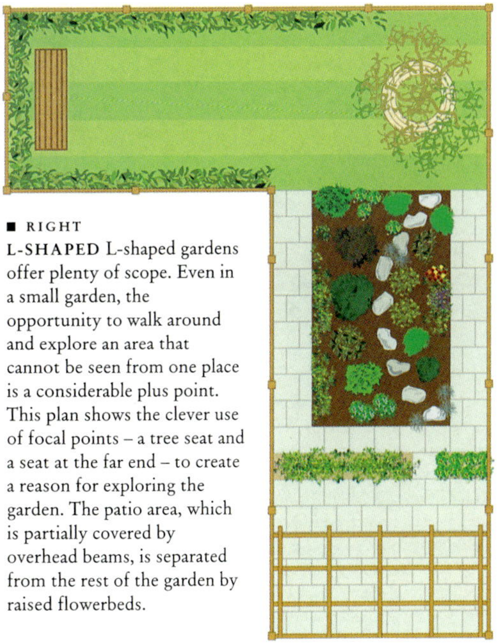

■ RIGHT

L-SHAPED L-shaped gardens offer plenty of scope. Even in a small garden, the opportunity to walk around and explore an area that cannot be seen from one place is a considerable plus point. This plan shows the clever use of focal points – a tree seat and a seat at the far end – to create a reason for exploring the garden. The patio area, which is partially covered by overhead beams, is separated from the rest of the garden by raised flowerbeds.

Coping with Slopes

Sloping sites are particularly difficult to plan on paper, and they are much more challenging to design in general than flat sites. As sloping gardens vary so much in the degree of slope – whether the garden slopes down from the house or upwards – as well as size and aspect, it is also more difficult to adapt designs created by others. Although sloping gardens are difficult to design, the drawbacks can be turned into advantages. Changes of level can add interest and provide an excellent setting for rock gardens and cascading "streams".

KEY TO PLAN

1 Patio
2 Wall fountain with small pool
3 Bricks or clay pavers
4 Rock garden bank sloping downhill and towards a flat paved area
5 "Stream" with cascades
6 Pond, disappearing behind shrubs
7 Small retaining wall
8 Shed for tools and mower
9 Shrubs
10 Summerhouse with views across garden and attractive view below garden
11 Lawn
12 Gravel with alpines
13 Gravel area with natural paving
14 Pavers mixed with paving slabs
15 Trees and shrubs
16 Ornament (on plinth)
17 House

■ **ABOVE RIGHT**
SLOPING DOWN A downward-sloping garden with an attractive view is much easier to design successfully than an upward-sloping one. If the outlook is unattractive, however, it may be advisable to screen the lowest part of the garden with shrubs and small trees and use it as the main sitting area.

This plan demonstrates several important principles when designing a sloping garden, and unusually combines terraces with a natural slope. Terracing is expensive and time-consuming: it involves earth-moving, and retaining walls on strong foundations have to be built. Moving the topsoil from one area to lower down the slope is unsatisfactory as part of the garden will be left with subsoil at the surface for planting – a recipe for disappointment. Topsoil should be set aside, the ground levelled, and then the topsoil returned, which is labour-intensive.

Terracing provides flat areas on which to walk and relax, and this design includes flat areas along the length of the garden. As these have been used for hard surfaces, the problem of subsoil and topsoil does not arise. Retaining the natural slope for a large part of the garden reduces the amount of structural work required and cost.

Although there are some retaining walls, the two walls that zigzag down the garden are stepped so that they remain just above the surrounding ground.

Retaining a large area of naturally sloping ground also provides an ideal setting for rock outcrops and an artificial stream with a series of cascades.

Taking a path across the garden at an angle makes it seem less steep. A path that runs in a straight line down the slope only serves to emphasize the drop.

■ LEFT
If the slope falls away from the house suddenly, building a raised patio like this will provide a level area and avoid the use of steps immediately outside the door.

■ RIGHT
SLOPING UPWARDS An upward slope is a challenge. Distant views are not a possibility, and even upper floors may look out on to a bank. Terracing in this situation can look oppressive, but a "secret" garden full of meandering paths flanked by shrubs is an effective way of dealing with the slope. Some retaining walls are usually necessary, but if planted with shrubs, the effect will be masked and the plants on the lower terraces will hide the upper walls and banks.

Lawns are difficult to accommodate on a steeply sloping site, and difficult to mow too, as mowers are awkward to carry up steps and steep ramps for access. It is generally best to avoid grass lawns, but use a grass "alternative" in a small levelled area. Chamomile and thyme require only an occasional trim with shears, which for a small area is not an onerous job.

KEY TO PLAN

1 Small tree
2 Shrubs
3 Natural stone paving slabs set in gravel
4 Ornament on plinth as a focal point
5 Dwarf shrubs on bank
6 Retaining wall
7 Brick edge
8 Lounger or deckchair
9 Thyme or chamomile lawn
10 Plants in containers
11 Wall fountain with small pool beneath
12 Patio
13 Shrub or small tree in large tub
14 Seat
15 Natural stone paving set in gravel
16 Natural stone path
17 House

FRONT GARDENS

Front gardens have special problems – especially if they have to accommodate a drive for the car. Perhaps for that reason they frequently lack interest and look uninspiring, yet it's the front garden that visitors see first, so it's worth making a special effort to create a good impression. Even enthusiastic gardeners with delightful back gardens are often let down by a dull front garden. Here two small front gardens with typical problems have been transformed by a little creative thinking and careful planning.

COUNTRY COTTAGE LOOK

Gardens don't come much more uninspired than this: a concrete drive, a small narrow flowerbed on the paved patio in front of the window, a narrow border along the edge of the garden, and a single flowering cherry tree placed in the centre of a rectangular lawn. However, the solution for this garden was a simple one, as the redesigned garden on the right shows. The cottage-garden style includes plants of all kinds which grow and mingle happily together with minimum intervention.

Besides being a short cut to the front door, the stepping stones encourage exploration of the garden and its plants. You actually walk through the planting, which cascades and tumbles around the paving slabs. The garden design has been reversed, with plants forming the heart of the garden rather than being peripherals around the edge. Don't be afraid to dig up a lawn – you can retain the year-round colour by planting evergreen shrubs and seasonal flowers.

PROBLEMS

- Although the cherry is spectacular in flower, and provides a show of autumn colour, it is attractive for only a few weeks of the year. Its present position precludes any major redesign, so it is best removed.
- Unclothed wooden fences contribute to the drab appearance.
- Small flowerbeds like these lack impact, and are too small for the imaginative use of shrubs or herbaceous perennials.

SOLUTIONS

- The lawn and tree have been removed, and the whole area planted with a mixture of dwarf shrubs, herbaceous perennials, hardy annuals, and lots of bulbs for spring interest.
- Stepping stones have been provided for those who want to take a short cut (they also make access for weeding easier).
- The fences have been replaced by low walls to make the garden appear less confined.

IMPACT WITH PRIVACY

Being on a corner, this garden is a jumble of shapes and angles, and as originally constructed lacks any sense of design. With its new look, the old curved path has been retained because its thick concrete base and the drain inspection cover within it would have made it difficult to move, but all the other lines have been simplified and more appropriate plants used. The curved, flowing stream along the right-hand side adds movement and sound to the garden.

PROBLEMS

- The bed along the left-hand side was a rock garden, but rock gardens are seldom successful on a flat site in a small garden.
- The tree would have grown large, eventually casting considerable shade and dominating the garden.
- Small beds like this, used for seasonal bedding, are colourful in summer but can lack interest in winter. This curve sits uneasily with the straight edge at one end and the curve of the path at the other.

SOLUTIONS

- The rock garden has been paved so that the cultivated area is not divided by the drive.
- Gravel replaces the lawn. This requires minimal maintenance and acts as a good foil for the plants.
- Dwarf and medium-sized conifers create height and cover, and therefore a degree of privacy. Using species and varieties in many shades of green and gold, and choosing a range of shapes, makes this part of the garden interesting throughout the year.
- Stepping stones add further interest. Because it isn't possible to see where the stepping stones lead to from either end (the conifers hide the route), a sense of mystery is added which tempts the visitor to explore.
- The existing path has been retained but covered with slate crazy paving to make it more interesting.
- A pond creates a water feature and also attracts wildlife.
- The awkward, narrow curving strip has been turned into a stream with circulating water flowing over a cascade into the pond at one end.

■ LEFT

Instead of a lawn with a few flowerbeds around the edge, this small front garden has been planted in cottage-garden style. It is packed with interest throughout the year.

CREATING ILLUSIONS

Sometimes it's good to deceive – at least deceive the eye into thinking your garden is bigger or better than it really is! Try some of these simple devices to solve some of those difficult problems. The few simple forms of visual deception described here should enable you to make your garden look larger than it really is, helping to distract the eye from unattractive features by making the most of the positive.

■ RIGHT
First impressions here are of a large garden extending beyond the arch, yet it's an illusion done with a mirror!

■ ABOVE LEFT AND ABOVE RIGHT
A small garden will seem box-like if the boundary is clearly visible, especially if it is plain and man-made like a fence or a wall, and the boundary will dominate. Simply adding a narrow border with masking shrubs will not help because the boundary, although better clothed, will still be obvious. Bringing the border into the garden in broad sweeps, with a hint of the lawn disappearing behind a sweep towards the end of the garden, will blur the boundaries, giving the impression of more garden beyond.

■ ABOVE LEFT AND ABOVE RIGHT
Straight lines can be uncompromising, and a dominant feature at the end of a straight path will foreshorten the visual appearance. Curving the path slightly, and perhaps tapering it a little towards the end, will create the illusion of greater depth. If the focal point is also diminished in height or stature, the optical illusion will be increased.

■ ABOVE LEFT AND ABOVE RIGHT
A long, straight path will take the eye to the boundary unless the garden is very large, so try to introduce a feature that will arrest the eye part of the way along the path. A curve around an ornament, a large shrub or small tree will keep the eye within the garden. If you do not want to move an existing path, try erecting an arch over it, planted with an attractive climber to soften the outline and perhaps extended along the length of trellis on either side.

PREPARING A PLANTING PLAN

The hard landscaping described so far in this chapter acts like a skeleton and gives the garden structure, but it is the choice of plants that gives shape and character to a garden. It's important to think about structure first, but getting the planting plan right is equally important if your garden is to have real impact throughout the year.

CREATING THE OUTLINE

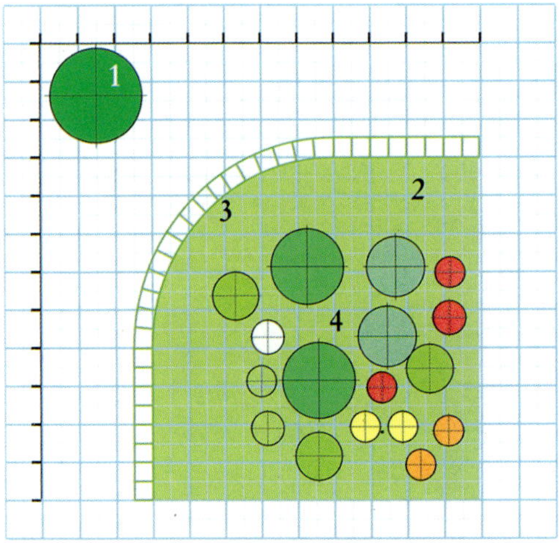

Start with the outline of the area to be planted, with distances marked on the graph paper to make positioning easier. Some good plant catalogues and books include plenty of pictures, and give likely heights and spreads for the plants. Treat heights and spreads with caution, however, as much depends on where you live, as well as on climate, soil and season.

If your plant knowledge is good, you may be able to draw directly on to your border plan, but if you find it easier to move around pieces of paper than use a pencil and eraser, cut out shapes to represent the plants that you are planning to include. Write on their height, spread and flowering period if this helps, and indicate their name on the back. Try colouring them, perhaps using stripes for variegated plants, and using green for evergreens. This will help form an overall picture.

KEY TO PLAN

1 Existing flagpole cherry (*Prunus* 'Amanogawa')
2 Lawn
3 Mowing edge
4 Cut-out plant symbols to position in border

ADDING THE PLANTS

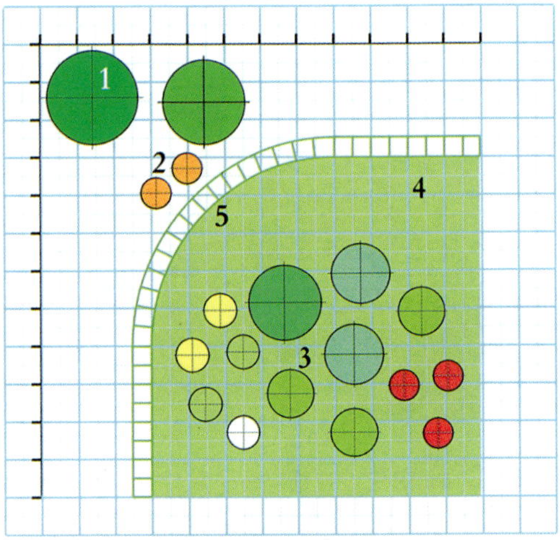

Position the symbols on your plan, starting with tall or key plants. It may be necessary to adjust them as other plants are added, but it is important that the key focal-point plants are well positioned as they will probably dominate the bed or border. Bear in mind the flowering periods, and ensure that evergreens are well distributed rather than clumped together, leaving large areas that will be bare in winter.

KEY TO PLAN

1 Existing flagpole cherry (*Prunus* 'Amanogawa')
2 Plants in position
3 Plants still to be positioned
4 Lawn
5 Mowing edge

FILLING OUT THE DESIGN

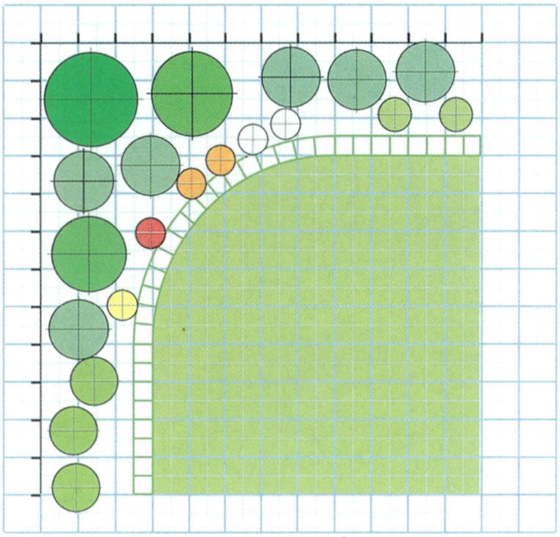

After placing the key plants, including tall ones best placed towards the back of the border, add the mid-height plants, but make sure some of these appear to drift towards the back of the border between the taller ones, to avoid a rigid, tiered effect. Finally, fill in with low-growing plants. The larger the drift of these, the more effective they are likely to be. Individual small plants often lack impact, and can be swamped by more vigorous neighbours.

COMPLETING THE DESIGN

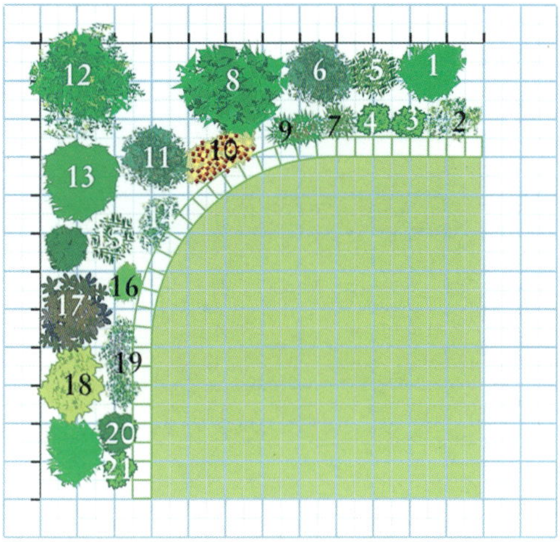

The initial plans can be fairly crude as they merely explore the possibilities of various combinations and associations. To visualize the final effect more easily, draw your final planting plan in more detail.

KEY TO COMPLETING THE DESIGN PLAN

1 *Perovskia atriplicifolia* 90cm/3ft
2 Bergenia (evergreen) 30cm/1ft
3 *Diascia barberae* 30cm/1ft
4 *Houttuynia cordata* 'Chameleon' 30cm/1ft
5 Kniphofia 120cm/4ft
6 Rosemary (evergreen) 120cm/4ft
7 *Artemisia* 'Powis Castle' 90cm/3ft
8 *Choisya ternata* (evergreen) 120cm/4ft
9 Dwarf Michaelmas daisy 60cm/2ft
10 Cistus 45cm/1½ft
11 *Cornus alba* 'Sibirica' 120cm/4ft
12 Existing flagpole cherry (*Prunus* 'Amanogawa') 10m/30ft
13 *Camellia* 'Donation' (evergreen) 200cm/6ft
14 Agapanthus 75cm/2½ ft
15 Hosta 45cm/1½ft
16 Bergenia (evergreen) 30cm/1ft
17 *Anemone* x *hybrida* 75cm/2½ft
18 *Potentilla* 'Princess' 75cm/2½ft
19 Lavender (evergreen) 30cm/1ft
20 *Stachys byzantina* (almost evergreen) 30cm/1ft
21 *Mahonia* 'Charity' (evergreen) 240cm/8ft

Low-maintenance Gardens

Low-maintenance gardens can be high on impact, and they can be just as stylish as gardens that demand regular attention.

This style of gardening is great for busy people who want a stunning garden but simply don't have the time or inclination to devote to regular watering or mowing, or routine chores like weeding and deadheading. Anyone with a disability, infirmity or simply suffering the effects of age will also be tempted by the appeals of low-maintenance gardening.

With low-maintenance gardens, you should be able to go on holiday for a week or more and come back without apprehension. They can fend for themselves for long periods. These are gardens where most of your time is spent relaxing rather than working.

■ ABOVE
Paving is low-maintenance, but it needs plenty of plants to soften the effect.

■ OPPOSITE
This strongly patterned design shows excellent use of line and form, mass and void – all elements of good design. A few select evergreen plants are used to create the maximum effect with the minimum of effort.

Inspirational Ideas

Low-maintenance gardens are often created using only a few striking plants, yet it is also possible to have a garden full of plants. It is the choice of plants as much as the number that determines how much time you need to lavish on them.

■ ABOVE
Gravel and stone gardens are low-maintenance, especially if you plant them with drought-tolerant plants such as lavenders. A few plants go a long way in this kind of garden, and maintenance is limited to trimming back any plants that begin to outgrow their space. This garden was created by Hilliers for the Hampton Court Flower Show, England, and has swirls of different-coloured gravel for extra effect: in your own garden, subject to regular foot traffic, you may prefer to use only one kind of gravel.

Weeds should not be a problem if the gravel is laid thickly. A plastic sheet laid over the ground first will prevent deep-rooted perennial weeds becoming a problem. Where necessary, it's possible to plant through the plastic sheet by making slits in the appropriate place with a knife.

■ ABOVE

Sometimes being big and bold within a small area can be extremely effective. Apart from the paving and brick raised bed, this garden contains little more than some large pots and plenty of pebbles and boulders. The use of large plants like *Phormium tenax*, arundinaria (a bamboo), and even a larch (larix) tree, provides plenty of impact. The use of a little colour, like the red nicotianas at the back, works all the better for being set among the greenery.

The choice of a bamboo fence gives the plants sufficient light for good growth while ensuring a good degree of privacy.

■ LEFT

You don't need a large space for a big impact. A small walled area can look stunning if the design is bold enough. Only a few different kinds of plants have been used here, but the varied textures of the garden floor compensate. The straight lines of the decking create an effective contrast with the organic shapes of stone and gravel. Mainly tender plants have been used in this dry garden, which is also a sun-trap. Most of these, like the echeverias in the blue bed in the foreground, will have to be taken in for protection where there are winter frosts, as this is essentially a summer garden.

The use of colour, on the walls and the edges of the beds, combined with the warm tones of the gravel, make this a garden of pleasing textures, colours and shapes even without the plants.

Inspirational Ideas

Whether formal or freestyle, minimalist or packed with features, successful low-maintenance gardens need careful planning.

■ BELOW
Courtyard and enclosed gardens can be cosy and private, especially if surrounded by high walls. By keeping the central part open, an impression of space is given, but a strong sense of form and structure is essential to create a "designed" look.

A strong focal point helps to give a garden a sense of design: here a row of lion mask water spouts commands attention. A design like this can look stark without plants, however, so the planting needs to be strong. Potted trees and shrubs have been used to soften the effect while retaining a formal style. Bear in mind that plants in containers require watering every day in dry weather, so it's worth considering an automatic watering system to save on the labour.

■ OPPOSITE TOP

These plants will tolerate dry conditions and do not demand regular watering. As well as making a pleasing backdrop for them, the gravelled surface should suppress weed growth.

The daisy-like annual dimorphothecas are easy to grow and bloom prolifically. Succulents such as echiums and *Agave americana* 'Variegata' should be placed in a frostproof place for the winter.

■ RIGHT

This strongly patterned design shows excellent use of line and form, mass and void – all elements of good design. It was created for the Chelsea Flower Show, London. Granite slabs have been set into the fine gravel, but for economy paving slabs could be used instead. Roof tiles set on edge have been used to create a strong, unusual pattern. The blocks of low-growing box (*Buxus sempervirens* 'Suffruticosa') can be achieved in a short space of time if a generous number are planted close together. This may appear extravagant, as box is fairly costly, but very few other plants have to be purchased for this style of garden.

■ LEFT

In contrast to the rigid formality of classical gravel gardens, this dry garden evokes a wild landscape. The seemingly random placing of the rocks and the sloping site without visible boundaries are cleverly planned to suggest that this garden is free from the rigours of design. Lavender, santolina and grasses have been planted in between the rocks for colour and a change of texture.

Know-how

THE GARDEN FLOOR

Although it may be the beds and borders that provide the initial impact in a garden, it's often the "floor" of the garden – lawns and paved areas for example – that occupy the largest area. This has a huge impact not only on time if you have to mow a lawn, but also in visual terms.

There are lots of ideas for hard surfacing (such as paving, decking and gravel) on these pages, with suggestions for plant alternatives to grass. Ground-cover plants are also important "carpets" for suitable beds and borders. It's important to get this aspect of the garden right, as, initially, it will be the most time-consuming and costly part of planning your garden. Also, consider carefully how much time you have to spend on maintenance, as your choice for the "floor" will eat into your time, as will maintaining the borders.

■ OPPOSITE

DECKING Consider timber decking instead of paving. If suitable timber is used, and it is treated with a good preservative, it can be long-lasting, attractive and practical.

DESIGN TIP *Stain the decking a colour that suits your style of garden or ties in with the interior decoration in your home. Although there are limits to the colour range of wood preservatives, there are many appropriate wood stains that can be used on already preserved timber. The size and spacing of the boards, and their colour, all change the visual impact on the garden as a whole.*

■ ABOVE

GRAVEL The gravel surface is useful for suppressing weeds (a path weedkiller, very carefully applied, should control weeds for a season if they do become a problem because of inadequate preparation or because the gravel is not deep enough). A large expanse of gravel is not to everyone's taste. Sometimes a mixture of gravel and paving looks better than either material on its own.

DESIGN TIP *Gravel can be enhanced with paving. Rather than position the paving slabs in straight rows or a regular pattern, try to introduce a sense of randomness for a more informal style.*

UNDERSTANDING GRAVEL

Gravel comes in many forms. Some gravels are angular, others have more rounded edges, they come graded in different sizes (the larger ones are more difficult to walk on, but very fine ones can also be a problem), and colours vary enormously. As well as grey, gravels can be shades of brown, red, almost green, and even with a hint of yellow. The colour of all of them changes depending on whether they are wet or dry when viewed, and whether in shade or sun. Very pale gravels can cause a strong glare in bright sunlight.

Coloured gravels are sometimes sold in plastic sacks in garden stores, and these may be adequate for a small area. If buying gravel for a large area however, have it delivered to your home in bulk to save on cost. If possible, obtain small samples of those you think might be appropriate and try them out in a small area in your own garden.

■ BELOW

GRAVEL Gravel is an excellent "flooring" for displaying plants and pots to their best advantage. Coloured gravel can be used to co-ordinate with containers.

DESIGN TIP *Empty decorative pots, grouped together or piled up, can be surprisingly pleasing and avoid the almost daily chore of watering. Position them by or near plants.*

DON'T BE BORING

Large areas of the same kind of hard landscaping material will look boring. Be prepared to mix different kinds of paving materials, perhaps timber and brick, natural stone paving slabs and bricks, or concrete paving slabs broken up with small areas or ribbons of gravel.

■ RIGHT

PAVING Unless the area to be paved is very large, consider bricks or clay pavers instead of concrete paving slabs. You can create different images with different laying patterns – a herringbone design has been used in this picture. Bricks and clay pavers often have a "warm" appearance that goes well with plants. Always check with the supplier that the bricks are suitable for paths – some are not and may crumble after frequent wetting and freezing.

DESIGN TIP *Try to soften the edging of paved areas with plants that will cascade or spread over the edge – but avoid those that will encroach too far and may become a hazard underfoot.*

Know-how

Alternatives to Grass

Some gardeners enjoy the physical effort of mowing the lawn – it's a useful form of exercise – but even the most energetic may begin to resent the time it takes in summer, or be dismayed at the visual impact an unmown lawn has on the garden if cutting has to be missed for a week or two through holidays or simply other pressures on time.

All-paved gardens are an option for small areas, but are not to everyone's taste, and most of us instinctively want to cover a large paved area with containers to add colour and interest – a course of action that necessitates the even more demanding task of frequent watering. For many of us, however, only a green lawn can set off a garden, giving it a natural kind of softness and beauty, and an attractive feature all year round. If you simply must have a lawn, don't despair – consider one of the alternatives to grass.

■ ABOVE

MOSS This may be a surprising choice for anyone who regularly buys mosskillers to treat their grass lawn. But there are many kinds of mosses, and some are attractive in the right setting. Normal lawn grasses would not do well in this shady area, for instance, but the moss thrives.

DESIGN TIP *Use moss for a damp and shady area where grass does not usually do well. It's not easy to buy moss, so you may have to encourage wild mosses and be patient.*

NEAT AND TRIM

With the exception of moss and the creeping thymes, occasional mowing or trimming with shears will be necessary for alternatives to grass. This will ensure low, dense growth, and keep the lawn looking smart and tidy, but it will be a less frequent job than for grass.

Chamomile will produce white daisy-type flowers if the plants are not trimmed, which some gardeners find detracts from the effect. The variety 'Treneague' is usually used for lawns as it produces fewer flowers than other varieties.

Don't forget that edges will also have to be trimmed occasionally to produce a neat finish and prevent the plants straying into neighbouring beds or borders.

■ OPPOSITE

CHAMOMILE Chamomile (*Chamaemelum nobile*, still often found under its older name of *Anthemis nobilis*) is a popular first-choice alternative to grass. It's readily available as plants, it looks attractive, and it's aromatic when walked upon. It also requires only infrequent trimming. It's not without its drawbacks, however, as it's not as tough as grass, and you won't be able to use selective lawn weedkillers on it (a problem that applies to the other grass alternatives too), so weeding can be tedious.

DESIGN TIP *Avoid using chamomile for large areas. It will be easier to maintain and keep weed-free if used for a small area like the one shown here, which is walked upon only for access to a sundial. It's not a good choice for an area of the garden that takes heavy traffic.*

■ RIGHT

CLOVER Clover may sound like an unlikely candidate, especially as many of us spend time and money trying to eradicate it from our grass lawns. However, anyone who has a lot of clover in their lawn will know that it often remains green for longer in times of drought, and it can make a dense, ground-hugging carpet. You'll need to mow it occasionally to remove the flower heads and to keep the growth tight and compact.

DESIGN TIP *Clover looks best as a small decorative area like the area shown here. It can create a lush-looking, ground-hugging carpet.*

BE PREPARED

Prepare the ground well before planting or sowing these grass alternatives, paying special attention to the elimination of weeds. Because the effective weedkillers sold for grass lawns cannot be used on these alternatives, hand-weeding will remain a chore until the plants are established and have knitted together to suppress new weed seedlings.

■ ABOVE

THYME Thyme is another popular alternative to grass for a small area, its aromatic leaves being part of the attraction. There are many kinds of thyme, however, and the bushy ones widely used as a kitchen herb are best avoided. The more ground-hugging *Thymus serpyllum* is a good choice. Here thyme is in flower, its purple blooms providing an attractive contrast with the granite path.

DESIGN TIP *Try using thyme for small areas near a garden seat, or allow it to meander between beds provided traffic over it will not be heavy. It is also attractive when used in combination with paving slabs: plant it in crevices between the paving.*

Know-how

IN PLACE OF CONTAINERS

Low-maintenance gardens often have large areas of paving or gravel, with ground-covering plants or shrubs in the borders. The temptation is then to use lots of containers to make up for the lack of seasonal colour otherwise provided by bedding plants and other flowers. Resist the temptation until you've first considered the alternatives.

HOW TO PLANT THROUGH GRAVEL

If planting through an already established gravel bed, pull back an area of gravel to expose the soil, then plant normally if the soil is fertile. If the topsoil has been removed during construction of the gravel bed, remove some of the poor soil and replace it with fertile topsoil or potting soil before planting. If the gravel has been laid over a plastic sheet, make crossed slits with a knife and fold back the flaps far enough to plant. Water well before returning the gravel around the crown of the plant.

■ ABOVE

PLANTING THROUGH GRAVEL

Instead of planting in containers to relieve a large expanse of gravel, plant directly through the gravel into the soil. Make sure the ground is well prepared in the planting area, so that the plants will grow strongly and require only infrequent watering. The plants in this picture need no attention at all, except for annually cutting back any that have outgrown their space.

DESIGN TIP *If planting through gravel, plant in bold groups, which will have much more impact than isolated plants dotted around.*

■ RIGHT

PLANTING THROUGH DECKING

Plants can be planted through spaces left in decking, just as easily as in a paved area. Although yuccas do not require regular watering, the greater depth of soil than that offered by a container will ensure a better specimen.

DESIGN TIP *If planning to plant directly into the ground, it's much easier to incorporate the planting spaces at the design stage, than to lift paving slabs or cut decking afterwards.*

■ RIGHT

PLANTING THROUGH A PATIO

Instead of planting in a container on a patio, try lifting a few paving slabs to make a small planting area. Maintenance will be cut down to a minimum, and it makes a more "planned" feature if worked into the original design.

DESIGN TIP *Don't leave the soil exposed, or weeds will spring up. Fill any exposed areas with gravel and pebbles. It will look more stylish.*

AGAINST THE WALL

Planting spaces left in paving are much better than containers for climbers, especially large ones such as wisterias and roses. Whenever possible, leave a planting area in the paving, then train climbers against the wall or fence. It may be possible to build up the edge slightly with bricks or walling blocks, to make the planting area a more positive feature, but always ensure the soil does not come too high and bridge the damp-proof course in the brickwork of your home.

■ LEFT

RAISED BEDS

A better way of introducing plants to a paved area than a number of containers. They usually hold a greater depth of soil than do pots or tubs, so plants are less likely to dry out, and it should not be necessary to water a raised bed daily during hot weather. Also, a single raised bed will have more visual impact than a group of containers.

DESIGN TIP *In a small area, a bed that is not elevated much beyond the surrounding ground may be as effective as a taller bed would be in a larger area, but in this case make sure the roots can penetrate the ground.*

Know-how

ORNAMENTATION

If you love terracotta and ceramic pots, or simply enjoy collecting interesting or unusual containers, don't assume you have to fill them with plants. Display them as ornaments in their own right. Those with a classic outline and a patina of age are ideal. Ornaments of all kinds can be used to give a garden that vital sense of "character".

FROST WARNING

Always check that terracotta or ceramic containers are frost-proof before leaving them out through the winter. Although empty containers are less prone to damage than filled ones, they can still crack or flake if not suitably fired when they are manufactured.

■ RIGHT
RUGGED ROCK Areas of ground cover like this patch of bergenia can look a little flat and boring. An ornament can often help by providing height and acting as a focal point. In this instance, a piece of rock serves the purpose admirably.
DESIGN TIP *Use ornaments to give height to a flat area or to act as a focal point in parts of the garden that otherwise lack sufficient impact.*

■ LEFT AND BELOW
GRAVEL TRANSFORMED Low-maintenance surfaces such as gravel and self-sufficient plants such as conifers can appear monotonous after a while, as the picture on the left shows. Experiment with a few ornaments – even a simple pot like the one below can transform the scene.

■ OPPOSITE
ELEGANT RESTRAINT If you have been seduced by a stunning terracotta container, don't feel that you have to plant it – you will be committed to regular watering. Try using such containers as ornaments in their own right, perhaps in a shady position where most plants would not thrive anyway.
DESIGN TIP *Although these containers are large, small ones will work just as well if used where their size looks in proportion to the surroundings.*

Planning and Planting

PRETTILY PAVED

A town or city garden, especially if enclosed by walls, often looks more stylish if the emphasis is on structure rather than masses of plants. Wall-to-wall concrete paving can look harsh and uninteresting, but warm-coloured bricks, laid in a pattern, provide a pretty background for plants as well as a practical surface for garden entertaining.

PLANNING

KEY TO PLAN

1 Garden shed
2 Climbers against walls and side of shed
3 Foliage plants in pots and tubs
4 Wooden bench seating
5 Table
6 Small-leaved ivy around edge of pool
7 Pool with waterlilies
8 Pedestal fountain
9 Brick paving
10 Shrub border
11 Sun-room
12 Stone finial
13 Brick steps
14 House

↑ Direction of steps down

Viewpoint on photograph

This town garden demonstrates how even a simple design consisting of basic rectangles can be transformed by the use of suitable landscaping materials and plants into a superb garden full of charm and character. The bricks, laid to an attractive basket-weave pattern, give colour and warmth to what could have been a dull garden. A built-in bench makes the most of limited space, and using a circular pond rather than a rectangular one, as the rest of the garden might suggest, provides a larger area of paving and more walking space, especially around the sitting area.

The small size of the bricks in comparison with paving slabs, coupled with the extra area created by the circular pond, helps to give

PLANTING

the impression that the garden is larger than it really is.

The circular pond could be converted to a sandpit if you have small children, or it could start out as a sandpit and be made into a pond as the children get older.

The many containers have the potential of negating the time saved by not having a lawn. Even though shrubs that don't need daily watering during warm weather have been chosen in this plan, they still require regular watering. An automatic watering system is the best solution, otherwise it might be better to convert the standing area for the containers into shrub beds.

PAVING PATTERNS

The pattern to which bricks and pavers are laid alters the overall impression created when viewed en masse. Three common bonds are illustrated below. The stretcher bond is usually most effective for a small area and for paths. The herringbone pattern is suitable for both large and small areas, while the basket weave needs a reasonably large expanse for the pattern to be appreciated. Always confirm that the bricks chosen are suitable for paving – those intended for house-building may be unsuitable.

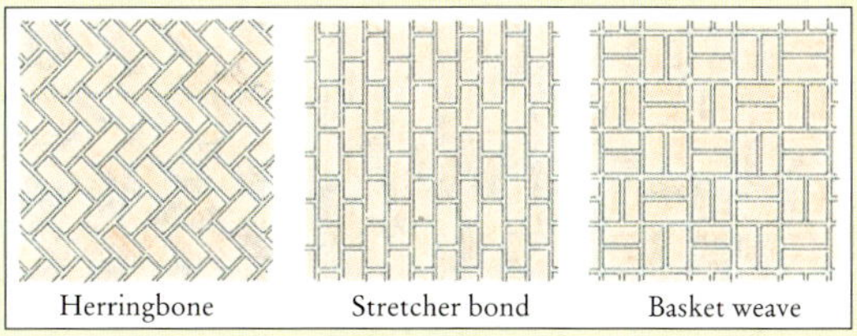

Planning and Planting

SETTING A STYLE

This low-maintenance garden uses granite setts to create an architectural tone, with a cabbage palm (*Cordyline australis*) as a centrepiece to add an exotic feel to regions where the winters are cool. Walling has been cleverly used to mask the garage.

KEY TO PLAN

1 Shrubs
2 Ground cover
3 Seat
4 Plant shelf
5 Raised patio with slabs
6 Garage
7 Fountain
8 Low-maintenance shrubs
9 Steps
10 Low-growing shrubs and ground cover in elevated bed
11 Tubs with dry-tolerant plants such as pelargoniums
12 Alpines and low-growing border plants
13 Paving slabs
14 *Cordyline australis*
15 Granite setts
16 Shrubs and ground cover
17 House

↑ Direction of steps up

Viewpoint on photograph

PLANNING

In the absence of a lawn, a large area of paving can sometimes appear oppressive. In this garden, the paved area has been divided into three separate sections, with granite setts used in one for a change of texture, and a variation in height introduced to help break up the garden visually. Raised beds at the end of the garden are an effective screen to the garage.

In spring and summer months, low-maintenance shrubs and ground-cover plants ensure plenty of visual interest, but focal points, such as the fountain at the end of the garden, are essential to make this an interesting garden at other times of the year, when the plants have died back.

As this is an enclosed garden, the eye has to be drawn inwards, rather than out towards an attractive distant view, so an "architectural" plant such as a *Cordyline australis* is needed to provide a focal point and an axis around which the garden hangs. This plant is not completely hardy in cold climates, but it will tolerate frost, especially once established. In colder areas, a large *Yucca gloriosa* could be used instead.

PLANTING

CHOOSING PAVING

There are many more paving materials available from garden centres, builders' merchant and specialist mail-order suppliers than many people realize. Each type will bring its own colour and texture to your patio or paved area, so it's worth studying a variety of catalogues and visiting a number of suppliers before ordering.

Concrete paving slabs are perhaps the most widely used form of paving. The vast range of sizes, shapes, and finishes can make choosing a bewildering task, but bear in mind that many of the bright colours tone down with the effect of dirt, age and weathering, so finish and texture may be more important. Some have a finish that resembles basket-weave bricks, others resemble real stone slabs.

Clay and concrete pavers are often rectangular but come in other shapes. They are usually bedded on sand and vibrated in. Pavers fit together closely, whereas bricks have to be mortared, leaving a seam around each one. Bricks have the advantage of being available in many warm colours, and it's easier to match the brickwork used for garden and house walls.

Stone setts, like the granite ones used in the garden illustrated above, create a strong sense of texture but may be a little more uneven to walk on. They mellow beautifully with age.

■ LEFT
The top row shows (from left to right) natural stone sett, clay paver, brick, artificial sett. The centre row shows a range of the different shapes of concrete paving blocks available. The bottom row illustrates some of the colours available in concrete paving slabs.

Planning and Planting

STUDY IN SYMMETRY

This is a town garden to sit and relax in, a place to meditate or relax rather than work in. Once constructed and planted, a garden like this demands little maintenance provided a self-watering system is used for the shrubs in containers, yet it's eye-catching and full of impact.

PLANNING

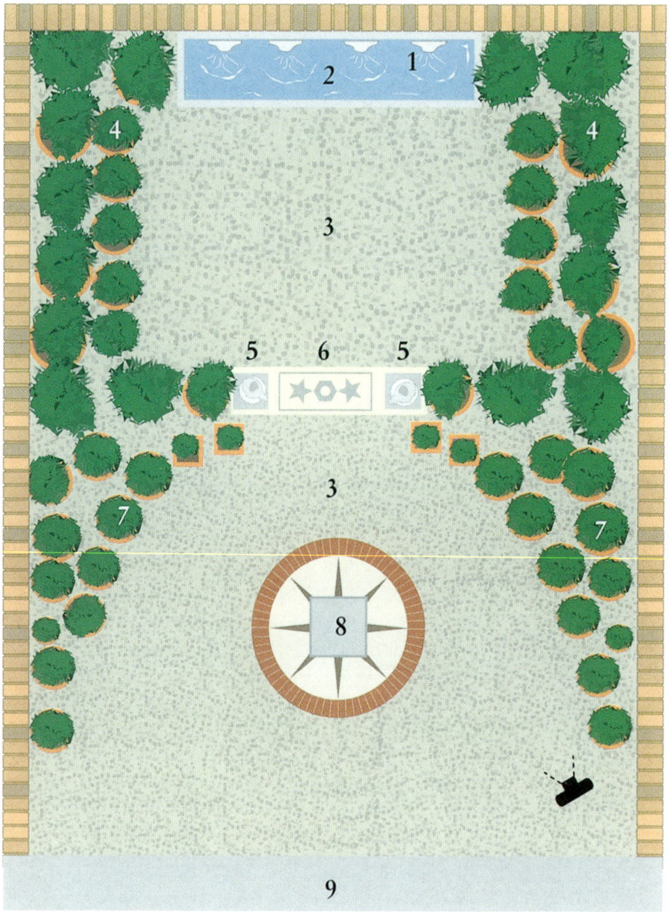

AKEY TO PLAN

1 Lion's head fountains
2 Raised pool
3 Gravel
4 Formal shrubs
5 Matching statues
6 Mosaic floor
7 Clipped box in containers
8 Ornamental pedestal on mosaic floor
9 House

Viewpoint on photograph

A very formal style like this depends on symmetry and bold features like wall fountains, mosaic, and matching statues to make a statement. This kind of garden will appeal to someone who enjoys shapes and a sense of order. Even the plants have been chosen for their shape and texture rather than for an intrinsic sense of beauty or colour.

A sense of artistry is used in the mosaic paving that links the two parts of the garden and the floor on which the ornament has been placed. These strong visual images break up the garden so that the eye is arrested and there isn't a void in the centre.

Clipped box (*Buxus sempervirens*) emphasizes the formal style of this garden, and it is not especially labour-intensive to maintain. Two or three clips during the growing season will suffice to keep the plants looking reasonable – a few more trims will maintain a smarter appearance, but still less time and effort than the weekly mowing required for a lawn. Box are also reasonably tolerant if they cannot be watered regularly, but it's best to use an automatic watering system if possible. This will ensure the garden is truly minimum-maintenance, and the box will thrive that much better.

PLANTING

COLOUR AND SIZE

Gravels are available in many colours, depending on the rocks from which they were derived, and the grade or size also affects the appearance. Look around to find a gravel with an appearance that you like. Make sure you see it both moist and dry, because it can look very different.

HOW TO LAY GRAVEL

1 Excavate the area to a depth of about 5cm (2in). You can make the gravel deeper, but it means more soil-moving and extra cost.

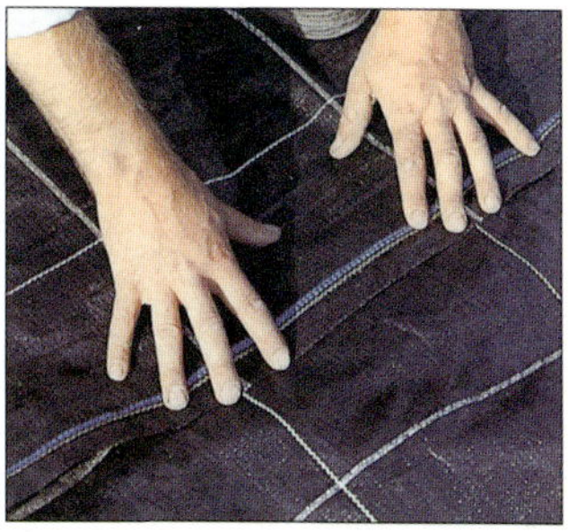

2 To prevent deep-rooted weeds appearing, lay a mulching sheet or heavy-duty black polythene (polyethylene) over the area, overlapping the strips by about 5cm (2in).

3 Barrow the gravel into position, then distribute it over the surface, making sure it is about 5cm (2in) thick. Use a rake to level the surface, then consolidate it by walking over it or rolling it. Re-rake if necessary.

Planning and Planting

FRAMING A FOCAL POINT

A dry garden like this benefits from a water feature such as a bubble fountain, which emphasizes the arid conditions all around and seems even more refreshing for that. Eye-catching structural features, like the moon gate and the ornament it frames, render the lack of bright plants unimportant. They give the garden high impact while still being low-maintenance, an impact that will be retained throughout the seasons.

PLANNING

KEY TO PLAN

1 Shed
2 Shrubs
3 Ground cover
4 Ornament
5 Gravel
6 Access door in wall
7 Moon gate (circular "window" in wall)
8 Low-growing shrubs
9 *Cedrus deodara*
10 Phormiums and yuccas in pots
11 Millstone water feature with pebble surround
12 Shrubs and ground cover
13 Patio with paving slabs
14 House

Viewpoint on photograph

Dividing the garden into smaller sections is a good way to add interest and encourage a sense of exploration. In this garden plan, the construction of a wall with a marvellous moon gate, a circular hole built into the wall, not only provides an outstanding focal point but gives the impression of more garden waiting to be explored beyond the wall. The ornament positioned against the back wall ensures the eye is taken not only to the moon gate but beyond it, and the fountain in the foreground echoes and balances it. The yuccas and phormiums positioned in pots on the right-hand side help to frame the window in the wall and require less watering than most container-grown plants.

PLANTING

A WALL WITH A VIEW

As a design device, "windows" set into a wall have the kind of magnetic attraction that seldom fails to inspire favourable comment. If the view beyond is attractive, then they work well in boundary walls; where the view is less enticing, they are better placed within internal walls.

The options are limited only by your imagination, but most "windows" are rectangular, oval, circular or arch-shaped. The material from which the wall is constructed may influence your decision. Unless you have experience of bricklaying, it's best to employ a professional.

■ ABOVE
Viewing "windows" can be built even into natural stone walls. Windows like the one shown above were once a popular design feature for the end of a long walk or alley within the garden.

■ ABOVE
When the view beyond a walled garden is an attractive one, make the most of it! Here an elegant fountain is framed by a classic brick arch, surrounded with pretty yellow flowers.

Planning and Planting

IN PLACE OF GRASS

Sometimes an existing garden can be transformed into a low-maintenance one simply by replacing the lawn. This is especially worth considering if the physical effort of mowing is a problem as well as the time element. In this garden the lawn was simply replaced by gravel. The effect is a garden that retains its interest throughout the year.

PLANNING

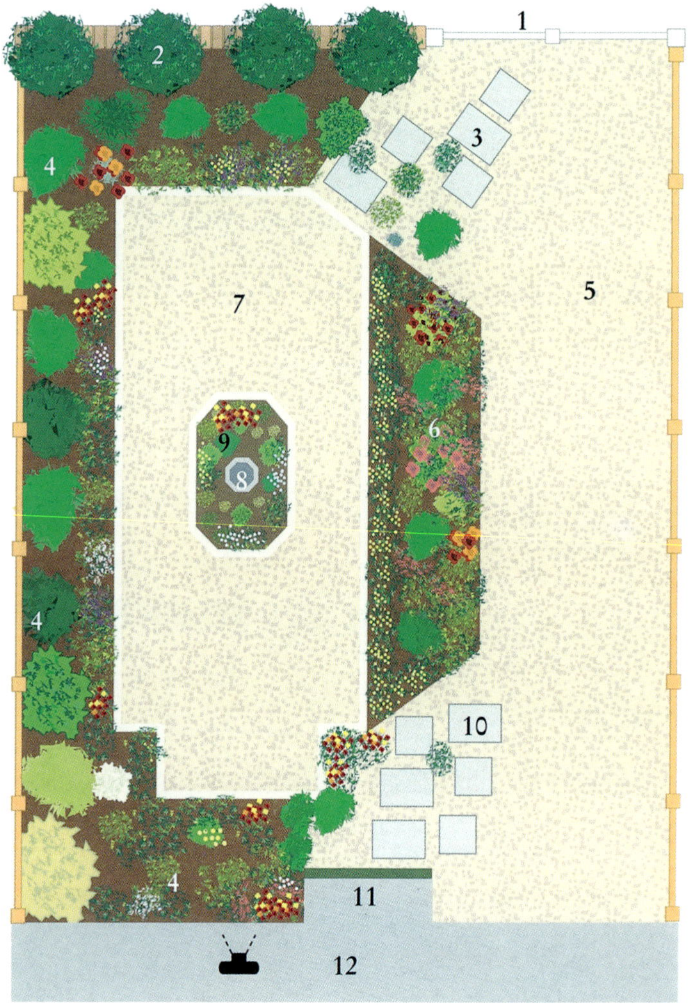

KEY TO PLAN

1 Picket gate
2 Conifers
3 Paving slabs and plants set in gravel
4 Mixed border
5 Gravel drive
6 Roses in mixed border
7 Gravel
8 Birdbath
9 Alpines and low-growing plants
10 Paving slabs set in gravel
11 Front door
12 House

Viewpoint on photograph

Not everyone wants to be involved in a major redesign in order to reduce the amount of time and effort spent on the garden. It may be possible to change a few labour-intensive features, and the lawn is often a priority in this respect. Here it was decided to replace the grass with gravel. Even though weeding and dead-heading would still be demanding at times, it was mowing the lawn that was becoming a chore. The existing beds were left, and the grass lifted and replaced with gravel. To prevent the gravel spreading on to the surrounding beds, an edging was added to keep it in place.

IN REVERSE

If you consider that a garden simply isn't a proper garden without a lawn, but are not too concerned about lots of flowerbeds to look after, you could keep the grass and fill the beds or borders with gravel instead. This will also suppress weeds in the beds. To reduce the amount of grass to mow, it may be worth cutting some new beds into the lawn.

PLANTING

HOW TO MAKE A GRAVEL BED

1 Start by marking out the shape with a rope, hose, or sand sprinkled where the outline should be. Oval-shaped beds are ideal for small gardens.

2 Cut the outline of the bed around the hose or rope, using a half-moon edger, or use a spade if you don't have an edging tool.

3 Lift about 10cm (4in) of grass with a spade. Add 7.5cm (3in) of gravel. Leave 2.5cm (1in) gap below lawn level to protect the grass from loose gravel.

4 For planting through gravel, fork in a generous quantity of rotted manure or garden compost, together with a slow-release fertilizer.

5 Allow the compost to settle before adding the gravel. Spread 5–8cm (2–3in) of gravel evenly over the firmed surface, and level it with a rake.

6 Gravel is best planted sparsely with a good space in between plants. Try adding a few stones or pebbles to enhance the effect.

Planning and Planting

CORNERING IN STYLE

Corner sites are always difficult to design, but if you can build a wall it's possible to isolate yourself in a very private garden.

KEY TO PLAN

1 Garden wall
2 Timber decking
3 Shrubs and ground cover
4 Raised bed
5 Bamboos
6 Plants in gravel
7 Raised timber patio
8 Pots on stand
9 Stepping stones
10 Rock feature
11 *Festuca glauca*
12 Conservatory
13 Gravel
14 House
Viewpoint on photograph

PLANNING

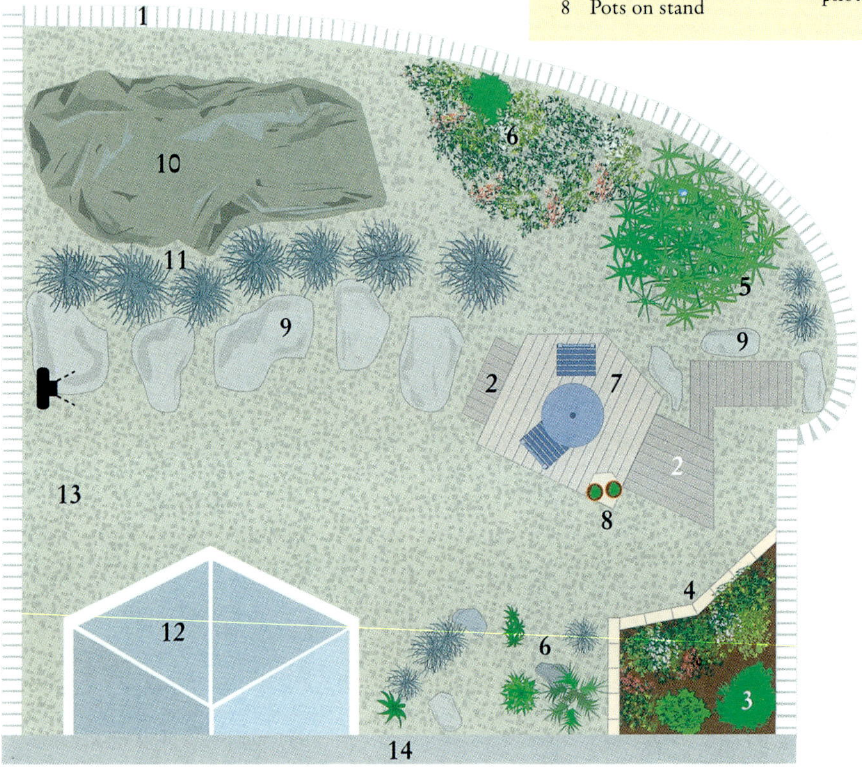

Here, a tall wall provides seclusion and privacy, creating an oasis in which a striking dry garden has been created. The white-painted finish helps to reflect light so that it doesn't look gloomy despite being enclosed.

In some places there may be restrictions on the height of wall that can be constructed in certain positions, mainly if they are likely to limit the view of traffic emerging from the road at a junction, so always check with the relevant authority if in doubt.

INEXPENSIVE GROUND COVER

Low-maintenance gardens often require lots of ground-cover plants to suppress weeds at the same time as clothing the ground. As they should be planted close enough to produce a carpet of foliage, a large number of plants are usually required. If gardening on a budget, keep down the cost by buying a few large plants and taking plenty of cuttings or dividing them if appropriate. Pachysandra is an example of an excellent ground cover that's easy to divide, even if the plant is still young.

HOW TO PLANT GROUND COVER

1 Ground-cover plants that spread by underground runners or have a crown of fibrous roots can be divided easily into three to four small pieces. Water the plant about half an hour before you start.

2 Gently knock the plant out of its pot. If it doesn't pull out easily, just tap the edge of the pot on a hard surface. It should then be possible to pull the plant without damaging the roots.

3 Carefully pull the root-ball apart, keeping as much soil on the roots as possible. Plants with a crown of fibrous roots can be prised apart into pieces using a couple of small hand forks.

4 If the crown is too tough to pull or prise apart with a fork, try cutting through it with a knife. If this is done carefully using a sharp knife, the plant should not be damaged too much.

PLANTING

5 It has been possible to divide this plant into eight smaller ones, but the number you will be able to achieve depends on the size of the original plant.

6 Replant immediately into the gravel or soil, if you don't mind starting with small plants. Otherwise pot up the pieces and grow them on for a year before planting out into the garden. Keep new plants well-watered until they are established.

Choosing Plants

Low-Maintenance Plants

Low-maintenance plants should not require attention more than once a year, and most trees and shrubs qualify on this score. Many play a more proactive role, by covering the ground with foliage and suppressing weeds – so-called ground-cover plants.

SUPER SHRUBS

Most shrubs are low-maintenance, but if you want to avoid annual pruning, choose evergreens, few of which require annual attention. *Viburnum tinus* flowers from mid-autumn to early spring, but it can grow tall and require pruning. Many hebes are compact and lots have attractive flowers, but some are vulnerable to cold winters.

Hebe 'Purple Picture' is a good example of a low-maintenance shrub. It's evergreen, compact and rarely needs pruning. Like most hebes, however, it is not suitable where winters are severe.

SHRUBBY GROUND COVER

Ivy, though a climber, makes a good ground cover for shade, but more interesting are prostrate cotoneasters, such as *C. dammeri*, with red berries, the variegated forms of *Euonymus fortunei* and, of course, the many kinds of heathers (especially callunas and compact ericas). *Pachysandra terminalis* 'Variegata' produces a smooth carpet of green-and-white foliage even in dry shade.

Euonymus fortunei 'Emerald 'n' Gold' will grow in sun or shade, cover the ground horizontally or grow up a wall or the trunk of a tree, yet it's not so vigorous that it's difficult to control. Its striking variegated leaves will provide winter colour.

BEAUTIFUL BORDER PLANTS

Choose border plants that do not require staking, are not prone to pests such as aphids or diseases like mildew, and do not spread so rapidly that they require frequent division. Pleasing all-round performers include astilbes, hemerocallis, kniphofias, and rudbeckias and *Sedum spectabile* for late flowers.

Sedum spectabile will bring a border alive in autumn just as most of its neighbours appear to be dying back for the season. There are several varieties and hybrids, in shades of pink and red. These succulent-like sedums require practically no attention and do not need staking.

HERBACEOUS GROUND COVER

Although most non-woody ground-cover plants die back to the ground for winter, they are more likely than shrubs to have bright summer flowers, and they suppress weed growth in summer. Among the plants used for summer ground cover are hostas and geraniums such as *G. endressii*.

Hardy geraniums are popular border plants, and many of them make pleasing ground-cover plants for the summer. Although they die back for the winter, they are more colourful than most ground-cover plants when in flower. Geraniums come in a wide range of colours.

ALL-SEASON TREES

Most trees are low-maintenance, so it's really a matter of choosing what you like the look of and have space for. Good trees for medium or small gardens with a long season of interest are ornamental crab apples (malus), hawthorns (crataegus), flowering cherries (various prunus), and small mountain ash such as *Sorbus vilmorinii*. *Acer griseum* is pretty and will still look good in winter with its cinnamon-coloured bark.

Acer griseum is one of several small acers that are unlikely to outgrow their welcome. They are slow-growing and well-behaved plants and look attractive in their dress of autumn colour. The cinnamon-coloured peeling bark makes an attractive feature throughout the year.

COMPACT CONIFERS

Dwarf and slow-growing conifers are great for low-maintenance gardens, but bear in mind that some will grow large or wide with time and some may eventually require moving. They form attractive "architectural" shapes, which can provide interest in sparsely planted gardens. There are narrow, upright growers, among the brightest being the golden *Taxus baccata* 'Fastigiata Aurea'; rounded shapes like the green *Chamaecyparis lawsoniana* 'Minima'; ovals like the golden

Thuja orientalis 'Aurea Nana' is a good choice for low-maintenance heather and conifer beds, with its golden foliage and oval outline, coupled with compact growth. It's slow-growing, usually reaching little more than about 60cm (2ft). The foliage turns almost bronze in winter.

Thuja orientalis 'Aurea Nana'; and prostrate ground cover conifers such as the 'blue' *Juniperus horizontalis* 'Bar Harbor'.

ALPINES FOR GRAVEL

Most alpines thrive in gravel, as the majority appreciate the good drainage. However, some alpines can be rampant and spreading, so

Armeria maritima, popularly known as thrift, is often grown in the rock garden, but it also makes a pleasing display when planted in gravel. Large areas of gravel are usually greatly improved by the introduction of plants such as this.

go for clump-formers such as thrift (*Armeria maritima*) and rock dianthus for low maintenance. There are many more ideal candidates, as well.

TROUBLE-FREE HEDGES

Hedges are excellent plants to define and give structure to a garden. However, many are tedious and time-consuming to trim, so avoid quick-growers such as privet (*Ligustrum ovalifolium*) or shrubby honeysuckle (*Lonicera nitida*). Give tall, fast-growing conifers such as x *Cupressocyparis leylandii* a miss too, as they will require a lot of maintenance.

Restrained hedges that demand little more than a single annual trim include *Berberis thunbergii*, beech (*Fagus sylvatica*), holly (*Ilex aquifolium*), and, for a conifer, yew (*Taxus baccata*) or *Thuja plicata* 'Atrovirens'.

Berberis hedges usually require clipping once a year, though for a more formal outline a couple of clips will improve the profile. Several berberis planted close together make pleasing hedges and form an effective boundary to a garden. They can also mask out noise or disguise unattractive features, such as a garage, refuse or compost area.

PATIOS, BALCONIES AND ROOF GARDENS

No garden should be designed without a place to sit, and, although garden benches and attractive seats tucked away in an arbour or alcove are always inviting, it's worth including a patio or an area where a group can sit and relax together, and perhaps enjoy a light meal or a drink surrounded by the sights and sounds of the garden.

If your garden is very small, or virtually non-existent, a patio or even a balcony may serve as the garden, in which case it is your extra room, the room outside. Where there's space, patios offer plenty of design scope.

It's natural to place a patio near the house, which is practical if you use the patio for meals, but it doesn't have to be a rectangle placed directly outside the patio doors. You could angle the patio around the corner of the house. It doesn't even have to be close to the dwelling – the design may be more impressive if the patio is at the end of the garden, or even to one side.

■ ABOVE
A shady retreat for dining al fresco, combining natural wooden benches with a sturdy stone table.

■ OPPOSITE
Where space is at a premium, a small curved bench can provide an attractive sitting area. Position it where you can enjoy the fruits of your labours.

Inspirational Ideas

You should consider carefully whether you want a patio filled with plants and flowers or something more structural or "architectural", with few plants and a big impact. A successful patio is often an extension of the style of the house.

■ LEFT
Balcony gardens can be striking in their simplicity. This one is large and has the benefit of a solid wall, which offers privacy as well as shelter from wind. A similar style could be used for a patio if you have plenty of space in the rest of the garden to indulge your taste in plants. This design shows strikingly the effect of form and shape, and the design value of "void", an area left uncluttered by garden furniture or tall plants.

■ OPPOSITE
A contemporary garden for a warm climate. Tall cacti grow out of the gravel, and rocks and stones are positioned among the beds to add interest. This truly is a garden for relaxing and enjoying the sun. The black furniture suits the modern, minimalist style of the garden.

■ ABOVE
The style of this sitting area could not be a greater contrast to the white-walled balcony shown opposite, top. Here, the garden is wrapped around the seating, a kind of mini-patio tucked away within the main planting areas. This is not the kind of area suitable for entertaining or for the family to relax together, but is a cosier, more intimate, place where a couple can rendezvous, or two or three friends can relax to discuss the pleasures of gardening.

INSPIRATIONAL IDEAS

If gardening on a balcony, in limited space, you'll want to cram in as many plants as possible, but in a large garden with plenty of flowerbeds you may prefer not to be bothered by bees and insects attracted by flowers while you are relaxing or eating.

■ LEFT
A secluded sitting area surrounded by plants has a special appeal. It becomes part of the garden proper rather than an isolated patio. White-painted furniture helps to make a statement in an area that could otherwise become cluttered visually. The white-painted trellis also helps to make a visual boundary and creates the impression of a more designed and integrated area by picking up the colour theme from the white garden furniture.

■ ABOVE
In a large garden, an area like this makes an ideal, sheltered retreat. The overhead beams not only create the illusion of an outdoor room but also provide support for a variety of evergreen climbers. Although climbers provide a wonderful natural canopy, bear in mind that the support must be high enough for trailing shoots not to become a nuisance below. This is especially important if climbing roses are planted, as the thorns are a potential hazard.

■ RIGHT
Balconies can be exposed to the elements, and sitting on a balcony can be a public experience. Using plenty of plants, including climbers, helps to overcome these problems, and from a gardening viewpoint transforms a barren area of paving into a haven of beauty. Here, vertical curtains of green have been achieved by planting climbers and wall shrubs against the dwelling wall, and by fixing a climbing frame to the edge of the balcony.

Know-how

Somewhere to Sit

Gardens should be places to relax in as well as to work in, and although a deckchair or lounger on the lawn is a good way to while away a few sunny hours, a patio or balcony garden room should be designed for relaxation and recreation, planned and furnished to become an enticing place to eat or drink al fresco.

No patio or balcony garden is complete without somewhere to sit, and the style and materials of the garden furniture used can have a profound effect on how the feature is perceived. No matter how cleverly designed and well constructed the patio, an inappropriate table and chairs can spoil the effect, while well-chosen seats and tables can make even a mediocre patio look good.

■ ABOVE

FOLD-AWAY CHAIRS Balconies pose a special problem as space is usually limited. Rather than normal garden chairs, consider directors' chairs, which can be folded to take indoors.

DESIGN TIP *Design a balcony garden so that there is good access and an area where several people can gather to sit together without fear of falling over plants or pots. This may mean grouping containers together into a few choice areas, but the impact will not be diminished.*

■ OPPOSITE LOWER LEFT

ALUMINIUM Cast aluminium alloy furniture has the appeal of the old cast-iron types that it replicates, with the huge advantage of light weight. This type of garden furniture is available in a range of colours.

DESIGN TIP *Greens and browns will blend into the garden, whereas white will stand out. Choose a colour that reflects the effect you want to create.*

■ LEFT

WOOD Informal wooden garden furniture like this blends in beautifully. Here, the seat is arranged much as it might be in an indoor room, which helps to give it the impression of being an extension of the home.

DESIGN TIP *Position your furniture to take advantage of the garden's colours, scents and view. A fragrant climber will add to your enjoyment of the garden as you survey your handiwork.*

■ BELOW

BENCH SEATS Bench tables with integrated seats can be reminiscent of public picnic places, but small stylish ones will banish any suggestion of lack of taste. This one has been varnished to keep its natural appeal, which makes it attractive as well as practical.

DESIGN TIP *Avoid placing a rectangular table at right angles to the wall or edge of the paving. It will probably look more pleasing if angled, like the one illustrated.*

■ ABOVE

NATURAL MATERIALS Cane and wicker furniture is not ideal for leaving out in poor weather, but it is usually light enough to be carried under cover. It is also a good choice for a balcony. This type of chair adds to the impression that your patio or balcony is just an extension of the home.

DESIGN TIP *White furniture stands out well from a background of plants. However, in a bright, sunny place with lots of paving and few plants, white can look stark. Choose a colour that's appropriate to the setting.*

MATERIAL MATTERS

Patio furniture varies widely in price and quality, and there should be something to suit every taste and pocket. The starting point, however, should be what looks right rather than a prejudice about a particular material or concern over price. It may be better to buy one really good piece of furniture rather than several cheaper pieces, but sometimes inexpensive furniture is perfectly adequate for a particular situation.

Plastics and resins are often dismissed, but some types make strong furniture that lasts well and is easy to wipe clean, stack and store. If those qualities, especially portability, are important, don't dismiss these materials.

Timber furniture is always a popular choice, but here you probably do pay for quality. Hardwood furniture that is well made to last for years is not cheap, and it can be heavy to move around. It will also require annual cleaning and treating with a suitable oil or preservative if its colour is to remain strong and bright.

Cast-iron garden furniture is still available, and looks right where a period atmosphere is being created, but it's extremely heavy to move. Cast-aluminium alloy imitations look as good yet are light and easy to move. They are worth the extra cost.

Aluminium alloy furniture is usually painted or coated in a special resin. White is a popular colour, but it shows dirt easily. Browns, greens, even blues, are colours that do not show the dirt so readily, and look stylish too.

Know-how

A Suitable Position

Be imaginative about where you position the sitting and outdoor dining area – it doesn't necessarily have to adjoin the house, and it doesn't have to be a conventional patio shape. There are many other options, and the possibilities are limited only by imagination.

■ RIGHT

CLOSE FOR COMFORT There's much to be said in favour of a patio close to the house – especially if you do plenty of entertaining. It is also convenient for watering containers from the kitchen tap, and handy for harvesting culinary herbs planted in containers.

DESIGN TIP *Angling a patio at 45 degrees to the building makes it that little bit more distinctive and takes full advantage of the sun as it moves around.*

■ BELOW

A SHELTERED SPOT This is a traditional patio, in a sheltered position close to the house. It is purely functional, but for many gardeners that's what's required, and in this country cottage setting it blends in with the rest of the garden. The slight change of level between paving and lawn helps to delineate the patio area.

DESIGN TIP *Choose a position that's sheltered from too much sun or rain, and not exposed to cold winds. Shade for part of the day is not a drawback, and is often welcome, but make sure that the patio receives sun for at least part of the day.*

■ ABOVE

THE CENTRE OF ATTENTION

Few would think of a sitting area in the centre of the garden, but it gives the impression of a garden designed for, and built around, people. Tasteful garden furniture is essential in this position, as it will become part of the main focal point of the garden.

DESIGN TIP *Don't be afraid to be different. It may bring that special quality to your garden that makes it personal, individual and powerful in a design sense.*

■ OPPOSITE

A PERMANENT OASIS This distinctive feature packs all the punch you could wish for. It's been sited away from the house, where the garden can be viewed in its full spendour, and is positioned to take advantage of the sun during the afternoon. Its position in the centre of the lawn acts as one of the focal points of the garden. The lightweight seating is easy to move around when required, while the fixed table, with its special planting area in the centre, looks good at all times.

DESIGN TIP *Don't be afraid to make your garden look lived in, or to be daring when it comes to built-in furniture! It can be a gamble that pays off.*

OBSERVATION PAYS

It's important to get the patio position right, and what appears to be a good position when planned on paper may have serious shortcomings in reality. It pays to sit out in the garden a few times, on different days, and ideally at different times of year, to assess whether it's a comfortable position as well as one that works in design terms.

You will soon discover whether shade, drips from trees or chilling winds caused by a wind-funnel effect between buildings are likely to be a problem. It will also give a better idea of privacy – if you don't want to be overlooked, it may be necessary to erect a screen or reposition the patio. A wall or a hedge might provide a private or sheltered position, or a patio overhead of beams supported on posts may give a sufficient degree of privacy. These can all be worked into the design and should be incorporated at the planning stage.

Know-how

EATING OUT

A meal outdoors always seems to taste better than the same food served at the dining-room table. A barbecue may be a bit smoky from time to time, and there may be the odd wasp to contend with, but it's all so much more fun. It isn't necessary to design your patio with meals in mind, but if you plan to do a lot of eating out it makes sense to consider the practicalities.

PORTABLE BARBECUES

Built-in barbecues look stylish and give the impression of a well-planned garden, but where space is limited, they may not be the best solution. Portable barbecues that can be wheeled out for a particular occasion work satisfactorily, and some of the kettle barbecues (those with a lid that closes over the food) are inexpensive, colourful and attractive. If you are designing a built-in barbecue, add a storage cupboard if possible, and also somewhere to place plates and kitchen accessories. If buying a portable barbecue, you may wish to consider a trolley barbecue with sufficient surface space for serving.

■ OPPOSITE TOP

TWO-IN-ONE Almost anyone with a barbecue will tell you that it is an uninteresting feature when not in use. Why not transform it into a seat? Remove the grill and metal plate, brush away any ash, then slot in the wooden seat. Add a cushion, and the transformation is comfortable and complete.

DESIGN TIP *If you have a small garden, make every part of it work. Look for multi-purpose features like this barbecue seat, or use a portable barbecue that can be stored away when not in use.*

■ OPPOSITE BELOW

DESIGNING WITH LIGHTS Lights positioned under a tree will cast a subtle light for dining, as well as dramatic, enchanting shadows.

DESIGN TIP *Consider electric lighting at the design stage, so that it can be planned without dangerous trailing cables. Low-voltage systems are the safest, but high voltage lights are more powerful and safe if installed by an expert. However, the cost of laying mains cable electricity lines in conduit will be cheaper if close to a mains supply.*

■ ABOVE

BUILT-IN BARBECUE If outdoor entertaining is high on your list of priorities, a built-in barbecue and seating is worth designing into your patio. This is an unexciting feature when the barbecue's cold, but here a white seat helps to enliven what could otherwise be a drab corner once the guests have left.

DESIGN TIP *Build the barbecue in a position that is unobtrusive when it's out of use, and away from a fence or other potential fire risk. For the same reason, avoid a position near overhanging trees.*

■ TOP

CANDLES Patio lights extend the hours of pleasure to be derived from your patio, and allow you to enjoy warm evenings to the full. Candles and flares lend atmosphere to an evening in the garden, as do lanterns.

DESIGN TIP *Position candle flares and lanterns where their light will cast evocative shadows around the garden. Grouped together, they will provide sufficient light for an atmospheric meal. Never leave candles, flares or lanterns unattended in the garden.*

Know-how

LOOKING DOWN

The surfacing material for a patio is usually chosen after the basic shape and position have been decided, but never overlook the relevance of this important choice. It will make a difference to the image your patio creates. Mistakes will be expensive and hard to hide. There are many materials from which to choose, and dozens of combinations to experiment with; here are just a few.

■ OPPOSITE ABOVE

PAVERS Bricks and clay pavers are popular for small patios, and they look especially effective if combined with brick pillars and low retaining walls. Not all bricks suitable for building walls are appropriate for paving, however, so check with your supplier or use a suitable brick that's a close match.

DESIGN TIP *Terracotta pots look good with bricks or clay pavers, but try using a group of them together rather than dotting them around: this will have more impact and look less fussy.*

DECORATIVE DECKING

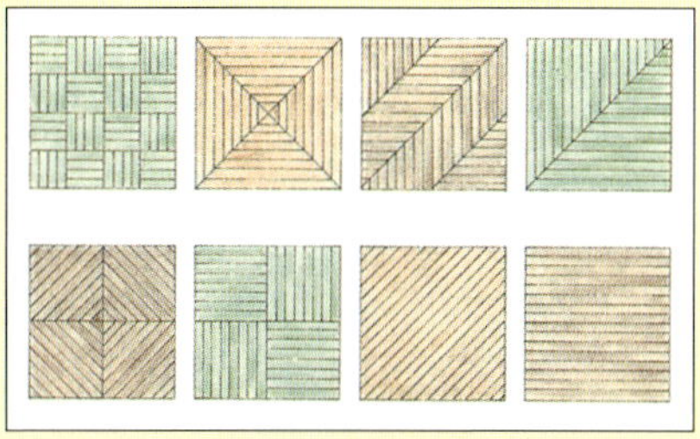

The way the planks are arranged changes the appearance of decking, as these eight variations show. Not all patterns are suitable for an irregularly shaped deck. Those that form a number of symmetrical squares are more appropriate for a rectangular deck.

If in doubt, try laying out various patterns before you cut and secure the timbers.

■ OPPOSITE BELOW

DECKING Timber decking is easy on the eye and harmonizes well with most plants. There are many decking styles, some of which are illustrated in the box above, and by using different wood stains or colours, even more effects can be created. It's advisable to experiment with a small area, or draw up a plan before buying and laying decking, to make sure that the pattern you like will suit the shape and style of your patio. Decking is also good for covering up uneven or irregular surfaces and will provide a sense of cohesion.

DESIGN TIP *Wooden furniture blends well with decking, but other materials can be used. If you are using trellis as a boundary to a decked patio, staining this a matching colour will help to produce a co-ordinated look.*

■ ABOVE

COMBINED EFFECTS Modern concrete-based paving materials and walling blocks mixed with brick can look pleasing and are especially useful where a modern image is desired. Don't be too tempted by brash colours, as they can look garish when new and weather to a muted colour anyway.

DESIGN TIP *Give an area of concrete paving an edging of bricks, clay pavers or tiles. It gives the paving a more definite edge and the contrast provides a clean, sharp look.*

■ LEFT

CONCRETE Don't dismiss concrete as a material. Concrete pavers can work well in the right setting. Here they blend with the concrete blocks used as seats.

DESIGN TIP *Consider how materials will blend with other features on the patio. Here, concrete blocks give the patio a modern image, but they might have looked incongruous with aluminium alloy furniture in traditional style.*

Planning and Planting

Sophisticated Courtyard

Quarry (terracotta) tiles can work better than bricks or paving slabs in a courtyard like the one shown here, as they help to create the impression of an outdoor room. A garden like this is very much an extension of the indoor living area.

PLANNING

KEY TO PLAN

1 Trellis overhead
2 Formal pool
3 Fountain
4 Quarry (terracotta) tiles
5 Quarry (terracotta) tiles, laid diagonally
6 Climbers along fence
7 Trees and shrubs
8 Specimen tree
9 Table and benches
10 House
11 Upright trellis
Viewpoint on photograph

The type of paving used will set the tone of a patio or courtyard. These warm-looking quarry (terracotta) tiles reflect the warm-climate feel of this garden. Water plays an important role in this kind of design, but the formal pond does not have to be large, and a gentle fountain is more appropriate than a gushing water feature.

Even the most attractive paving can look overpowering if there's too much of it. Using a strip laid diagonally introduces the necessary visual break without damaging the sense of unity and harmony within the garden.

The long trellis overhead and the trellis enclosing the garden provide useful shade and a sense of privacy.

Here are instructions for building an upright trellis arbour, which can be adapted if you want to erect an overhead trellis.

CONSTRUCTING A TRELLIS ARBOUR

1 Gather together the trellis panels and "dry assemble" to ensure you are happy with the design. Two of the 200 x 60cm (6 x 2ft) panels are for the sides and the third is for the top. The two narrow panels and the concave panel are for the front and the 200 x 90cm (6 x 3ft) panel is to be used horizontally at the top of the back. Trim the wooden posts to length. They should be 200cm (6ft) plus the depth of the metal "shoe" at the top of the metal spike that will hold the post.

PLANTING

■ ABOVE
An upright trellis painted in a co-ordinating colour, and surrounded by colourful, fragrant plants in bed and pots, makes a perfect secluded retreat.

2 Start with the back panel. The posts need to be placed 200cm (6ft) apart. Mark their positions, then, using a club hammer, drive in a spiked metal post support (protect the top with a piece of wood or special metal insert). Drive a ready-trimmed post into each of the metal "shoes". Using the galvanized nails and the hammer, temporarily fix the top of the trellis to the top of the posts. Using a No. 8 bit, drill holes for the screws at intervals down each side of the trellis. Screw in the screws.

3 In the same way, position the front outside posts and fix the side panels, then the inside front posts and front panels. Fix the concave panel into the panels either side of it. Finally, fix the roof in position, screwing it into the posts. Paint the arbour with exterior decorative wood stain and leave to dry.

TOOLS AND MATERIALS

For a 200cm (6ft) long trellis:
- Lattice (diagonal) trellis in the following panels:
  - 3 panels 200 x 60cm (6 x 2ft)
  - 2 panels 200 x 30cm (6 x 1ft)
  - 1 concave panel 200 x 45cm (6 x 1½ft)
  - 1 panel 200 x 90cm (6 x 3ft)
  - 6 timber posts 8 x 8cm (3 x 3in), each 2.2m (7ft)
- Saw
- 6 spiked metal post supports 8 x 8cm(3 x 3in), each 75cm (2½ft) long
- Club hammer
- 10 x 5cm (2in) galvanized nails
- Hammer
- Electric drill with No. 8 bit, screwdriver attachment
- 40 x 2.5cm (1in) No. 10 zinc-coated steel screws
- 2.5 litre (½ gallon) can exterior woodstain
- Small decorating brush

Planning and Planting

SURROUNDED BY FRAGRANCE

Instead of making your patio formal and structural, try building it into the edge of a border. You will feel more immersed in your garden, and if you use plenty of scented plants it will be a wonderfully fragrant experience too.

PLANNING

KEY TO PLAN

1 Shed
2 Compost area
3 Specimen tree
4 Large screening shrubs
5 Mixed border
6 Ornamental varieties of native shrubs to link with woodland boundary beyond
7 Woodland boundary
8 Sundial
9 Lawn
10 Ornament on plinth
11 Bank of thyme behind seating area
12 Table and chairs
13 Patio of clay pavers
14 Pots of lavender
15 Stepping stones to lead around corner
16 House

Viewpoint on photograph

If the formality of a rectangular patio conventionally positioned by the house does not appeal to you, and you want your sitting area integrated more naturally into an informal garden style, try building a small sitting area into one of the borders.

The bank of thyme surrounding the seating area will be fragrant when touched or the leaves are crushed, and the pots of lavender will enhance the aromatic delights of sitting in this enchanting part of the garden. Bear in mind that these aromatic plants will also attract lots of bees, which could be an inconvenience.

SITTING PRETTY

Instead of buying garden furniture, you could give some old tables and chairs a lick of paint, and you may be able to colour co-ordinate them with the surrounding plants. Wooden furniture will look best. You can be sure of perfect toning as paints are available in hundreds of shades. If you don't have any suitable old chairs, try junk shops. To maintain the chairs in good condition, keep them indoors when not required outside.

PLANTING

■ ABOVE
These bright Caribbean colours may not harmonize with many plants, but your garden certainly won't be dull with a chair like this.

■ ABOVE
A combination of grey and white looks cool and elegant and will blend with most garden settings. Natural or muted colours contrast well with the bright blooms of seasonal flowers.

■ ABOVE
Prettily decorated with the bright colours typical of a summer garden, this chair would look wonderful surrounded by bright bedding plants such as fiery red pelargoniums.

■ ABOVE
The chair shown above blends in sympathetically with the painted shed behind. The delight of this project is that you can choose shades and colours to blend or contrast.

Planning and Planting

ON THE ROOF

Roof gardens have limited scope for radical overhauls as structural and load-bearing considerations will determine the scope. Furniture and plants are elements that will set the style.

PLANNING

KEY TO PLAN

1 Decorative light
2 Timber decking
3 Wire supports for climbers
4 Skylight to floor below
5 Table and chairs
6 *Aucuba japonica* 'Variegata'
7 *Fatsia japonica*
8 Standard box (*Buxus sempervirens*)
9 Ivy
10 Timber walkway
11 Rails
12 Building
Viewpoint on photograph

Roof gardens offer more scope than balconies as they are often larger, but the problems are the same. The physical structure dictates the basic shape and limits of what you can do. Choose furniture and plants carefully to evoke atmosphere. Here, a formal garden has been created with box and other "architectural" evergreens in a simple planting scheme. These shrubs tolerate the winds more readily than less robust plants.

This roof is able to take the weight of the numerous clay pots, but with other roof gardens it may be necessary to use plastic containers and lightweight potting soil. Make sure they are heavy enough to withstand severe winds. If in doubt about your roof's load-bearing capacity, consult a structural engineer.

CLASSIC TOPIARY

Topiary is easy to maintain. When trimming, don't get carried away. Little and often with an ordinary pair of scissors is better than the occasional dramatic gesture with a pair of shears.

PLANTING

■ BELOW
left to right:
Ball topiary, corkscrew topiary, three-ball topiary and classic standard ball topiary. With patience and skill, box topiary can be trained from young plants. Buying ready-trained specimens will create instant impact.

POTTING TOPIARY

1 Knock the plant out of its original pot. Place into the terracotta pot containing broken crocks, and fill the space around the rootball with potting soil.

2 Push the potting soil down the side of the pot firmly, to ensure that there are no air spaces. Scatter the surface of the soil with plant food and water well.

3 To conserve moisture and create an elegant finish, especially on standard topiaries, cover the top with a generous layer of chipped bark or gravel.

Planning and Planting

CENTRE OF ATTRACTION

Your patio or sitting area will probably have far more character if you break with tradition and move it to a more central position, away from the house. A patio like this places you at the heart of the garden where you can admire the view.

PLANNING

KEY TO PLAN

1 Specimen tree
2 Mixed border
3 Climbers on wall
4 Specimen shrubs
5 Rear door to garage
6 Mixed planting
7 Climbers on garage wall
8 Garage
9 Granite setts
10 Granite sett steps
11 Drive
12 House

↑ Direction of steps down

Viewpoint on photograph

It is the clever use of meandering paths of granite setts combined with masses of plants that make this tasteful garden a delight for the plant enthusiast. Positioning the main sitting area slightly away from the house, so that it is surrounded by shrubs and mixed planting, makes it a magical place to sit and have a meal.

The structure of this garden does not follow any of the common grids based on rectangles or series of circles, which amply demonstrates that design "rules" should be interpreted flexibly. Some of the best gardens give the impression of having simply evolved, with one part melting into the next. Curves and straight lines do not usually mix happily, however, and this garden is full of circles, arcs and gentle curves.

SITTING COMFORTABLY

Garden seats should be practical as well as pretty whenever possible. Charming and elegant seats are available in practical cast-aluminium alloy (they look like wrought iron from a distance, but are much lighter and more practical for use outdoors), but even old seats from around the garden and home can sometimes be renovated and used to give your garden character.

PLANTING

■ RIGHT
The old Lloyd loom chair illustrated had been given a new look a few years earlier with two shades of blue spray-on car paint. Even though the finish has become worn, the chair exudes a comfortable, cottage-garden feel. This kind of chair is not really weatherproof, but it can sit in a conservatory and be brought out for special occasions.

■ ABOVE
Metal benches are often unattractive, but this one was given a new lease of life when it was painted a bright Mediterranean blue. Used with a couple of co-ordinated cushions, it would add charm to any sitting area.

Planning and Planting

ELEGANT FORMALITY

Even city gardens like this one offer scope for a sense of spacious elegance, combining a long, open view to a distant focal point with plenty of interest-packed areas of restrained formality.

PLANNING

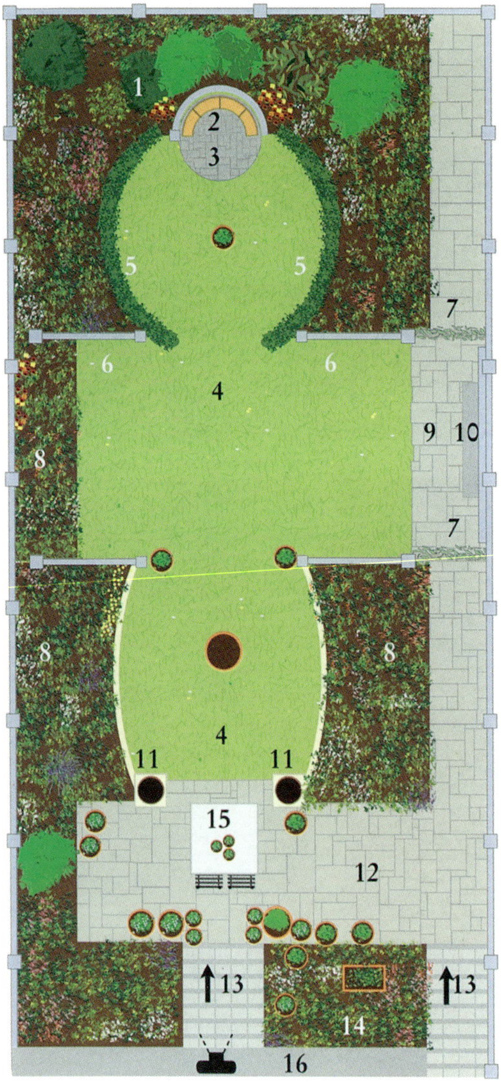

KEY TO PLAN

1. Shrub border
2. Curved trellis with seat
3. Circular paved area
4. Lawn
5. Box (*Buxus sempervirens*) hedge
6. Downcurving trellis with climbers
7. Archway with climber
8. Mixed border
9. Random-slab seating area
10. Trellis arbour
11. Urn
12. Random-slab patio
13. Steps
14. Dwarf shrubs
15. Seating area
16. House

↑ Direction of steps up

Viewpoint on photograph

A design with many interesting features, this garden illustrates how effectively a simple device like a trellis can break up the garden visually. Shaped trellises have been used to divide the garden into a series of compartments. A trellis adds height and structure without blocking the view or casting a heavy shadow in the way that a hedge or wall does. Trellises can also be painted or stained in various colours to create a particular mood or emphasize a style.

It's possible to buy ready-made shaped trellises from specialist suppliers, but they can also be made to suit a specific need.

The curved trellis at the end of the garden encloses a small sitting area, something that balances the patio at the house end of the garden and also provides a focal point. It's a good idea to have more than one patio, so that you always have a sunny place to sit as the sun moves around. The secondary sitting area does not have to be large. This kind of design is easily achieved without a great deal of construction if there is already an existing central lawn.

PLANTING CLIMBERS

Trellises of all kinds, whether grand like the ones shown in the picture opposite or modest and erected specifically for a climber, demand to be clothed. It's not necessary to cover the whole trellis with climbers (sometimes the exposed structure strengthens the sense of design), but a good degree of cover avoids it looking too bare.

If the trellis is close to a wall or fence, it's very important to plant a little distance away, to avoid the worst of the "rain shadow".

PLANTING A CLIMBER

1 Excavate a hole twice the diameter of the rootball. The centre of the plant should be 30cm (1ft) away from the wall or fence, otherwise the roots will be too dry. Dig in a generous amount of rotted manure or garden compost, to help hold moisture in the soil as well as add nutrients.

2 Water the plant, then gently knock the bottom of the container to remove the plant from its original pot. Carefully tease out some of the fine roots from around the edge of the rootball, to encourage them to grow into the surrounding soil. Return the soil to the hole and firm.

3 Loosen the stems if they have been tied to a support cane in their pot, and spread them out evenly, spreading them wide and low. Tie in.

4 Water thoroughly after planting, and continue to water carefully until established. Apply a mulch to reduce water loss and suppress weeds.

Planning and Planting

SIMPLE ELEGANCE

Often simple shapes well executed have the most impact. This garden is based on rectangles around a large lawn. The patio is situated a distance from the house, linked by herringbone paving, which gives it a strong "architectural" element.

KEY TO PLAN

1 Hedge
2 Compost area
3 Shed
4 Gravel path
5 Specimen tree
6 Mixed border
7 Pergola on brick piers
8 Brick patio
9 Climbers over pergola
10 Lawn
11 Brick-edged pond
12 Brick path
13 Small specimen tree
14 Dwarf shrubs
15 Brick paving
16 House

Viewpoint on photograph

PLANNING

The choice of materials as well as the basic shape of the garden helps to create a sense of unity. In this garden, brick has been used extensively to link the various parts, and particularly the house and patio. Brick pillars for the patio overhead continue the theme and make the feature a more substantial element in the overall design.

Lighting has been built into the pillars as part of the patio lighting, to make this an area of the garden to be enjoyed for relaxing or dining after dusk as well as by day.

LAYING CLAY OR CONCRETE PAVERS

Bricks are usually bedded on mortar with mortared joints, but clay or concrete pavers are bedded directly on to sand. Their dimensions ensure they lock together simply by vibrating or tamping sand between them. They can be used instead of bricks, for patios or paths.

PLANTING

HOW TO LAY CLAY OR CONCRETE PAVERS

1 Excavate the area and prepare a sub-base of about 5cm (2in) of compacted hardcore or sand-and-gravel mix. Set an edging along one end and side first. Check that it's level, then mortar it into position, and lay the pavers.

2 Lay a 5cm (2in) bed of sharp sand over the area, then use a straight-edged piece of wood between two height gauges, notched at the ends so the wood strikes off surplus sand and provides a level surface.

3 Position the pavers in your chosen design, laying about 2m (6ft) at a time. Make sure they butt up to each other tightly, and are firm against the edging. Mortar further edging strips into place as you proceed.

4 Hire a flat-plate vibrator to consolidate the sand. Alternatively, tamp the pavers down with a club hammer used over a piece of wood. To avoid damage do not go too close to an unsupported edge with the vibrator.

5 Brush loose sand into the joints of the pavers with a broom, then vibrate or tamp again. It may be necessary to repeat the vibrating process once more for a firm, neat finish. The patio should be ready to use straightaway.

Choosing Plants

Patio, Balcony and Roof Garden Plants

The majority of plants can be grown in pots. Use shrubby and annual climbers to clothe patio walls, and a few striking "architectural" shrubby plants as focal points, but make the most of bedding plants, tender perennials and containers for masses of summer colour.

CLIMBERS AND WALL SHRUBS

Patios and balconies almost always have a wall boundary on at least one side, which would be more attractive if clothed with attractive climbers or wall shrubs. Ivies are ideal for clothing a large wall, but try to include plants with flowers or attractive berries to make it more interesting. Large-flowered clematis are ideal if supported on a trellis, but avoid rampant ones such as *C. montana*. Avoid thorny climbing or rambling roses if the space is confined. Pyracanthas are ideal wall shrubs as they can be trained and confined easily.

Clematis Large-flowered clematis are among the most popular and spectacular climbers to grow up a trellis. These varieties are 'Nelly Moser' (top) and 'Lasurstern' (bottom), but garden centres will have many to choose from.

"ARCHITECTURAL" SHRUBS

These are plants with a strong profile such as a spiky appearance or large bold leaves, which act as a focal point or a clearly defined shape. Avoid plants with spine-tipped leaves, such as *Yucca gloriosa* for example, as these can be dangerous, especially for children. *Cordyline australis* has a spiky appearance but softer tips, and there are prettily variegated varieties. Phormiums make striking plants for beds or large containers, and are available with variegated and coloured leaves.

Cordyline australis 'Albertii' is one of several variegated forms of this architectural plant, useful as a focal point. It is likely be less hardy than the all-green species, so it may require winter protection in cold areas.

BORDER PLANTS FOR CONTAINERS

Few border plants are used in containers other than hostas, but it's worth experimenting if you have spare pieces of border plants left over when you divide them. Because they are not usually grown in containers, the impact of potted border plants can be greater. *Lychnis coronaria* can be very pleasing, and *Ligularia dentata* 'Desdemona' can be impressive with its large, almost purple leaves. Generally, foliage plants are a better choice than those grown mainly for flowers.

Hostas come in many forms. Most are attractively variegated, and some have pleasant flowers. They do surprisingly well in containers if watered regularly. This makes them highly desirable foliage plants for a patio.

TREES AND SHRUBS FOR CONTAINERS

Patio colour is usually provided by summer-flowering seasonal plants, but it's worth growing a few evergreen shrubs in large containers, so that your patio or balcony does not look too bleak in winter. *Viburnum tinus* is especially useful because it flowers all winter. *Fatsia japonica* is grown mainly for its striking foliage, but mature plants do have ball-like heads of whitish flowers in late autumn. Small trees such as laburnums and some acers can be grown successfully in large pots.

PATIO ROSES

Most roses can be grown in large containers, but they will be much happier in beds beside the patio or cut into a patio. There are, however, patio roses – really dwarf and compact floribunda (cluster-flowered) varieties – that perform well in pots and in patio beds. 'Sweet Dream' and 'Top Marks' are particularly good, but there are many more.

Trailing pelargoniums, with their bright, vigorous blooms, can be used to great effect in both window boxes and hanging baskets. They are particularly good plants for containers as they will tolerate a period of dry soil better than most plants.

Argyranthemum frutescens is probably still better known as *Chrysanthemum frutescens*. There are many varieties with daisy-like flowers in shades of pink, yellow and white, produced over a long period. This is is 'Sharpitor'.

Patio roses do best in flowerbeds or raised beds on the patio, but will usually put on a respectable performance in a container too. This one is 'Top Marks', one of the most highly regarded varieties among professional rose growers.

POPULAR BEDDING PLANTS

Any of the popular bedding plants can be used in patio containers, and which you grow is purely a matter of personal preference. Pelargoniums (bedding geraniums) should be on the short list, however, because they have that Mediterranean look and thrive in a hot position. They are also less demanding regarding watering than most other bedding plants. Busy Lizzies (impatiens) are also priority patio plants because they are so long-flowering and tolerate shade or sun. The New Guinea hybrids, which have larger flowers and sometimes variegated leaves, are not generally used for mass bedding, but they make excellent patio plants.

INTERESTING TENDER PERENNIALS

The group of brightly coloured summer flowers loosely called tender perennials, to distinguish them from bedding plants raised from seeds, are always worth including. They have to be propagated vegetatively and overwintered in a frost-free place, so if you don't have a greenhouse it's usually necessary to buy fresh plants each year. Fuchsias are a popular example, but try some of the bright daisy-like plants too, as these suggest a warm climate. Argyranthemums, venidioarctotis, and osteospermums are good examples and will continue flowering over a long period.

A TOUCH OF THE EXOTIC

A sheltered patio or balcony may provide the right environment for some of the plants more usually grown in a greenhouse or conservatory, where winters are frosty. Coleus are easily raised from seed, so can be discarded at the end of the season. Try putting some of your houseplants on the patio for the summer, after careful hardening off (acclimatizing).

Coleus are often grown as pot plants, but they can be grown very successfully in the garden. They are easy to raise from seed, started into growth in warmth in mid or late winter.

The Japanese Influence

Authentic Japanese gardens are constructed according to strict rules, and features carry a significance that is seldom appreciated by Westerners. This in no way detracts from our ability to enjoy the style and aesthetics, and to incorporate some Japanese features into our own gardens, even if they lack the underlying significance of "authentic" Japanese gardening.

Whole books are written on the subject of Japanese gardening, but most of our designs seek only to capture the mood. Gardens have to be adapted to suit the environment and culture in which they are built. In our Western gardens, we may wish to introduce the Japanese influence only into part of our garden, or use a few key features as garden ornaments. Japanese votive lanterns, for example, are widely bought and positioned without regard to their original significance and are enjoyed purely as attractive garden ornaments. On the other hand, an area set aside as a Japanese-style garden will have a sense of peace and tranquillity that's special and supremely relaxing. Even if you are not persuaded to convert the whole of your garden, a Japanese corner will certainly add grace and elegance.

■ ABOVE
A simple feature like this evokes images of Japanese culture.

■ OPPOSITE
A Western interpretation of the style, using Japanese features and plants.

Inspirational Ideas

Japanese influences can be introduced to your garden in varying degrees. You won't have to completely redesign your garden for it to take on an oriental air. A bamboo screen, fountains, or lanterns can all add to the effect if chosen and positioned with care.

■ OPPOSITE
The space at the side of a town house is often neglected because it's so difficult to persuade plants to thrive there, and the scope for a strong design is severely limited. This design shows how Japanese images and features can be put to good use in a most unpromising position. Note the use of bamboo and reed screens to help mask the surroundings, which would certainly have lessened the impact of this type of garden.

■ BELOW
A garden like this won't demand much maintenance, other than clipping the domes two or three times a year, yet it has as much impact as one packed with flowers. This genuine Japanese garden may not be to the taste of gardeners more used to a rainbow of colour and a garden packed with as many different kinds of plant as possible, but it has a different function.

■ BELOW
Although there are Japanese influences in the water garden, this is clearly a hybrid with a more traditional Western style. For many gardens, this may work better than a stricter interpretation of the Japanese style.

Inspirational Ideas

The starkness of Japanese-style gardens may be unappealing to gardeners who expect to see greenery and colourful blooms. However, as these pictures show, the appeal of natural materials compensates with a serene style, which often requires the minimum of care.

■ LEFT
This is typical of a garden where elements of Japanese gardening have been mixed with normal Western elements, without attempting to follow authentic Japanese gardening philosophy. There's nothing wrong with this, as any garden should reflect personal preferences, which may involve borrowing from many styles.

■ BELOW
In a small or town garden it may be possible to devote only a corner to a collection of Japanese images. This inevitably means compromises, but the message is received clearly even in this small corner. It has been helped by creating a background that doesn't detract from the illusion. Painting the brickwork white helps enormously, and the bamboo fence is infinitely better than the traditional wooden fence that was probably there before the transformation.

■ OPPOSITE
Though created far from Japan, this garden shows strong oriental influences. The surrounding fences and buildings could have killed the illusion, but reed screens have been used cleverly to mask a potentially distracting background, and they make an uncluttered backdrop against which to view the various features to advantage.

Know-how

THE MAGIC OF LANTERNS

You don't have to be a student of authentic Japanese garden design to use and appreciate many of the features associated with this style of garden. Votive lanterns can be used as attractive ornaments if you are content not to look for deeper significance. Specialist catalogues offering lanterns and features such as deer scarers and water basins may use the Japanese names, but you will be understood if you ask for them by their English equivalent.

Lanterns are widely used in Western gardens merely as garden ornaments, but in traditional Japanese gardens the different kinds each have a particular significance, and they are always positioned with great care. If they are used as ornaments, however, do not be afraid to position them where they look pleasing.

■ LEFT

POSITION Make the most of winding paths in a large garden by positioning lanterns to show the way. Lanterns were used to light the way to an evening tea ceremony or to draw attention to a particular scene.

DESIGN TIP *Small Japanese acers and moss-covered ground will emphasize the oriental theme. Avoid plants that might look alien in a traditional Japanese garden.*

■ BOTTOM

PAGODA-SHAPED LANTERNS *Kasuga*-style lanterns, with their pagoda-shaped tops, are named after a shrine in Nara, Japan. They make a bold focal point and can often dominate the scene.

DESIGN TIP *Position the lantern at the edge of a pond if possible so that its long reflection is cast across the still water for a dramatic effect.*

■ OPPOSITE ABOVE

PEDESTAL LANTERNS *Rankei*-style lanterns are set on an arching pedestal so the light extends out over the water, the better to reflect the image.

DESIGN TIP *Position the lantern so that it looks pleasing close up but also so that it forms a focal point across the water, at a distance or from another part of the garden. By giving careful consideration to positioning, it's usually possible to achieve both these aims.*

■ OPPOSITE BELOW

SNOW-VIEWING LANTERNS *Yukimi-doro* or snow-viewing lanterns are often placed close to water. This position is used because when snow covers the wide top and the lamp's light reflects on the water, the effect can be particularly beautiful. The large roof also represents the shape of a Japanese farmer's rush hat. Lanterns were traditionally used near bridges to light the way.

DESIGN TIP *Lanterns, bridges, water, rocks, and gravel are all strong elements in Japanese gardens, so if space is limited try to introduce them in close proximity if possible. Do not cram in so many elements that it looks cluttered, however, as a sense of space is equally important.*

BUYING AND FIXING LANTERNS

Top-quality stone lanterns, made from materials such as granite, are expensive and heavy to handle. Consult specialist suppliers, and take your time choosing. Consider where you will be placing the lantern before you order.

Genuine stone lanterns are heavy and are likely to be shipped from Japan in sections. It's important that these are fixed together securely for safety reasons. Follow the suppliers' advice on assembly and fixing materials.

Reconstituted stone versions are cheaper, but perfectly adequate if viewed from a distance, perhaps across a lake or pond.

Lightweight resin reproductions are surprisingly good and perfectly adequate for a budget garden.

Lanterns should strictly be positioned at certain critical angles, to your home for instance, but your specialist supplier should be able to offer advice if you desire to lay out your garden in an authentic Japanese design.

Know-how

Water Features

Ponds, lakes and streams form the heart of many large Japanese gardens, but in a small garden the scope for these may be limited. Fortunately, water is used in many other ways, most of which can be incorporated into even a modest-sized garden.

■ LEFT

DISPLAY PLATFORMS You can make a small pond look oriental if it's accompanied by suitable bridges and rocks. Here, a couple of charming bonsai, displayed on a platform that reflects the materials and style of the bridge, bring out the essential "Japanese" ambience.

DESIGN TIP *Don't use rocks only around the edge of the pond. Try to position a few rocks in the water as well. Try covering them with moss and perhaps planting a bonsai in a suitable crevice. Be careful not to puncture the liner (use pieces of off-cuts beneath the rocks), and don't forget that your bonsai will still require regular watering despite being surrounded by water.*

■ RIGHT

WATER BASIN

Water basins capture the essence of a Japanese garden, and are small enough to feature in any garden. Traditionally, the water is fed through a bamboo flume.

DESIGN TIP *Don't be tempted to elevate the basin higher than suggested by the manufacturer. The low-level placement is symbolic, requiring a low stooping position to use it, as a gesture of humility for the ritual cleansing before the tea ceremony.*

■ LEFT

BRIDGES Water provides an ideal excuse for including a wonderful Japanese bridge, bright red being the usual colour. These are focal points in their own right, but also cast enchanting reflections.

DESIGN TIP *Whether making the bridge or buying it, it makes sense to span the narrowest part of the pond or stream. If necessary, just make a small inlet that extends a little way past the bridge to give the illusion that the water flows beyond.*

PUMPS

Most small water features, such as deer scarers and water basins, require only a very gentle flow of water. An inexpensive, small, low-voltage pump is adequate, and this can be housed in a small hidden reservoir beneath the feature, water trickling through pebbles supported on a strong mesh base, to be recirculated.

■ RIGHT

ORNAMENTS This large pond benefits from this focal point. Ornaments should be simple but striking, and have relevance to the scene.

DESIGN TIP *Don't overdo the ornaments, especially if you have used lanterns around the garden. Too many focal points will clash with each other. A few striking features usually work better than many mediocre focal points.*

Know-how

ROCK AND STONE

From early times, the Japanese have had a deep and abiding affinity with rock. Rock forms an important element in their landscape, and it symbolizes durability. It is possible to construct a Japanese garden without rocks, but it would be a pity not to include this most attractive of materials.

■ BELOW

CHOOSING ROCKS Consider colour, texture and size when choosing rocks. Here the different surfaces and sizes look as though they have been deposited naturally beside the stream.

DESIGN TIP *Random positioning of rocks and pebbles will create a natural look, enhanced by clusters of water plants.*

■ ABOVE

LARGE ROCKS A couple of large rocks have transformed a potentially dull corner of this Japanese garden. Whether you view them as symbols or simply as an ornament, they are a striking focal point and make a feature of a part of the garden that would otherwise go almost unnoticed.

DESIGN TIP *Rocks like this are heavy to move. To help get the positioning right without too many attempts, make a number of sketches to show the selected rocks in a number of positions. Begin to position them only when you have a sketch that looks convincing.*

■ BELOW

FEATURE FOUNTAIN A drilled boulder through which water is pumped so that it trickles gently over the surface creates a wonderfully calming and refreshing feature, especially on a hot day. By surrounding it with gravel topped with smaller boulders or beach pebbles a rock landscape is achieved. Adding a few other large rocks ensures this looks more like an erupting volcanic island set among a sea of pebbles.

DESIGN TIP *A feature like this can form part of a larger Japanese garden, but it would also make a pleasing water feature in another style of garden, to bring interest to an otherwise dull corner, perhaps where plants struggle to thrive.*

■ ABOVE

PATHWAYS Rocks with a suitably flat surface are sometimes used as stepping stones – through either lawn or water. They form a path that leads you through the garden, and the size and spacing of the stones are specially selected and positioned to dictate the pace at which you make the journey.

DESIGN TIP *Stepping stones placed close together slow up the speed of travel. Wider spacing will tend to speed up the pace. You can use different spacing to determine the rate at which the garden is to be explored, or vary the pace to meet the needs of different parts of the garden, perhaps dwelling on a feature of which you are specially proud.*

Buying Rock and Stone

Garden centres and builders' merchants are likely to stock only a limited range of rocks and stones. Look in local directories for stone merchants – these should have a reasonable selection.

For a large feature it may be best to visit a suitable quarry, and perhaps select your rocks there. However, bear in mind that carriage is substantial on such a heavy material, so if possible use a local rock rather than one found perhaps in another part of the country, to save on carriage.

Know-how

SAND AND GRAVEL

Dry landscapes, with the emphasis on the element of stone, have their origins in the Zen style of gardening, its history originating from a form of Buddhism. This is a fascinating garden form to explore in specialist books on the subject, but you can imitate some of the elements in your own garden without an in-depth knowledge of the symbolism.

■ LEFT
GRAVEL OR SAND CIRCLES
Long straight lines of raked gravel or sand usually suggest calm water, and wavy lines evoke flowing water. Concentric circles in gravel also imply a sense of movement, perhaps where the water flows around an "island". DESIGN TIP *To prevent gravel spilling over on to beds, borders, lawns or paths and ruining the design, it is important to have a firm, raised edge to a dry garden whenever possible.*

■ RIGHT
GRAVEL LINES
Where space is limited, a Japanese-style garden can be achieved by combining raked sand, rock and boulders and lantern in a vacant corner. The bridge here is for aesthetic purposes, rather than for practical reasons. DESIGN TIP *Be cautious about using raked sand or gravel close to deciduous trees. Maintaining this neat appearance will be far from easy in autumn.*

■ ABOVE

COMPLEMENTING GRAVEL
The area of raked gravel or sand is usually limited, and here the path in the foreground is created from flat rounded stones, toning in with the almost mountain scree landscape of the rocks beside it.
DESIGN TIP *Be cautious about raked gravel where it might be used as a path or short-cut – it only takes one pair of feet to ruin the effect! Here a paved area has been provided around the edge to avoid this risk and provide a pleasing contrast.*

■ RIGHT

DRY BRIDGES Bridges can be built over dry garden "rivers" and "cascades", but these may spoil the scale of the landscape unless used with care.
DESIGN TIP *Dry gardens are striking features, but they can look a little barren to Western eyes. Plenty of plants in the background will help.*

Planning and Planting

A Hint of the Orient

A garden created totally in authentic Japanese style may not be appropriate for Western gardens, especially where the surrounding environment makes it seem alien. Some of the designs that follow on later pages show the Japanese influence more strongly, but this is one for anyone looking for a compromise with a strong Western influence.

PLANNING

KEY TO PLAN

1 Bamboo screen
2 Covered patio in style of Japanese tea house
3 Paving slabs
4 Step
5 Granite setts
6 Specimen shrubs and herbaceous plants
7 Rocks and moss-covered pebbles
8 Stockade fence
9 Pond
10 House

↓ Direction of steps down

Viewpoint on photograph

This garden is an ideal compromise between a family recreational area and a Japanese-influenced garden. Gardens often have to be a compromise between the conflicting requirements of different family members. Try to visualize what the garden will look like in winter. The use of a few choice evergreen shrubs and trees like rhododendons and acers will ensure vital shape and form maintained throughout the year.

USING GRASSES

Grasses and small bamboos look effective in gravel or stone areas of borders. There are many varieties with interesting shapes and colours. Try planting contrasting groups for extra impact.

PLANTING

HOW TO PLANT GRASSES

1 Water the plants well and then knock them out of the pot and plant in well-prepared weed-free soil. If there are a lot of roots tightly wound around the edge of the pot, gently tease out some of them to encourage growth.

2 Some grasses are fast growers, so check first. If using a rampant grass, plant it in a large pot to restrict its spread. Dig a hole large enough to take the container, which must have drainage holes in it.

3 For spreading grasses, partly fill the container with soil then plant normally, with the rootball at the correct level. Firm the plant well, with your hand or heel, and add more soil if necessary.

4 Make sure the rim is flush with the surrounding soil (not below it, otherwise the grasses with creeping roots may escape). Water well, and keep well-watered until the plants are established.

Planning and Planting

STONE AND WATER

Two elements of symbolic importance in Japanese gardens are stone and water, both of which feature strongly in this design. This is a garden for contemplation and quiet admiration – not a family garden for children to play in. It's important to have a clear idea of what you want from this style, and to modify the degree of authenticity to suit.

PLANNING

KEY TO PLAN

1 Timber decking
2 Mat-forming ground cover
3 Rock island with lantern
4 Water lilies
5 Pond
6 Specimen shrub
7 Specimen tree
8 Climber on wall
9 Dwarf shrubs
10 Japanese lantern
11 Raked gravel
12 Rocks and bamboo
13 House

Viewpoint on photograph

This stylish Japanese garden makes extensive use of raked gravel, with rock "islands" and associated plants. In our plan, extensive use has also been made of water, another very pleasing visual and aural element that features strongly in the Japanese style of gardening. Plants have been used to create shapes and textures, and foliage effect is more important than colourful flowers. Before setting to work on this kind of garden, it's worth spending time doing some in-depth reading on Japanese gardens and their symbolism.

Although raked gravel is a very visual device, and highly attractive, you should bear in mind that the family dog and local wildlife or

PLANTING

playful children will quickly make re-raking an urgent priority if you are to keep it looking good. In addition, the area will require regular clearing and raking during the autumn to remove fallen leaves.

UNDERSTANDING LANTERNS

Japanese lanterns make a fascinating study worth reading up on or sending for catalogues from specialist suppliers. Their form and function are steeped in ancient conventions and traditions. In the meantime, it might be helpful to understand some of the basic terms: the parts of the lantern, the variety of styles and how the lantern should be positioned in relation to the house, if you want to be precise.

POSITIONING LANTERNS

■ ABOVE
Although most Western gardeners simply position their lanterns where they look pleasing, they should be angled towards a point where the centreline meets the house, as shown in the illustration.

THE PARTS OF A LANTERN

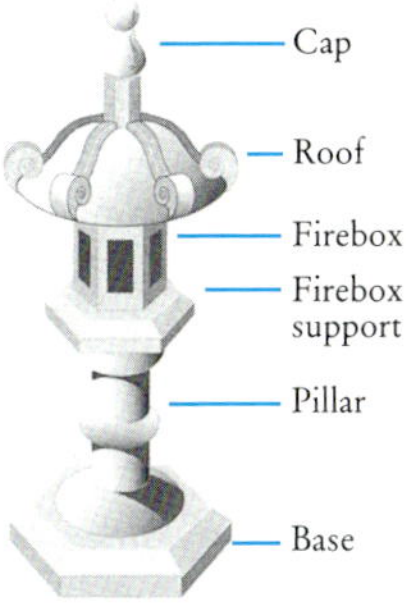

■ RIGHT
Lanterns may not have all the six parts illustrated here. The base may also be described as legs, pedestal or earth ring; the pillar called the trunk or shaft; and the roof referred to as the umbrella.

KNOW YOUR STYLES

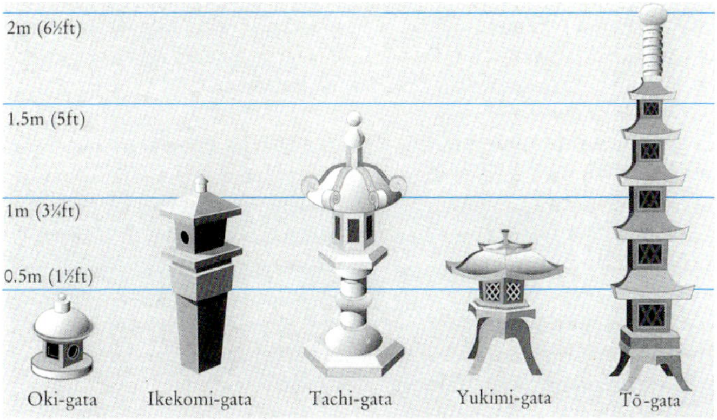

Planning and Planting

A Garden of Elements

Symbolism is important in a Japanese garden, and here rock, water and wood, all strong forces in nature, help to give this garden strong imagery.

PLANNING

Because many features in Japanese gardens, such as water, rock and gravel mingled with plants, are designed to be viewed rather than sat among, it's important to provide suitable viewing areas. Decking blends in unobtrusively, and here it has been used on three sides to provide ample viewing angles as well as somewhere to sit and entertain.

A water feature like this, with a combination of rectangles and curves, and rocks placed within the pond, makes construction difficult for an amateur. It is worth taking professional advice when thinking about a creating a water feature of this size and complexity. Positioning heavy rocks also calls for teamwork.

DECIDING ON DECKING

Complicated decks with several changes in level or which project over water, for example, as here, require special construction techniques. There are companies who specialize in making and installing decking, and these should be consulted if you are in any doubt.

KEY TO PLAN

1 Bamboo screen
2 Climbers
3 Mound-forming plants
4 Bamboos
5 Japanese lantern
6 Rocks
7 Pebbles and gravel
8 Pond
9 Water irises
10 Timber decking
11 Dwarf shrubs
12 House

Viewpoint on photograph

PLANTING

HOW TO MAKE SIMPLE DECKING

1 Level the area to be decked, then position bricks or blocks on which the bearers will be supported. Bearers must be clear of the ground so that they are not in contact with damp earth and to allow air to circulate freely beneath the decking. If the ground is unstable, set the bricks or blocks on pads of concrete. Make sure they are level, or the final decking will not be stable.

2 Apply an additional coat of preservative to all fence posts. Lay out the posts provisionally, to check that the supports are spaced closely enough together and to ensure that they are cut so that two lengths butt over a support block. Lay heavy-duty polythene over the ground to prevent weeds growing though. Water will drain away where the sheets overlap.

3 Lay the posts over a waterproof membrane where they come into contact with the supporting bricks, and ensure that any joins are positioned over the support. Cut gravel boards to size and coat with preservative. Fix these to the posts using galvanized nails. Leave a gap of about 6mm (¼in) between each board to allow water to drain and the wood to swell safely.

Planning and Planting

SHADES OF GREY AND GREEN

Japanese-style gardens make their statements in a more subtle way than many of us are used to, often to stunning effect. Rocks like grey granite and grey gravel and pebbles have a bold yet restrained visual impact, and make a wonderful backdrop for the many shades of green foliage.

PLANNING

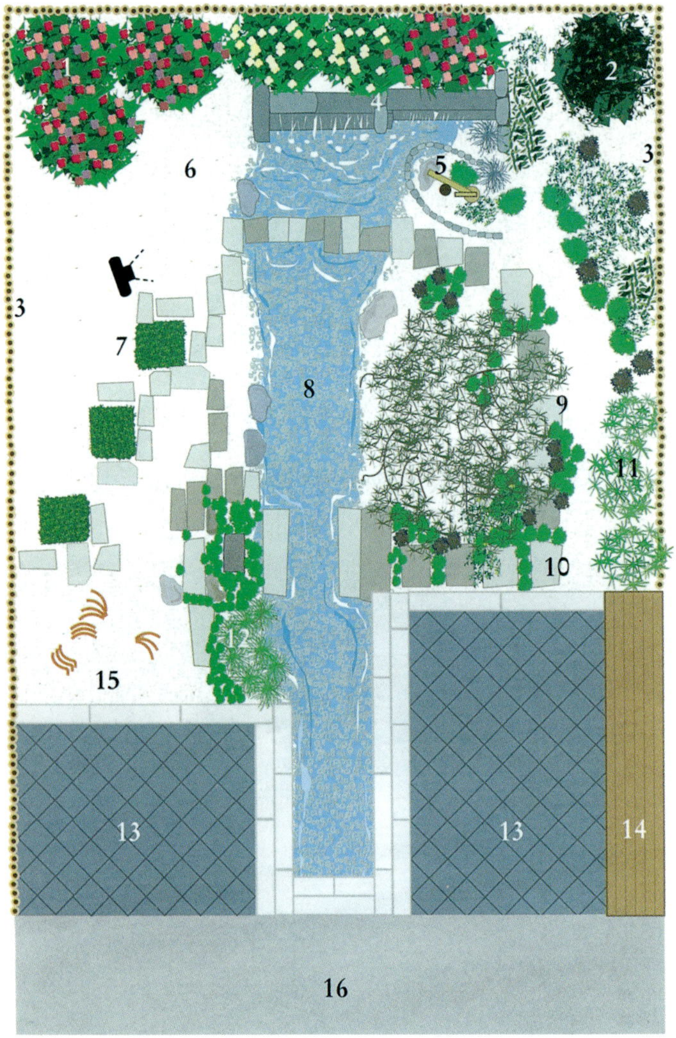

KEY TO PLAN

1 Rhododendron banks
2 Specimen tree
3 Bamboo fence
4 Granite retaining wall incorporating cascade
5 Deer scarer
6 Gravel
7 Clipped box squares
8 Stream with gravel bed
9 Pine tree with ground cover beneath
10 Stepping stones set into gravel
11 Bamboos
12 Dwarf rushes
13 Patio
14 Tea house
15 Terracotta tiles vertically embedded into gravel
16 House

Viewpoint on photograph

Water and rock play their usual important roles in this design, with the "stream" that runs the length of the garden being the central feature and holding the garden together. It draws the eye inward rather than to the boundaries, and the uncluttered open space generates an impression of size in a limited space. These are qualities that make the Japanese style suitable for gardens of all sizes, even small ones.

For a design like this to work properly, it's important to use appropriate materials. It is advisable to have a complex and possibly expensive garden like this constructed professionally, or at least take the advice of specialist suppliers before you start.

PLANTING

■ RIGHT

EASY-TO-MAKE TEA HOUSE This professional-looking tea house was made by an amateur from inexpensive and scrap wood, and shows what can be achieved with a little imagination and enthusiasm.

The side panels were made from a sheet of white material secured behind a home-made trellis constructed from battens, and the other walls were constructed from scrap timber. To make it visually acceptable and light on the inside, rolls of tied reeds were secured in position. The roof "tiles" are easy to make from feather-edged fencing boards, and the flashing around the finial at the top makes it weatherproof. As the wind can swirl into the open front, it is important with this kind of structure to secure the upright posts well into the ground. The seat was made from old railway sleepers (railroad ties), supported on short off-cuts of the same material. A black wood preservative on the exterior timber ensures this home-made structure has a really professional and authentic finish. Although the detailed construction of this kind of feature depends on the materials available, it shows what an excellent project a tea house makes for a do-it-yourself enthusiast.

Planning and Planting

Merging with Nature

Japanese gardens often reflect the natural world and its forces symbolically, but traditionally Japanese gardens are often designed to give a spectacular natural view from a vantage point, perhaps glimpsed as one bends down at a water basin. This garden simply becomes part of the landscape, natural and made-made merging almost imperceptibly. The large central pond is a striking central feature, but will need a regular care and maintenance to keep it looking its best.

KEY TO PLAN

1 To open countryside
2 Bamboo hedge
3 Ornamental grasses and wild plants
4 Timber decking pontoon
5 Pond
6 Bog plants
7 Grasses and sedges
8 Marginal pond plants
9 Japanese lantern on pedestal
10 Bamboo water spout
11 Planted containers
12 Paving of granite setts
13 Gravel
14 House

Viewpoint on photograph

PLANNING

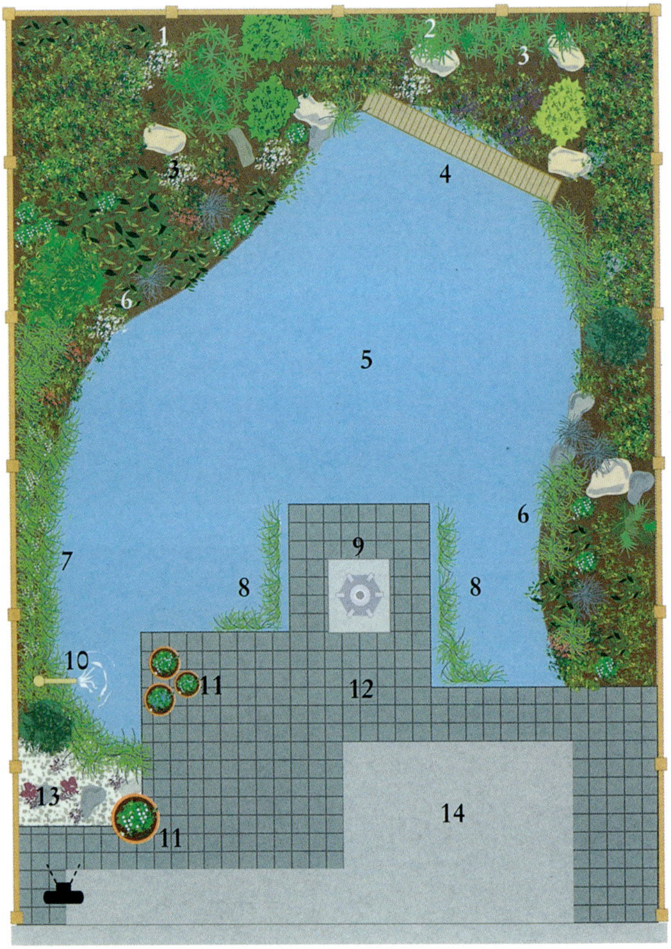

This garden almost merges with the landscape, but the mountains in the distance are in Switzerland, not Japan. Wherever there's a superb view, this kind of garden should appeal.

The whole garden revolves around the pond, the banks of which provide an opportunity for growing plenty of bog plants, blended with grasses and wild plants further back. This enables the garden to merge into the natural setting beyond, with no clear boundary when viewed from the house.

The more structured part of the garden, with its hard edges and rigid shapes, is confined to the area immediately outside the house. It is from this part of the garden that the view will be enjoyed, surrounded by the sights and sounds of nature. The bamboo spout adds to the musical sounds associated with water.

■ RIGHT

HOW TO MAKE A BAMBOO WATER SPOUT A water spout is quite easy to make. You may find it difficult to obtain lengths of bamboo of suitable thickness, but you can buy the spouts ready-made.

Buy a small plastic or glass-fibre reservoir, and sink this into the ground, a little below surface level. Place a small low-voltage pump in the reservoir, standing it on a brick to reduce the risk of the filter clogging with debris. Cover with a piece of strong metal mesh, larger than the reservoir.

Fix a length of flexible hose to the outlet of the pump, long enough to feed through the bamboo. Hollow out the bamboo if necessary, and cut a hole in the upright piece large enough to take the spout as a tight fit. Secure with a waterproof adhesive, then bind and tie black twine around the joint. Thread the hose through the spout and down the main stem, making sure it does not show. Then secure the bottom of the hose to the pump with a Jubilee clip.

Fill the reservoir, then test. It may be necessary to adjust the flow with a valve fitted to the pump – a gentle trickle is often more effective than a torrent. Make sure the water is not thrown beyond the reservoir. If it is, reduce the flow or lay pond liner around the area with the edge covered to channel the water back into the tank.

Cover the strong metal mesh with large pebbles completely. Heap up pebbles around the base of the bamboo to keep it stable.

As water will be lost through evaporation and splashes blown in the wind, check the reservoir periodically. The level must always cover the pump. Use a dipstick to tell you when it requires topping up without having to remove all the pebbles.

WATER PUMP

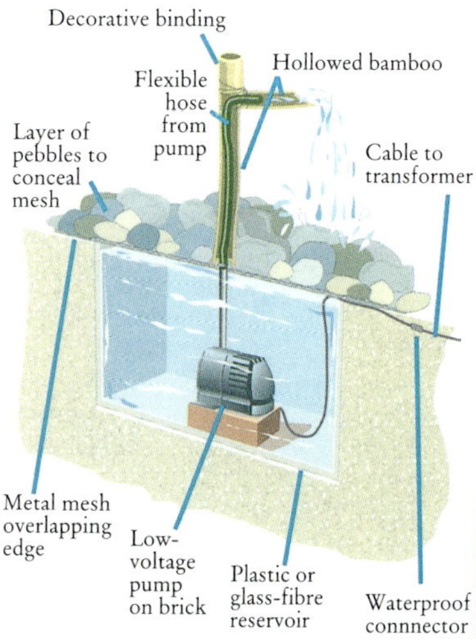

PLANTING

Planning and Planting

FORCES OF NATURE

Not all oriental gardens are gentle and tranquil. Some use rocks and the forces of water in a more dramatic way. This garden uses the drama of rock banks and forceful cascades, as you might find on a wild mountainside.

KEY TO PLAN

1 Decorative trellis
2 Clump of bamboo
3 Shrubs and Japanese acers
4 Japanese lantern
5 Rock bank
6 Cascade
7 Stone bench
8 Rocks and pebbles in gravel
9 Pond
10 Gravel
11 Shrubs
12 Gateway to side garden
13 Slab path set in gravel
14 Japanese acer
15 House

Viewpoint on photograph

PLANNING

Rock features like the one shown here are difficult and expensive to construct, and professional assistance will probably be required, but the effect is stunning by day and enchanting at night if the cascades are illuminated. A pond as large as this will also suit fish such as koi, which bring their own fascinating charm as they come up to feed. They also emphasize the Japanese theme.

To introduce a sense of calm to the rest of the garden, a large area of gravel has been used, together with restrained planting with bamboos and Japanese acers in key focal points.

ALONG THE GARDEN PATH

Paths in Japanese gardens tend to meander rather than lead in straight lines by the shortest route. Stepping stones are popular, as they affect the pace at which you proceed through the garden, as well as adding so much more character than ordinary paving slabs. These are a few ideas for stepping-stone paths.

When choosing stepping stones, an irregular shape is often more appealing than rectangular slabs of stone, but in the interests of safety try to ensure the actual stepping surface is reasonably flat and even.

PLANTING

STEPPING-STONE PATHS

■ ABOVE
Reasonably flat and evenly spaced stones make this an easy path to traverse, but these stones and the curve form an essential part of the design of the garden, and are much more interesting than a strictly functional garden path.

■ ABOVE
These stones project high above the surrounding ground and are irregularly spaced. Exploring this path, which is heavily planted on each side, is a more adventurous experience. It suggests a journey down a river full of obstacles, with dark and mysterious banks.

■ ABOVE
These stepping stones lead enticingly through a border of small shrubs, crossing a ribbon of pebbles that suggest a dried-up river bed. This use of paths makes even a short and simple journey to the bottom of the garden an exciting experience.

Choosing Plants

PLANTS FOR JAPANESE GARDENS

Make your Japanese garden more authentic by using mainly plants that originate in Japan. This is a part of the world that has given us many beautiful plants, and those illustrated below are only a tiny fraction of the wonderful plants available.

GRASSES AND BAMBOOS

Many bamboos are native to Japan and China, but some of them will grow too tall for a small garden. Where space is very limited, try the gold variegated *Pleioblastus auricomus* (*Pleioblastus viridistriatus* or *Arundinaria viridistriata*). Among the grasses native to Japan are several varieties of *Miscanthus sinensis*.

Pleioblastus auricomus is a plant of great beauty. It may also be found under its two synonyms *Pleioblastus viridistriatus* or *Arundinaria viridistriatus*. This gold and green variegated bamboo is compact and slow-growing.

JAPANESE MAPLES

Numerous acers are associated with Japan, but especially *Acer palmatum* and *A. japonicum*. There are many fine varieties of both species. *A. palmatum* makes a smaller tree, so it is a better choice.

There are many varieties of *Acer palmatum;* they all provide an effective display throughout the year and can be relied upon for some truly magnificent autumn colour.

CONIFERS

Among the conifers associated with Japan are some splendid varieties such as *Pinus densiflora*, *P. parviflora* and junipers such as *Juniperus chinensis*.

Pines come in many shapes and sizes, so be sure to choose an appropriate one for your Japanese garden. This is *Pinus densiflora* 'Jane Kluis'.

RHODODENDRONS AND CAMELLIAS

Many rhododendrons (including azaleas) and camellias are native to Japan, or have been bred there. There are large numbers of excellent varieties available. Both plants require an acid soil.

Rhodendrons and azeleas (which are types of rhododendron) are very popular Japanese shrubs, and readily available in garden centres, but they must have an acid soil to grow well. This one is an azelea called 'Ima-shojo' also known as 'Christmas Cheer'.

GROUND COVER

Ground-cover plants are used extensively in Japanese gardens, but of those grown mainly for foliage rather than for flowers, *Pachysandra terminalis* is typical, and it makes a green carpet about 30cm (1ft) high. There is also a variegated form. The grass-like, black-leaved *Ophiopogon planiscapus* 'Nigrescens' is often found in Japanese gardens.

Mosses feature as a ground cover in many genuine Japanese gardens, but these are difficult to cultivate to order in some climates, and not easily bought. *Sagina subulata*, still widely found under its older name of *S. glabra*, is a ground-hugging plant that resembles moss from a distance. There is a golden form called 'Aurea'. It will tolerate some frost but is not hardy in cold areas.

Ophiopogon planiscapus 'Nigrescens' is very distinctive with almost black grass-like foliage. It needs careful positioning in a light area of the garden otherwise it can be lost against a dark background. Use individual plants in juxtaposition with green foliage plants or flowering shrubs or plant it in a bold drift.

HOSTAS

These universally popular plants are widely grown in Japan, and some species are native to that country. There are dozens of readily available species and hybrids that would make excellent herbaceous plants for a Japanese garden, and they look good reflected in water.

Hostas are widely grown in Japan, and they are available in a wide range of leaf forms, many atractively variegated. They are a magnet for slugs; protect frequently.

JAPANESE IRIS

The iris most associated with Japanese water and bog gardens is *Iris ensata*. There are numerous varieties, all of which are attractive with big blooms that resemble a large-flowered clematis.

The Japanese iris is now called *Iris ensata*, but you may still find it sold as *I. kaempferi*. This attractive and popular variety is 'Mandarin'.

CLIMBERS

If you need to use a climber, choose one associated with Japan. The flowering climber *Wisteria floribunda*, sometimes called Japanese wisteria, is surely one of the most magnificent.

For foliage effect, try *Vitis coignetiae*, which has very large leaves with wonderful autumn colour. It looks especially pleasing growing over a bridge, but can be grown very successfully over a large pergola.

Only suitable for a large wall, but magnificent when its leaves turn crimson and scarlet before they fall, is the self-clinging *Parthenocissus tricuspidata*.

For something more unusual, try *Trachelospermum asiaticum*, an evergreen with creamy-white fragrant flowers, positioned against a warm, sunny wall.

Vitis coignetiae is a climber grown for its large leaves, which are especially beautiful in autumn when they turn crimson and scarlet. It is vigorous and can be grown through a tree, but can be confined by pruning if necessary.

ROCK AND WATER

Water has an almost magical attraction, holding a fascination for children and adults alike. Youngsters who show no interest in other garden construction jobs almost invariably become interested once a water feature is involved – a fact that may deter families with very young children. But water does not have to be deep and potentially dangerous: a flow just a fingertip deep along a rill can look cool and refreshing, and a pebble fountain will provide movement and sound with hazards reduced to a minimum. Wall fountains, especially self-contained ones where water flows into a shallow dish that forms part of the feature to be recirculated, make a wonderful focal point and are safe if small children are around.

Rock gardens, which are often combined with a pond, make interesting features in their own right and allow a large number of alpine plants to be grown in a relatively small area. Rock features work best on a naturally sloping site, but they can often be combined effectively with a pond or water course. The soil excavated from the pond can be used to form a raised bank, but be sure to cover any subsoil with prepared topsoil, otherwise the plants will languish.

■ ABOVE
A simple container full of pebbles can make a striking focal point.

■ OPPOSITE
Full of lush tranquillity, this city garden has only a small pond with little space for true water plants, but use has been made of border plants such as hostas and *Iris sibirica*, and the striking water hawthorn (*Aponogeton distachyos*).

Inspirational Ideas

Ponds and "streams" can form the centrepiece of your design. These will attract an amazing diversity of wildlife, and of course can be stocked with fish – which will become very tame if fed regularly during summer months.

■ ABOVE
A raised formal rectangular pond can be constructed from bricks or building blocks, rendered inside and out. It can be waterproofed using special resins or bitumen products obtainable from a pond supplier. The render on the outside can be painted a light colour to create a more attractive feature. Raised ponds are particularly useful for anyone who is disabled or infirm, or who finds bending difficult, as they bring the underwater wonders that much closer to eye level.

■ ABOVE

Imagine this scene as an ordinary lawn with just the borders at each side: pleasant but a trifle boring and without a strong sense of design. A simple pond in isolation would have been equally unappealing because there would be no sense of setting or height, and in winter it could look bleak and uninviting. Setting the pond in a larger circular area, however, with crescents of borders, paths and pebble areas, has given this section of the garden a sense of cohesion and design. The pebbles cleverly merge border and pond, and the sloping beach that drops away into the pond provides easy access for wildlife.

■ LEFT

In this water feature, the water flows directly into a submerged reservoir beneath a strong grille that supports the stone and boulders, making it safe for even small children. Occasionally, genuine millstones are used for this kind of feature, but these are extremely heavy to handle and support, as well as being expensive and difficult to obtain. Fortunately, convincing glass-fibre imitations that look just as good, and which are much easier to handle and install, are available. You can buy them as part of a kit that includes the reservoir, and all you have to provide are the boulders or pebbles.

Although these kinds of feature can be set among plants, they tend to look most effective in a courtyard or dry-looking area as shown here.

Inspirational Ideas

Rock and water features are perfect tools for gardeners fond of strong, bold statements of shape and form. They also offer the opportunity for growing a range of colourful water and bog plants.

■ BELOW
Making use of the strong textures of water and slate, this Japanese-style garden is a study in shape and form. Although this kind of water feature may not appeal to a plant-lover – the only water plants apart from a water lily are water hyacinths (*Eichhornia crassipes*), both of which will die down in winter – it will appeal to someone whose sense of design is stronger than their love of plants and bright flowers.

■ LEFT
Formal ponds can be pleasing but water can also be used in a natural way. The shape and dense planting around the edge of this pond create the illusion that it is a natural part of the landscape. Although close to the boundary fence, taking the pond beneath a bridge gives the illusion of water flowing far beyond. Bridges themselves are almost always focal points, and they usually entice visitors to walk over them to explore the garden on the other side. A pond or "stream" provides the justification for building a bridge.

■ RIGHT
A pond may not always be appropriate, but a small running-water feature like this one can have just as much impact. In this design, the circular basins reflect the curves in other parts of the garden, and although it would have made a pleasing feature anywhere, its impact is that much stronger because it clearly looks part of an overall design.

Know-how

FORMAL PERFECTION

Water features can easily be added to an existing garden, but they will look more integrated if you plan for them early on in the design process. Rock gardens are more difficult to add at a late stage without their looking like a very artificial mound of earth, and they almost always work best when landscaped into the basic garden plan.

If you want fish and flowers in your pond, choose an open site that will receive sun for at least half the day if possible, and is away from overhanging deciduous trees unless you are prepared to net the pond and clear the leaves from the water to prevent pollution. The majority of rock plants also require a sunny position.

Formal ponds, with their regular outlines and geometric shapes, look best in gardens designed to a rigid grid where the same lines are carried through to other parts of the garden. They offer less scope for pondside planting and associated bog areas than informal ponds do, but provide plenty of scope for aquatic plants and fish.

■ BELOW

BREAKING UP PAVING Although this pond is relatively small, it makes an impact because it forms a focal point in a strongly geometric design. Water can be a vital element in counteracting the potential harshness of a large amount of paving. The wall mask ensures the area will remain attractive even when the pond plants have died back.
DESIGN TIP *To avoid an expanse of paving appearing monotonous, use materials of a contrasting colour to pick out a design or to emphasize a change of level. Here, bricks and terracotta tiles have been used to provide contrast and to add a touch of colour to a large area of paving.*

■ LEFT

LONG AND FORMAL Formality is the essence of this style of garden, and water is the central feature around which the garden has been designed. It is essentially a garden for a warm climate, or at least where the illusion of a warm-climate garden is required, but a variation on this style of gardening could make a stunning town garden.
DESIGN TIP *Where water is a major feature, always consider how the garden will look in winter. Pumps will have to be turned off in very cold climates, and a pond's frozen surface can look bleak. To compensate, include plenty of evergreens and make lavish use of decorative pots and ornaments around the water feature.*

■ BELOW

UNUSUAL SHAPES Formal ponds are practical for even a small front garden, and the strong design and impressive planting in this one ensure it will be pleasing all the year round. The introduction of a stepping platform to connect the two ponds ensures they link the garden rather than divide it.

DESIGN TIP *If the visual aspects of gravel appeal but you are worried about the loose stones being kicked around on a path that is used frequently, consider bonded gravel, which has been used on these paths. The small stones are bonded to a resin instead of being laid loose. The effect is equally as attractive as loose gravel.*

■ ABOVE

CASCADES A garden created on a gentle slope provides scope for cascades and tumbling water, and in this garden the formal water chute and rectangular pond reflect the overall design, with its straight lines and right angles.

DESIGN TIP *Allow the overall design of the garden to dictate the style of pond you create. In this garden, with its dominant straight lines, an informal wildlife pond with meandering outline and shallow beaches around the edge would have looked incongruous.*

RECTANGULAR PONDS

Rectangular ponds can be constructed with a liner, but this involves pleating it at the corners, which can look unattractive unless masked by careful planting. It is possible to have box-welded liners made by specialist suppliers, otherwise render a concrete or building-block pond and waterproof it with a resin or bitumen-based product manufactured for the purpose.

Know-how

NATURAL INFORMALITY

Informal ponds are usually easier to construct than formal ones and are preferred by wildlife because access to the water is usually easier and the surrounding planting provides useful shelter. Informal ponds also provide an excuse to introduce a bog garden.

■ LEFT

NATURAL POND This garden is completely informal, yet it has a strong sense of design and structure, which the bridge and trellis help to emphasize. The irregular informal shape and rocks give the illusion of a natural pond, and the lush planting helps to mask neighbouring gardens.

DESIGN TIP *An informal pond can be used to encourage a sense of exploration and may make your garden seem larger than it really is. Having access around all sides, or a bridge linking paths, will appear intriguing.*

■ RIGHT

PEBBLES This kind of natural-looking water course can be created easily with a liner, the edge of which can be well hidden by beach pebbles. With this kind of covering, a drop in water level through evaporation will not be noticeable as there is no obvious water line. It must flow into a deep area at the end, however, so that the submerged pump remains covered.

DESIGN TIP *Don't think only in terms of fish ponds when introducing water. Features like this one can be even more effective if you want to create the illusion of a wild or natural garden. They will still attract lots of wildlife which will come to the garden to drink and bathe.*

CLEAR WATER

Even the most well-designed pond will be unattractive if the water is green. Most ponds turn green for a few days or weeks each year, usually in spring and early summer when the water is warming up, but the aquatic plants are not sufficiently grown to reduce the amount of sunlight reaching the water. A pond that remains green for long periods requires treatment.

Green water is caused by millions of free-floating algae, which feed on nutrients in the water, multiplying rapidly in warm, sunlit water. Avoid adding nutrient-rich soil to the pond, and do not use ordinary fertilizer on pond plants.

There are chemical controls of various kinds, but they vary in effectiveness, their effect can be short-lived, and the dead algae can cause problems with falling oxygen levels as they decay (which may kill fish). The most satisfactory way to deal with green water is to install a UV (ultra-violet) clarifier. This will require a power supply for the special lamp and a pump to circulate the water. Provided you choose a unit powerful enough for the capacity of your pond (consult your supplier), the water should begin to clear within days.

■ ABOVE

STREAM-FED POND Regular clearing and planting with a range of water lilies and other plants has transformed this natural stream-fed pond into a wonderful garden feature. The banks have been planted for year-round interest, and ornaments provide useful focal points in winter when most of the vegetation has died down.

DESIGN TIP *Don't forget to incorporate a few garden seats, even in an informal garden. You will get more out of your garden if there's somewhere to sit and relax. Here, the addition of a couple of colourful cushions has transformed an ordinary garden bench into a comfortable focal point from which to view your garden.*

■ RIGHT

CLOSE TO THE HOUSE This pond has been taken up to the conservatory, then a deck has been built out over the water. Pondlife, especially the fish, can be enjoyed from the deck on a sunny day and from the conservatory when the weather is less inviting.

DESIGN TIP *Use plants to create privacy and a sense of seclusion. Here the dense planting masks a busy road.*

Know-how

MOVING WATER

Still water brings calm and tranquillity to a garden, but sometimes a sense of vibrancy and life is needed. A tumbling "stream" introduces an authentic feeling of the wild to a garden, but sound and movement can be created with equal effect by a tinkling fountain, a tumbling cascade or a simple water spout fixed to a wall. Whichever you choose, moving water is almost certain to become one of the garden's most exciting focal points.

■ RIGHT

WATER STAIRS Although an ambitious project, a flight of water stairs can be attention-grabbing as well as musical. Building them on a curve makes the most of the limited space available, and in this case the feature makes a splendid centrepiece for the garden.

DESIGN TIP *Don't be put off by an ambitious project simply because you lack construction skills. Hire a contractor to do the building to your own specific designs.*

THINK ABOUT FLOW

Whether installing a cascade or a fountain, it's important to choose a pump with an appropriate flow rate (which is measured in gallons or litres an hour). This is a complex area as it also depends on whether the same pump has to share the operation of a biological filter, or perhaps another cascade or fountain. Go to a reputable water garden specialist for advice. Some will even allow you to exchange the pump if it does not do the job.

Large flows will require a high-voltage pump, but most small fountains operate satisfactorily from a low-voltage pump.

■ LEFT

SMALL FOUNTAIN Without moving water, even well-designed small patio ponds may lack impact. A fountain will add to the formal atmosphere, and in a small garden the sound will not be as potentially overpowering as that from a cascade.

DESIGN TIP *Corners can be difficult areas to fill creatively, but a corner pond with an attractive fountain will make excellent use of otherwise wasted space.*

■ OPPOSITE

MOORLAND STREAM It takes years of experience and a lot of effort to construct a moorland stream to this standard, including a knowledge of the natural landscape and the mechanics and flow rates of pumps, but a more modest version is within the scope of an enthusiastic amateur.

DESIGN TIP *Unless your garden is on a natural slope, keep the fall from top to bottom of the "stream" relatively modest. This will avoid too much earth-moving and reduce the need to manhandle heavy rocks, yet the effect can be just as stunning as cascades with large falls.*

■ RIGHT

WALL FOUNTAIN A wall fountain can transform any backyard or courtyard wall. A trickling spout of water will add to the visual and auditory pleasures of the garden. This one is particularly ornate, but in an area where there may not be much else to arrest the attention, being bold can bring rich rewards.

DESIGN TIP *Bear in mind that the higher the position of the water spout above the receptacle, the louder the sound will be. In a confined area, a strong flow from a height could become irritating for you or your neighbours. Fortunately, most pumps have a flow adjuster.*

Know-how

ON THE ROCKS

Rockwork can be difficult to work into a garden plan, and will be much easier on a sloping site than on a flat one. Don't think only of traditional rock garden banks, however, as rock outcrop beds can be equally pleasing and are much easier to construct in gardens without a natural slope.

PEAKS AND TROUGHS

Rock gardens are at their best in spring, and by comparison they can seem rather dull at other times of the year. Do not allow this commonly cited drawback to deter you from using rock features. By choosing plants that flower at different seasons, and including evergreens and winter-flowering bulbs for the bleakest months, a rock garden can be packed with interest every month of the year.

Try using annuals to fill in any gaps for the summer, even if they are not strictly alpines, but make sure they don't seed readily and thereby become a nuisance in future seasons.

■ ABOVE LEFT

ROCKERY BORDER An artificial mound in a flat garden does not always work as well as this example, especially if the mound is low and only small pieces of rock are used. This mound is substantial enough to make a positive feature, and it has plenty of evergreens and winter-flowering heathers to make it attractive the year round.
DESIGN TIP *To prevent a rockery from looking stark in winter, be sure to plant sufficient evergreens as well as alpines in this kind of rock garden.*

■ LEFT

SLOPING ROCK GARDEN A gentle slope like this makes an ideal natural-looking rock garden. A rock garden of this size will accommodate a large number of plants and is ideal for anyone who wants to specialize in alpines. A path through the rocks is perfect for viewing these small plants close up.
DESIGN TIP *The natural effect would have been spoilt if the steps had run up through the centre in a straight line. A staggered or meandering path is less obtrusive, and is likely to be less tiring to climb than one that goes straight up by the shortest route.*

■ ABOVE

ROCKY BANKS Rock and water make happy partners, and this weathered limestone is especially attractive. This garden is on the grand scale, but a smaller version could be constructed for a more modestly sized garden.

DESIGN TIP *Follow any natural contours in the ground wherever possible to minimize the amount of earth-moving required.*

■ LEFT

FEATURE ROCKERY This rock feature could be incorporated into most informal designs. It's simply a bed cut into the lawn, and even a small area like this can be densely planted. The rock is tufa, a soft, porous stone into which planting holes can be easily drilled if necessary.

DESIGN TIP *Keep the height of a rock bed in proportion to its size. A small bed should have only a low mound, a large bed can be higher. If you plant densely, as has been done in this rock feature, height is relatively unimportant.*

Planning and Planting

CHANGING LEVEL

Rock gardens are sometimes used as a design solution for a steep slope, where rock outcrops can look very convincing. If the slope is more gentle and the setting inappropriate for a large conventional rock garden, it may be possible to make the most of a raised rock bed. This one forms a natural break between a level upper lawn and a larger sloping lawn that leads to the rest of the garden.

KEY TO PLAN

1 Specimen tree
2 Hedge
3 Mixed border
4 Specimen shrubs
5 Outbuilding
6 Slope to lower lawn
7 Path
8 Rhododendrons
9 Lawn
10 Raised rock bed
11 To side garden
12 Patio of crazy paving
13 Crazy paving
14 Small specimen tree
15 Steps
16 Dwarf shrubs
17 Path around house
18 House
← Direction of steps and slope down
Viewpoint on photograph
× Garden continues

PLANNING

SLOPING GARDENS

Even gently sloping gardens pose the problem of how to integrate the various levels. Steep gardens are often terraced, although this is a labour-intensive and often expensive option. Where the height difference is small enough to make mowing a safe and practical routine, a gently sloping lawn is a sensible option. Here, a flat area of patio and lawn has been created at the front of the house, with the lawn falling away beyond the rock bed.

Rock beds make pleasing features, but they look best where they have a purpose. Here, the rock bed acts as a divider, with the ground falling away more on one side than the other.

MAKING A ROCK GARDEN

A raised rock bed like this one can be made on a level site if necessary, or you could build one at the back of a pond using the excavated soil for the basic mound. In either case good fertile soil should be used for the planting areas. Locally quarried rocks are usually cheaper and blend in with the area.

PLANTING

HOW TO MAKE A ROCK GARDEN

1 Build up soil to form a raised area of appropriate size. Always ensure there is a space between the soil and any fence or wall, and be careful not to bridge any damp-proof course in nearby brickwork.

2 Mix together equal parts of soil, coarse grit and peat and spread evenly over the mound. Lay the first rocks at the base, trying to keep the strata running in the same direction.

3 Position the next row of rocks. Use rollers and levers to move them. Ensure that the sides all slope inwards, and make the top reasonably flat rather than building it into a pinnacle.

4 Position the plants. As each layer is built up, add more of the soil mixture, and consolidate it around the rocks. Finish by covering the exposed soil with a thin layer of horticultural grit, to improve the appearance.

Planning and Planting

FOCUS ON CIRCLES

Circular themes are almost always distinctive, and they make striking gardens even with minimal planting. This kind of garden depends very much on structure for impact, and the focal point here is a fantastic water feature that uses both sight and sound to command attention.

PLANNING

KEY TO PLAN

1 Specimen tree
2 Ground-cover plants
3 Raised bed
4 Brick paving
5 Raised pool
6 Cascade
7 Dwarf shrubs
8 Specimen shrub
9 House

Viewpoint on photograph

Circular themes can make use of full circles or crescents and arcs, sometimes overlapping as shown here. The three corner beds make use of quadrants. There's a sense of symmetry about this kind of garden, but simple mirror images could make it a little too predictable, and another cascade opposite this one would probably detract from the impact. The sound of two tumbling sheets of water might also cross the threshold between being pleasant and irritating.

Although there are plenty of pots in this design, little other maintenance is required so it is not especially labour-intensive. Pots of seasonal plants help to provide that vital dash of colour.

The choice of paving and the bricks used for the raised beds is also important in a garden like this. Here colours and textures have been chosen that blend together well, but if bricks and paving had been chosen with colours that did not harmonize, the overall effect might have been much less pleasing.

PLANTING

■ RIGHT

WALL MASKS AND SPOUTS

This kind of cascade is really a job for a professional or very experienced amateur, but it is possible to create a water spout on a more modest scale. A high wall isn't necessary, as a gentle flow with a drop of 60–90cm (2–3ft) may sound more musical than a torrent from a high spout. Unless the feature is large, a low-voltage pump should be adequate, but choose one with a flow adjuster so that you have more control.

Metal pipework can be used, but plastic pipes are perfectly adequate. The difficulty lies in concealing pipes. Whenever possible, drill a hole through the wall and run the pipework up the back, bringing it back through the wall at the appropriate height. Disguise any unsightly pipes with an evergreen climber, such as ivy.

CROSS-SECTION OF A WALL MASK OR SPOUT

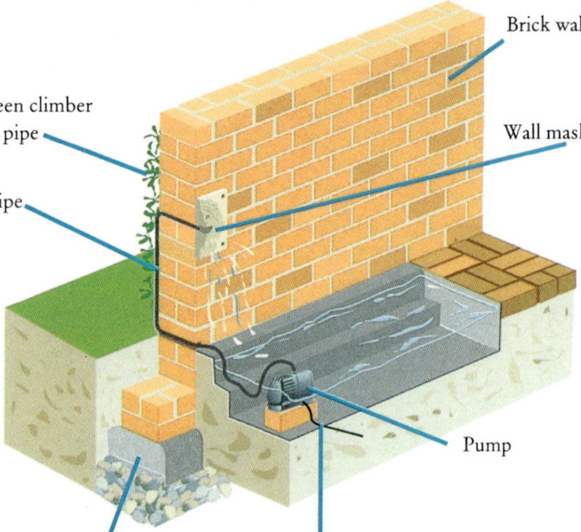

Planning and Planting

Classic Romance

With a little imagination you can bring a dream garden with classic connotations to life, even in a small town garden. All you need are some materials from a company specializing in reclaimed demolition materials and a vivid imagination.

PLANNING

KEY TO PLAN

1 Yew hedge
2 Shrubs and climbers
3 Specimen shrub
4 "Staircase" cascade
5 Plants and paving set in gravel
6 Formal pond
7 Herbaceous border
8 Lawn
9 Grass access strip to rear of border
10 Reclaimed classical pillar and plinth
11 House
Viewpoint on photograph

This is a garden for the romantic with a love of traditional gardens and a classical style. The "staircase" cascade forms the focal point, and it sets the tone for this part of the garden. Because it has been constructed mainly from reclaimed building materials from old houses, it has a timeless quality that can transform a town garden into a romantic piece of the past. The clever use of an old pillar, positioned so that it looks as though it fell from its pedestal many years ago, creates a wonderful sense of atmosphere.

Good old-fashioned herbaceous borders flanking the lawn reflect a formal style of gardening once popular, and the traditional yew hedges hold the two parts of the garden together.

When using reclaimed materials, it's best to have a flexible approach. Be prepared to modify your plans according to the materials you can obtain.

PLANTING

■ BELOW

CONSTRUCTING WATER STAIRS

The actual method of construction will depend on the materials used and the size of the feature, but the same principles can be applied to most forms of water stairs.

After excavating the pond area, form a consolidated slope of soil at an appropriate angle, taking into account the height of each step. On a natural slope you may only have to cut into the bank; on a flat site it will be necessary to build it up and compact the ground.

Lay the pond liner first. Then lay a sheet of liner along the slope, leaving enough material to fold up at the sides to ensure a watertight channel. Use a liner underlay to protect it from stones, and it is worth using an extra layer of liner as access, for repairs will be difficult once construction is finished.

Lay a concrete pad on the bottom of the pond to support the brick wall. Place a piece of spare liner over the bottom of the pond, folded over a couple of times, then construct a brick support wall to the height of the first riser.

Bed the first step on mortar, ensuring it has a slight slope forwards, but is level from left to right. Lay each of the other steps in the same way. At the top, make a chamber a couple of bricks high into which the return hose can be fed. Cover this with another slab or stone.

Ensure the liner comes up to the level of each step at the sides – it will be necessary to trim it to size. Be careful not to trim too short, and if possible leave it long enough to tuck into the soil mounded against each side. Plant lavishly with evergreens to hide the edges and any trace of the liner.

Once the mortar is completely dried, connect the pump and check for any leaks. A powerful pump will be required to ensure a fast flow of water over the edge of each lip. Consult an aquatic specialist for advice about the flow requirements before you buy. Also check on hose sizes and fittings. If in doubt, go for a larger size, as you can always turn down the flow if necessary.

CROSS-SECTION OF WATER STAIRS

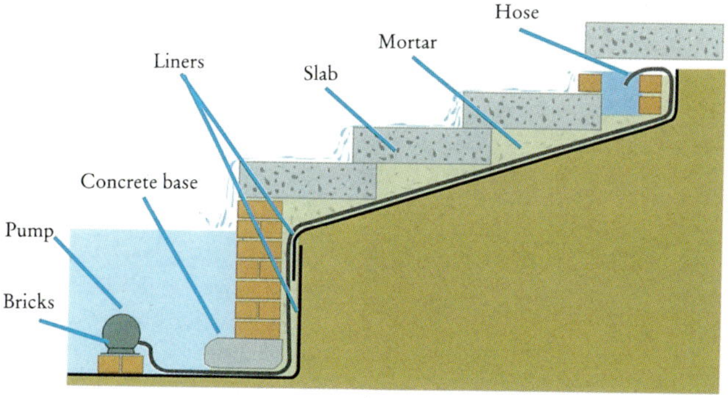

Planning and Planting

MODERN IMAGE

Instead of thinking of ponds and cascades when designing with water in mind, try visualizing water as a texture, rather like an area of paving or gravel. This garden shows how smart water can look in a modern setting. Don't be afraid to use water imaginatively: although the amount used in this garden is small, it's one of the most interesting and creative features in an already fascinating and exciting garden.

KEY TO PLAN

1 Bed with dwarf shrubs and border plants
2 Pergola with climbers over
3 Paving
4 Water
5 Raised bed under pergola
6 Island bed
7 Lawn
8 Small trees
9 Fern bed
10 Moisture-loving plants in pebbled planting bed
11 Steps
12 Grass strip
13 Ornamental stone feature
14 House

↑ Direction of steps down

Viewpoint on photograph

PLANNING

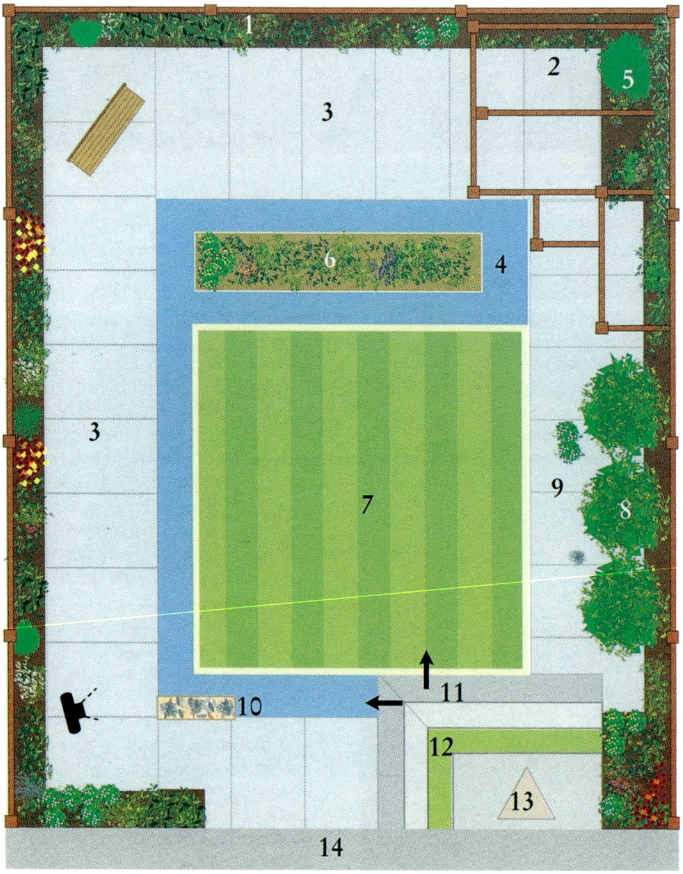

As this garden makes the most of shapes and textures, it is likely to appeal to someone who loves to explore design ideas rather than to a plant enthusiast. Apart from the lawn, which requires regular cutting, it's also very low-maintenance. The water-framed lawn is perhaps the main focal point, so it's essential that the grass is kept short and looking lush, and care must be taken not to allow grass clippings to fall into the watery surround.

Ordinary paving slabs could have been used for economy, but the choice of a natural stone such as slate gives it a more sophisticated appearance and a stronger sense of design. Where paving is a dominant feature in a garden, it is worth spending time and money to select the most suitable material.

Where natural stone forms an important part of the design, it is worth visiting a few stone merchants or quarries to discuss your requirements in detail. They may be able to advise and perhaps assist with the selection and cutting of the stone.

PLANTING

■ RIGHT

PERGOLA POSSIBILITIES Although rustic poles are often used for rose pergolas, in design terms a sawn timber (lumber) pergola is a better choice. It will also be able to support heavy climbers such as wisterias. Use preservative-treated wood (but avoid using creosote if planting soon after erection), and treat cut surfaces before assembling. Fix the uprights securely, setting them in concrete or securing them in post spikes, always using a spirit level to check verticals.

Assemble the overhead sections "dry" on the ground to make sure the joints all fit well, but don't nail them yet. Halving joints are suitable for the overhead beams, but the lower halves will have to be nailed to the uprights before the top halves are assembled.

The halving joints are best screwed together, but drill starter holes while the assembly is on the ground, as it will be difficult to drill at a height.

If the pergola is long, overhead beams will have to be joined, which should be done over a post. Use galvanized nails or zinc-plated screws.

FIXING A POST

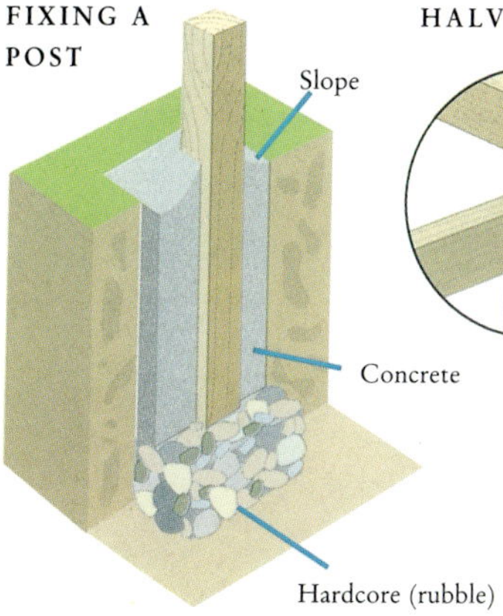

HALVING JOINT

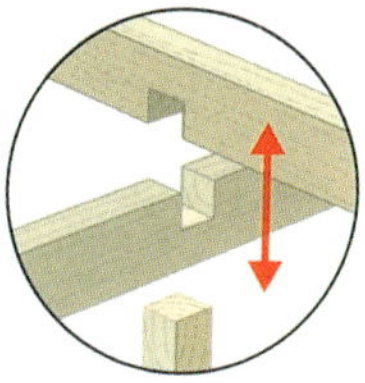

JOINING BEAMS

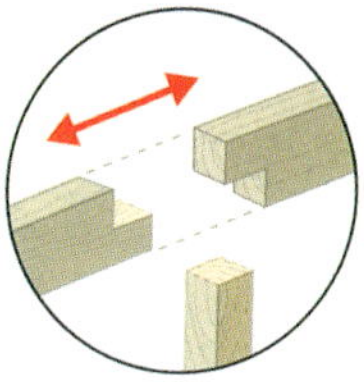

Planning and Planting

NATURAL SLOPE

Gardens with a gentle slope offer an ideal opportunity for constructing a natural-looking rock and water feature, with perhaps a stream and a small cascade. For ease of construction, these features may have to follow the natural contours of the site, and this may influence your design.

KEY TO PLAN

1 Garden bench
2 Lawn
3 Rock garden
4 Slope and step
5 Pond
6 Cascade
7 Stream
8 Mixed border
9 Header pool
10 Dwarf conifer
11 Patio
12 Plants in containers
13 House
↑ Direction of steps down
Viewpoint on photograph

PLANNING

A naturally sloping garden is ideal for a rock and water feature, but your design will be determined largely by the slope and profile of the ground. Where practical, choose a rock type found in your locality: it will look more natural, and it will almost certainly be cheaper than rock that has been transported over long distances.

Planting plans are difficult to devise for a rocky slope, so concentrate on a few key plants, such as dwarf conifers and dwarf evergreen shrubs. The smaller rock plants are usually best planted intuitively, choosing subjects that fit both the space available and the setting.

A meandering path is always more interesting than a straight one, and a combination of sloping path and a few steps changes the pace and makes the slope easier to cope with.

Seating also requires careful thought. It's worth providing a refuge large enough to take a seat part-way down to help those who find slopes difficult. Choosing a position that has an attractive view of the garden, or of the scene beyond, will encourage more use of the seat.

PLANTING

■ RIGHT

MAKING A ROCK STREAM

A stream can be constructed from a series of separate long, narrow ponds, with the liners overlapped and sealed where the levels change.

Use a good-quality liner over a proper liner underlay, and make small concrete slabs at each side of the level changes on which to bed suitable rocks. Fold over a piece of spare liner to form an extra cushion under the concrete pad.

The stream is made watertight at the cascades by overlapping the liner from the higher pond over that from the lower (see illustration opposite). This should prevent water escaping, but as an additional precaution seal the overlaps with special tape or adhesive. Consult your aquatic supplier regarding materials, as it depends on the type of liner used.

Bed the rocks firmly on each side of the cascade on mortar to ensure they are stable. You may, however, first want to have a test run, then drain the water to make any adjustments. An aquatic specialist should be able to advise on a suitable pump – it will need to be powerful to maintain a fast flow over a wide lip. A header pool is used at the top, fed by a return hose from the pump.

CROSS-SECTION OF A ROCK STREAM

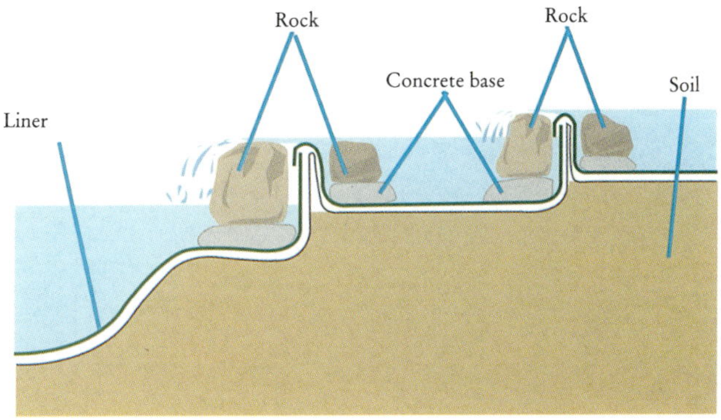

Planning and Planting

TRADITIONAL FORMALITY

Large gardens normally require large ponds to have any impact, but by creating a formal area to frame a small formal pond it's still possible to create a big impact.

Very large gardens are often difficult to design, especially if you want to introduce a formal style. Here the problems have been overcome by using an area near the house for a lawn, with a low clipped hedge to mark the boundary between the formal and informal areas. Within this formal part of the garden an enclosed mini-garden has been introduced with a central pond.

The disparate parts of the garden have been linked by the path layout within the enclosed formal garden. One of the main paths is aligned at right angles to the house so this is the feature you see as you leave the house. The other main path swings around the pool to leave in a direct line with the pergola in the corner of the lawn.

PLANNING

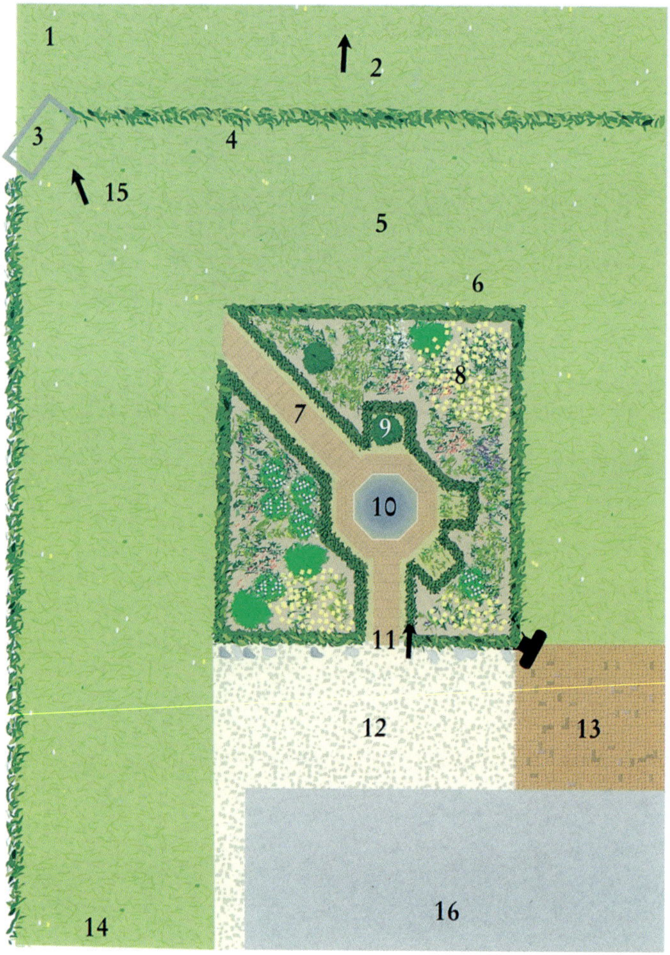

KEY TO PLAN

1 Woodland garden
2 Slope to woodland garden
3 Pergola over steps down bank to woodland garden
4 Low hedge
5 Lawn
6 Dwarf perimeter hedge
7 Brick path
8 Mixed formal planting
9 Dwarf box hedge
10 Formal pond
11 Step
12 Gravel
13 Brick patio
14 Garden continues
15 Slope to pergola
16 House

↑ Direction of slope/step down

Viewpoint on photograph

AN ALPINE WHEEL

If you have small children, you may prefer an alternative to the central circular pond in this design. Instead, you could build a fragrant herb wheel or a pretty alpine wheel. You will need: two lengths of wood, string, spade, garden compost and fertilizer, an old drain cover, bricks, fine gravel, pebbles and slates for decoration, and of course a selection of alpines.

MAKING AN ALPINE WHEEL

1 Dig over the soil and enrich with fertilizer and garden compost. Tie a piece of wood at each end of a piece of string the length of the radius. While someone holds the central peg, scribe the circle while keeping the string taut. Lay bricks around the circumference and to form the spokes of the wheel.

2 Position the plants on the wheel while still in their pots, to check the spacing, then plant. Plant each section of the wheel with a different variety so that, as they grow, they will help to define the design. A contrast of colours and textures of leaves will look most effective.

3 Cover the surface of exposed soil with gravel, then add decorative pebbles and slates to improve the appearance while the plants grow to their full potential.

Choosing Plants

Water and Rock Plants

Choosing water and rock plants can be bewildering: there are always more desirable plants to grow than there's space for. For a balanced pond, it's important to choose some submerged oxygenators even though they have little visual appeal, as well as deep-water plants such as water lilies to provide vital foliage cover over part of the surface. However, it's among the marginal plants (those planted in shallow water at the edge) and bog plants for wet ground outside the pond that the greatest variety can be found.

WATER LILIES

It's important to select suitable varieties. Some of the most vigorous ones are suitable only for lakes and very large ponds, while others are miniatures suitable for water features in sinks and tubs. If in doubt, always check with your supplier. Good ones for a small pond are 'Froebeli' (red) and 'Rose Arey' (pink). For medium-sized ponds, suitable varieties include 'Amabilis' (pink), 'Attraction', 'Laydeckeri Purpurata' (red) and 'Marliacea Chromatella' (yellow).

Nymphaea 'Amabilis' is one of many beautiful water lilies suitable for a medium-sized pond. Although water lilies are relatively expensive to buy, they will provide years of pleasure.

OTHER PLANTS FOR DEEP WATER

So-called deep-water plants are grown with about 30cm (1ft) or more of water above their crowns, although most will grow in water more than twice this depth. Water lilies are the best-known deep-water aquatics, but try the water hawthorn (*Aponogeton distachyos*), which has slightly fragrant white flowers that bloom from spring to autumn. It can be rampant if planted directly in mud at the bottom of the pond, but is suitable for any pond if planted in a container.

Aponogeton distachyos, the water hawthorn, is an amazing water plant that flowers from spring or early summer right through until ice covers the surface of the pond. Its white flowers are slightly fragrant.

PLANTS FOR SHALLOW MARGINS

"Marginal" plants are grown with only a few centimetres of water above their crowns. They are often planted on special marginal shelves around the edge of the pond, about 23cm (9in) below the water. Try *Acorus gramineus* 'Variegatus', *Caltha palustris* (marsh marigold), *Pontederia cordata* (pickerel weed) and *Veronica beccabunga* (brooklime).

Acorus gramineus 'Variegatus' can be grown with an inch or so of water above the soil, and has the merit of being semi-evergreen. The flowers are insignificant and it is grown for foliage effect.

OXYGENATING PLANTS

Few of these submerged plants enhance the pond visually, but they are invaluable for the health of the pond if you keep fish. They

Myriophyllum aquaticum is one of the most attractive oxygenating plants because it produces some of its feathery foliage above the water. It's also useful for masking off the edge of the pond.

increase the oxygen content of the water when the fish most need it, and by absorbing nutrients they may also help to control the algae that cause green water.

Lagarosiphon major (also known as *Elodea crispa*) is one of the best known but it's a rampant grower and may have to be thinned out periodically. The water milfoils or myriophyllums are some of the most attractive oxygenators because much of their feathery growth rises above the surface.

BOG PLANTS

Bog plants grow in mud or wet soil that does not dry out but is not permanently submerged. Some will also survive in normal border soil, others will soon die if the ground dries out. Many primulas, such as *Primula japonica* and *P. bulleyana*, make excellent bog plants, but the skunk cabbage (*Lysichiton americanus*), with its strange yellow spathes, is one of the most spectacular in spring.

Primula bulleyana is one of several excellent bog species, especially beautiful when planted in drifts to maximize the full impact of the flowers when they come out in spring. It needs damp soil to thrive.

EASY ALPINES

Some of the easiest alpines, such as aubrieta and *Alyssum saxatile* (now more correctly called *Aurinia saxatilis*), are also the most rampant. Plant them for a bright display, but not in close proximity to choice but less rampant growers. Snow-in-summer (*Cerastium tomentosum*) falls into the same category. The rock phloxes *Phlox subulata* and *P. douglasii*, along with many of the spring-flowering saxifrages, are examples of rock plants that make a bold show even from a distance but are not so invasive.

Phlox douglasii varieties produce sheets of colour in the rock garden in spring. This variety is 'Daniel's Cushion'. Although these plants form a carpet of growth, they are easy to control.

CHOICE ALPINES

There are so many choice alpines, both widely available and uncommon, that any selection must reflect personal preferences. Two that are definitely worth including, not only for their deep blue colour but also because they flower after the main flush of spring, are *Gentiana septemfida* (mid- to late summer) and *G. sino-ornata* (early to mid-autumn).

Gentiana septemfida is especially useful for colour in the rock garden in late summer and, since the foliage is evergreen, provides some winter interest too. It requires a humus-rich soil to do really well.

DWARF CONIFERS

Not everyone appreciates dwarf conifers and in a very small rock garden they may look out of place. However, they give it structure and interest in winter. One that's small enough even for an alpine trough is *Juniperus communis* 'Compressa', which makes a miniature column of grey-green foliage. If there's space, some of the larger ones are bright, including *J. communis* 'Depressa Aurea' and *Thuja orientalis* 'Aurea Nana'.

Juniperus communis 'Compressa' is one of the best dwarf conifers for a rock garden. It is relatively slow growing and even an old plant is unlikely to exceed about 75cm (2½ft) in height.

GARDENING FOR WILDLIFE

For many of us, wildlife such as birds and butterflies add immeasurably to the delights of gardening, bringing not only colour and beauty but birdsong too. Even the less spectacular wildlife, like insects and beetles, plays a vital role in pollinating flowers and fruit, and many act as a natural form of pest control.

Gardens designed purely with wildlife in mind can look uninspiring – even weedy if you encourage butterfly food plants such as nettles. The long grass and seeding wild flowers that attract such a diversity of wildlife may not be your idea of a neat garden. With compromise, however, it is possible to have the best of both worlds, especially if you give over only part of the garden to the wild flowers and long grass, and incorporate water features and plenty of shrubs and evergreen climbers in the more conventional parts of the garden, with flower borders that also include insect-attracting plants.

■ ABOVE
A birdbath or feeder is one of the simplest ways to attract wildlife.

■ OPPOSITE
An unremarkable garden in terms of size and shape has become a refuge for local wildlife. Borders densely planted with shrubs, and a few trees, offer shelter for many kinds of insects and animals as well as birds.

INSPIRATIONAL IDEAS

Simple structures, like nesting boxes and bird tables or feeding nets, will encourage plenty of birds, and even the compost heap and wood pile may afford the shelter and protection that many overwintering animals and insects require.

■ ABOVE
Wildlife will be attracted to a garden with lots of trees, shrubs and ground-cover plants, which will provide hiding places for birds, insects and other wildlife. Insects are an important link in the food chain and will in turn attract plenty of birds to the garden.

■ ABOVE
Anyone lucky enough to garden in the countryside starts off at an advantage, and often it is sufficient to grow plenty of cottage-garden plants and to provide sufficient cover and a supply of water, to encourage wildlife into your garden.

■ RIGHT
A wildlife haven can be created even in a very small front garden. Here, a bog garden has been built in place of a border, which has deliberately been left rather wild, with a small pond at the end. This attracts not only frogs, toads, newts, and spectacular dragonflies and damsel-flies, but a whole range of insects and small mammals. Such refuges are really worthwhile in small town gardens where natural habitats are increasingly under threat.

INSPIRATIONAL IDEAS

Gardening with wildlife in mind does not necessarily mean a wild-looking garden, just a balance of features that in total make your garden a nature-friendly place. Set aside parts of the garden for wildlife so you can have the best of both worlds.

■ ABOVE
A suburban or town garden can support a surprising amount of wildlife if it is planned with a good mix of trees, shrubs and open space. Putting out food for birds and other local wildlife, and planting flowers that attract butterflies and other insects will also ensure a garden packed with activity and interest.

■ OPPOSITE
Woodland gardens, especially those with open spaces as well as plenty of trees, will usually encourage a wide range of wildlife. Trees alone do not make a garden, however, so lawns and other open areas are important to introduce some sense of design and to encourage those creatures that prefer more open spaces.

■ RIGHT
Borders with lots of flowers will certainly attract bees, butterflies, and all kinds of insect life. Retaining a nettle patch in an unobtrusive position, perhaps at the back of a shed or boundary bank, for the caterpillars of attractive butterflies, need not mean a garden that looks neglected or lacking in colour. Some of the best wildlife gardens are a compromise between the wild and the beautiful.

Know-how

WAYS WITH WATER

Wildlife gardening is a compromise between creating a garden that we find aesthetically pleasing and one which wildlife finds attractive. Often these demands are in conflict, but with a little imagination it's possible to combine both aims.

Water is a magnet for wildlife of all kinds, not just amphibians and aquatics. For those with children, there are some simple, safe water features that will provide an opportunity for wildlife to visit to drink and bathe. Even a birdbath is better than no water at all.

■ BELOW

PONDS A pond like this makes an attractive feature in its own right, and can form the centrepiece around which the garden is designed, but it will also bring the bonus of wildlife that otherwise would not visit the area.
DESIGN TIP *An informally shaped pond with easy access from the edges is more likely to attract wildlife than a formal one which is difficult to reach.*

■ ABOVE
STREAMS Anyone lucky enough to have a natural stream running through their garden is fortunate indeed, and will almost certainly have plenty of visiting wildlife. For those less fortunate, it's possible to create a very convincing man-made stream like this one.
DESIGN TIP *To make an artificial stream look truly convincing, plant densely up to the water's edge, using plenty of native plants.*

■ ABOVE
SMALL WATER FEATURES Everyone has space for a simple wildlife water feature like this. It's only an old dustbin (trashcan) lid filled with pebbles and placed over a reservoir with a small pump that recirculates the water through the frog's mouth. Although it won't support amphibians or insect life, it will make a water hole for birds and many mammals.
DESIGN TIP *Use this kind of feature to bring movement and life to an otherwise dull part of the garden, perhaps in a very shady spot where few plants thrive.*

■ RIGHT
BANKS Don't be afraid to use native plants and garden plants together if it helps to create the right illusion. This pond bank has a very natural appearance despite being planted with many cultivated plants.
DESIGN TIP *The larger the expanse of water, the more important it is to plant the banks imaginatively unless it is intended to create a void or texture within a formal setting.*

Know-how

WILDFLOWER MEADOWS

Gardens recently created on grassland already rich in wild flowers are likely to have lots of flowers germinating everywhere. Elsewhere, it may be necessary to introduce them. There are companies that specialize in wildflower seeds (as separate species and as mixtures), and you can even buy young plants from some nurseries and specialist suppliers.

■ LEFT
WILD AREAS If the lawn is large enough, it's possible to have ornamental areas to enjoy as a traditional lawn, while in other areas the grass is left to grow long and wild flowers are allowed to seed naturally. In this garden, wild orchids are among the flowers that thrive in the unmown areas. Such diversity of flowers attracts a wide selection of butterflies and birds.
DESIGN TIP *For a more "sculptured" effect, a large lawn can be cut to several different heights, the shortest grass forming paths and broad drives through the taller zones.*

■ RIGHT
MEADOW MIXTURES This sown meadow mixture has a diversity of grasses and broad-leaved plants. Although mixtures where one type of plant predominate are often more spectacular for a short time, a wider range of plants may be more useful for attracting wildlife and may sustain flowering over a longer period.
DESIGN TIP *Meadow mixtures are intended for sowing in place of a lawn where there's room for a decidedly "wild" garden. They seldom look right in juxtaposition with more conventional beds and borders.*

■ LEFT

NATIVE PLANTS Wild and woodland areas can sometimes be left uncultivated in large gardens. They will be colonized by native plants some of which can be very decorative. The self-seeded red campion (*Silene dioica*) shown here is native to the area where this photograph was taken.

DESIGN TIP *These truly wild areas may look stunning for a relatively short time, and uninspiring at other seasons. For that reason they are appropriate only for the fringes of a very large garden.*

■ RIGHT

WILD BORDERS This group of wild flowers, allowed to grow as a natural drift between lawn and border, shows how colourful wild flowers can be. Later in the season, when they grow tall and untidy, they can be cut back to make the area tidier.

DESIGN TIP *Avoid positioning this kind of wild bank in a conspicuous place. It will be more acceptable tucked away in a quiet part of the garden, something wildlife will also appreciate.*

■ LEFT

CULTIVATED WILD FLOWERS Cultivated wild flowers have transformed an otherwise waste piece of ground into an eye-catching feature that is as bright and colourful as many carefully planted borders. Several seed companies offer wildflower mixtures, and some specialize in wildflower seeds.

DESIGN TIP *Use wild flowers to brighten up an uninteresting bank or strip of vacant land. These have been sown on a railway (railroad) embankment at the end of a garden, but the location could just as well be a roadside verge.*

Know-how

Orchards and Woods

Open woodland and orchards make ideal wildlife sanctuaries, and they form a natural transition between the formal parts of the garden and the truly wild areas.

BE OPEN

Open areas within woodland or around the edge are likely to have the greatest variety of wildlife and wild flowers. You don't require a very large garden, or need to think too long-term, to establish a small woodland glade or a copse. Choose quick-growing trees such as birch, especially *Betula pendula*, which can reach over 6m (20ft) in a decade, and space them out well so that they retain an attractive shape and do not cast too much shade. A small copse of about a dozen trees within a large lawn can be very appealing and provide excellent shelter for many types of wildlife.

■ ABOVE

UNDERPLANTING Woodland is not always dark and dreary – bluebells are among several woodland plants that spread readily once introduced. Cultivated bulbs like the tulips and muscari shown here can also be used, provided the shade is not too dense. If you have a large garden, a woodland area will make an ideal wildlife retreat. DESIGN TIP *If you are planting a new woodland, birches are quick-growing and, being deciduous, are ideal for under-planting with spring-flowering plants. These make most growth before the leaves of deciduous trees cast too much shade.*

■ LEFT

PATIOS

Woodland areas need not be positioned away from the house. A wild area near a patio looks charming, and will attract wildlife close to your door. Proximity to wildlife can be a blessing, but be prepared for unwanted intruders.
DESIGN TIP
Leave the edges of wildlife beds as natural-looking as possible.

■ LEFT

KEEPING IT TRIM If you have a large garden with space for an orchard, or a woodland area, you have the potential for an ideal wildlife habitat. Allow wild flowers to take over most of the area – the long grass can be cut only once or twice a year (provided there are no rare plants to be considered) to keep the area presentable. Just mow the grass paths regularly.

DESIGN TIP *Paths can be either straight or meandering. Aim to make the path natural- looking – not mown too closely, or trimmed too geometrically.*

■ RIGHT

WILDFLOWER ORCHARD Once part of an old orchard, this area is now studded with *Fritillaria meleagris* and wood anemones (*Anemone nemorosa*) along with daffodils. All these plants naturalize well in grassed orchards, and look very pretty in spring. Summer wild flowers continue the display, and wildlife is always abundant in this environment.

DESIGN TIP *Don't wait for nature to transform an old orchard. Be prepared to naturalize bulbs and plant or sow wild flowers if appropriate.*

Know-how

FEATHERED FRIENDS

Of all the wildlife that visits the garden, birds are perhaps the most ready to respond to a little coaxing. They will soon become regular visitors if you routinely leave out suitable food, and some may also become relatively tame. They also appreciate water, for drinking and bathing, and this too will ensure they return frequently.

■ ABOVE

ORNAMENTAL BIRD TABLES
Bird tables are usually practical rather than ornamental, but it doesn't have to be that way. This home-made bird house is an ornamental feature in its own right, though the finer points will probably be lost on the birds.

DESIGN TIP *Position a bird table where cats and other animals can't jump up on to it, but try to avoid the centre of the lawn if possible. Bird tables and bird houses soon begin to weather and can quickly become unattractive if left covered with unsightly droppings.*

■ ABOVE

DOVECOTE A dovecote should ensure the company of some elegant feathered friends, and it can become a charming ornamental feature in its own right.

DESIGN TIP *Dovecotes are often painted white and placed in a conspicuous part of the lawn, but they may look better sited towards the back of a border.*

■ OPPOSITE BELOW

BIRDBATHS: ADDING INTEREST
A birdbath simply placed in isolation on the lawn can look a little stark. Making an attractive base such as this one, which has alpines planted in the gravel, makes a more powerful focal point.

DESIGN TIP *Don't assume the centre of the lawn is the best place for a birdbath. It will often look more pleasing if it is placed to one side or not far from the edge of the lawn and close to a border. It will draw the eye across the garden, and birds may feel more secure with the shelter of trees and shrubs nearby.*

■ ABOVE

BIRDBATHS Birdbaths can help to break up a border and sustain interest at those times of the year when herbaceous plants are not at peak performance. Although birdbaths are frequently placed as focal points in a more formal setting, or within the lawn, in some styles of garden a border position may be more appropriate.

DESIGN TIP *Try planting a ground cover around the base of the pedestal to make it look a more integrated part of the design. When the border is bare, evergreen ground cover is particularly useful.*

Planning and Planting

A Sanctuary Garden

This garden is a sanctuary for wildlife of many kinds, but it's also a place where the gardener can retreat from the pressures of everyday life. It is a combination of wild and formal.

Three elements that are strongly attractive to many kinds of wildlife are woodland shelter, water and plenty of flowers rich in nectar and pollen. This garden is designed to provide all three.

As woodland adjoins the property, part of the garden boundary has been merged into the wooded area, and water has been introduced for the benefit of gardener and wildlife alike.

The pergola acts as a kind of natural bridge between the canopy of trees and the island beds. Although it's tempting to plant lots of wild flowers, in a garden like this, with a fairly rigid structure, it's best to concentrate on cultivated ornamentals that can be enjoyed by insects because they are rich in nectar or pollen. Although many annuals, and some outstanding herbaceous perennials, are ideal attractants, shrubs are essential to prevent the beds looking flat and uninteresting in winter. If you include berried shrubs such as cotoneasters, these will provide a source of food for birds in autumn and winter.

The adjoining woodland area provides the necessary shelter for wildlife of many kinds, but areas of long grass also ensure many kinds of wild flowers thrive that would be unable to survive in a closely mown lawn. These in turn will attract insects and birds.

KEY TO PLAN

1 Yew hedge
2 Animal ornament on plinth
3 Path of concrete pavers
4 Mixed island border containing shrubs, border plants and annuals to attract butterflies and other insects
5 Timber decking
6 Patio of concrete pavers
7 Pond
8 Adjoining woodland
9 Pergola
10 Shrubs
11 Boundary left open to adjoining woodland
12 Parking area
13 House

× Garden continues

Viewpoint on photograph

PLANNING

PLANTING

ISLAND BORDERS

■ ABOVE

ISLAND BORDERS Island beds are useful design elements for breaking up large spaces. They also look attractive from all sides. The two island beds in the plan opposite have four "faces", each offering a different perspective and groupings of plants. Island beds can be formal in shape, as shown in the plan opposite, or informal in outline, as in the illustration on the left. Large borders can be filled with herbaceous plants and bulbs, and benefit from the inclusion of a few shrubs. Even if they are not evergreen, the framework of stems gives height to the border in winter. Some flowering shrubs, such as hydrangeas, will look more interesting if the old flower heads are allowed to remain until the following spring.

Shrubs with colourful winter stems, such as *Cornus stolonifera* 'Flaviramea' and *Cornus alba* 'Sibirica' also help to sustain interest throughout the seasons.

KEY TO PLANTS

1 *Salvia guaranitica*
2 *Polygonatum* x *hybridum*
3 *Osteospermum jucundum*
4 *Origanum laevigatum* 'Herrenhausen'
5 *Iris pseudacorus* 'Variegata'
6 *Ligularia dentata*
7 *Persicaria amplexicaulis* 'Atrosanguinea'
8 *Cornus alba* 'Aurea'

Planning and Planting

WILD FORMALITY

The conflict between the needs of wildlife, which prefers a largely uncultivated area, and the gardener's desire for an attractive formal garden has been reconciled in this design.

PLANNING

KEY TO PLAN

1 Small trees
2 Shrubs
3 Rough grass
4 Bird table
5 Planted bank
6 Steps
7 Pond
8 Paved area with plants in crevices
9 Ornamental shrubs
10 Lawn
11 Weeping tree
12 Dwarf box (*Buxus sempervirens* 'Suffruticosa') hedge
13 Herbs
14 Brick path
15 House

↑ Direction of steps up

Viewpoint on photograph

Two distinct parts of the garden have been linked by a lawn and a large weeping tree. The tree acts as a midway focal point to assist the gradual transition that marries these two contrasting styles: a formal herb garden near to the house, with a wildlife area of rough grass, pond, shrubs and trees at the far end of the garden.

Wildlife areas can sometimes look overgrown and weedy. That's how things are in nature, but not necessarily how we like our gardens to look. You can have the best of both worlds by making the end of the garden a wildlife zone, while retaining a more formal style near to the house. A lawn is a good way of linking the two styles; rough grass with wild flowers at the back, and a formal, neatly mown lawn nearer to the house.

PLANTING

Added interest has been created in the brick paving around the formal beds by using two different bonding patterns.

RANDOM PAVING

The term random paving is a misnomer, as it actually needs to be carefully planned. A very regular pattern, where the slabs all align, can look a bit repetitive, especially when covering large areas. Staggering them, and perhaps using slabs of different sizes, will add character and interest. If you wish to plant in the crevices, between the paving, either leave large gaps unmortared, or space the slabs to leave a larger planting area.

Natural stone always looks particularly pleasing when laid in a random pattern, but you can also buy concrete slabs of different sizes to achieve a similar effect. The latter are readily available and generally less expensive.

HOW TO LAY RANDOM PAVING

1 Excavate your chosen area to a depth that will allow for about 5cm (2in) of compacted hardcore (rubble) topped with approximately 5cm (2in) of ballast (sand and gravel), plus the thickness of the paving stones.

2 Place five blobs of mortar where the slab is to be placed, one in the centre, the others near the corners. Alternatively, cover the area where the paving is to be laid with mortar, ensuring it is fairly level.

3 Bed the slab on the mortar and check with a spirit level. If laying a large area, lay on a slight slope to ensure water runs off freely. Use a wedge of wood under one end of the spirit level to check the slope.

4 *(right)* Use spacers of an even thickness to ensure regular spacing, and adjust the slabs again if necessary. If you are planning to plant in the crevices, leave large spaces between the paving. Remove the spacers before filling the joints with mortar. Wait for a day or two before mortaring the joints. Use a dryish mortar mix, and with a small trowel push it well down between the joints. Finish off with a smooth stroke, leaving the mortar slightly recessed. Wipe any stains off the slabs before the mortar dries.

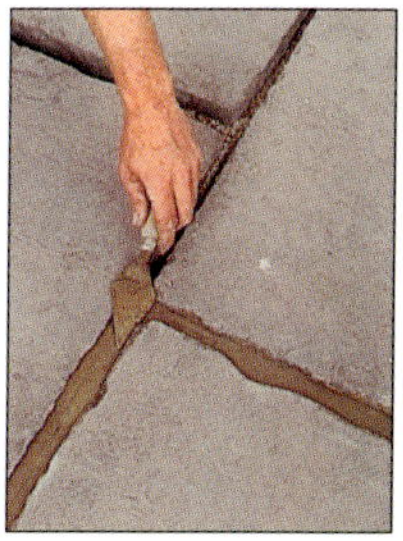

Planning and Planting

Squaring Up to the Problem

This garden successfully marries a formal garden with the informality of a wildlife area. A formal geometric-based design is combined with a woodland space accommodating the needs of both wildlife and gardener.

Woodland gardens make excellent wildlife refuges, but they can be unstimulating to look out on to from the house. This garden retains a strong sense of design in the area immediately in front of the house, combining differently shaped rectangles and squares, with the wildlife area containing rough grass and trees running along one side. Being at the edge of an area that contains some large trees, it receives a lot of shade, but the . strong sense of line and the different surface textures used in the formal area ensure the garden always looks interesting, with many shade-tolerant foliage plants playing an important role.

Water always attracts wildlife, so a small pool has been included, with a shallow sloping beach at one end for a bathing area for birds.

KEY TO PLAN

1 Hedge
2 Lawn
3 Trees and shrubs
4 Raised bed made from railway sleepers (railroad ties), with mixed planting
5 Gravel
6 Paving
7 Rough grass
8 Small wildlife pond
9 Woodland area
10 House
11 Seating area

× Garden continues

Viewpoint on photograph

PLANNING

PRE-FORMED PONDS

Your design may require a small informally shaped pool, and a pre-formed pond is a quick and easy solution. If the ponds are displayed on their sides, lay them on the ground before buying as they may look smaller from a normal viewing position.

PLANTING

HOW TO INSTALL A PRE-FORMED POND

1 Transfer your shape to the ground by inserting canes around the edge of the pond. Run a hosepipe (garden hose) or rope around the outside of the canes.

2 Remove the pond and canes and excavate the hole to approximately the required depth, following the profile of the shelves as accurately as possible.

3 Place a straight-edged piece of wood across the rim of the hole to check that it is level. Measure down to confirm that you have dug to the required depth.

4 Put the pond in the hole, then add or remove soil to ensure a snug and level fit. Remove any large stones. Check with a spirit level that the pond is level.

5 *(right)* Remove the pond, then line the excavation with damp sand if the soil is stony. With the pond in position, and levels checked again, backfill with sand or fine soil, being careful not to push the pond out of level.

6 *(right)* Fill with fresh water from a hose pipe and backfill further if necessary as the water rises, checking the levels frequently as backfilling often lifts the pond slightly. The pond is now ready to fill with plants and wildlife.

Planning and Planting

WILD AND WONDERFUL

A large garden in an attractive setting offers every opportunity for a really superb display that's pleasing for the gardener and an ideal habitat for many kinds of wildlife. The sloping ground on which this garden has been constructed offers plenty of scope for attractive landscaping.

Large gardens with a natural slope must be designed to make use of the natural contours of the land wherever possible. For this reason, gardens like this are almost always unique. However, you can take the general principles and design concepts to apply to your own garden, if it seems appropriate. Although this is a large garden, a smaller sloping site could be landscaped in a similar way.

A natural stream is a tremendous asset to any garden, but with a little ingenuity and a lot of energy you can make an artificial stream using a liner.

PLANNING

KEY TO PLAN

1 Coniferous woodland
2 Woodland
3 Grass path
4 Steps
5 Ornamental trees, shrubs and herbaceous planting
6 Grass
7 Bridge
8 Stream
9 Balustrade
10 Pergola over entrance to steps
11 Lawn (level)
× Garden continues
↓ Direction of steps down
Viewpoint on photograph

■ OPPOSITE

PLANTING IN DRY SHADE Wooded areas are always more attractive if they are underplanted with herbaceous plants and dwarf shrubs. The shady area beneath trees is often dry, however, so choose plants that can tolerate those conditions, and be sure to keep them well watered for the first season until they become established.

It may help to remove some of the lower branches of large trees (this is best done by a tree surgeon, who may also be able to thin the crown if it's necessary).

To keep woodland looking natural, use curved paths and not straight ones, and allow some of the plants to tumble over the edge. If planting a large area, individual plants may have little impact, in which case plant in drifts of the same kind of plant.

PLANTING

PLANTS FOR DRY SHADE

KEY TO PLANTS

1 *Ajuga reptans*
2 *Geranium magnificum*
3 *Geranium pratense*
4 *Deutzia x kalmiiflora*
5 *Rubus spectabilis* 'Flore Pleno'
6 *Geranium macrorrhizum* 'Album'
7 *Colchicum autumnale*
8 *Arum italicum*
9 *Myosotis sylvatica*
10 *Helleborus* hybrids
11 *Geranium macrorrhizum*
12 *Galium odoratum* (syn. *Asperula odorata*)

Planning and Planting

NATURE TRAILS

Where the garden is large enough to create an area devoted to informal walkways, which can meander between and around small streams, woodland and meadow-type grassed patches, the result can look very natural.

PLANNING

KEY TO PLAN

1 Specimen shrubs
2 Mixed border planted mainly with plants that attract butterflies and other wildlife
3 Mown grass path
4 Garden bench
5 Large sculpture or ornament
6 Rough grass with wild flowers
7 Woodland garden
8 Steps
9 Stone wall
10 Specimen tree
11 Bog garden
12 Stream
13 Grass paths
14 Mixed bed
15 Shrubs
16 Lawn
17 House
↑ Direction of steps down
Viewpoint on photograph

Although this garden appears to consist mainly of meandering paths that look perfectly natural, they have been planned for maximum impact. Apart from the point where the paths converge at the steps between wooded and open areas, paths split and merge, or go around in loops. This layout offers multiple choices for exploring the garden. The wildlife it attracts will be equally varied, with trees, water, long grass and wild flowers providing a wide range of habitats. The borders are planted mainly with flowers that attract insects and shrubs that provide birds with berries.

PLANTING

DECORATIVE DECKCHAIRS

■ ABOVE
In an informal garden like the one opposite, deckchairs are ideal for taking out on a sunny day for relaxing amid the wild flowers and birdsong. If you have old deckchairs that have seen better days, it's easy to give them a new lease of life by covering them with new canvas and getting to work with some stencil paints. You will need about 1.5m (5ft) of deckchair canvas, which should be washed, rinsed, dried and ironed before use.

You can buy stencils from art supply shops, or you can make your own, to stencil both canvas and surround. Alternatively, try staining the old wood with a coloured woodstain to co-ordinate or contrast with the decorated canvas.

■ ABOVE
Work out your design first, then fix the stencil in position using masking tape. Load the stencil brush with paint, removing any excess paint by dabbing up and down on a piece of newspaper, then apply the colour to the relevant part of the stencil. Move the stencil and repeat until all areas of that colour have been painted. Then reposition the stencil over the original colour and apply a fresh paint colour. Repeat until the design is complete. When dry, set the paint by covering it with a white cloth and pressing with an iron at its hottest setting, covering each part for at least two minutes. Use upholstery tacks to fix the canvas securely to the top and bottom of the chair.

Planning and Planting

MERGING WITH THE LANDSCAPE

A large garden in a rural setting can merge into the landscape if the boundaries are planted with shrubs and trees, rather like the edge of a woodland area. A garden of this size will have a lot of lawn, but by leaving some areas long for wild flowers and wildlife, the amount of time spent on maintenance is reduced.

KEY TO PLAN

1 Tree and shrub border
2 Garden seat
3 Paved area around seat
4 Lawn
5 Long grass and wild flowers
6 Shrubs and ground cover
7 Low-growing shrubs
8 Retaining wall
9 Patio
10 Brick paving
11 Courtyard of natural stone paving and dwarf shrubs
12 Formal pond
13 House
Viewpoint on photograph

PLANNING

Despite its large size, this garden has been planned for minimum work and maximum enjoyment. Cutting the grass is the only tedious chore, but leaving areas of grass long for wild flowers and wildlife reduces the area to be mown regularly, and a large powered mower can make short work of it. There are few seasonal plants in containers to be watered, and the trees and shrubs require no regular maintenance.

A small, formal pond has been introduced into the courtyard-like paved area between the two wings of the house. Although small, it is a secluded area that will be visited by plenty of wildlife, including birds, which will use it for drinking and bathing.

The slightly elevated large patio gives a good view across the garden, and emphasizes that this is a garden for relaxation and enjoyment rather than weeding and work.

INTRODUCING WILD FLOWERS TO THE GARDEN

You can encourage birds, butterflies and other creatures by having a wildflower lawn, instead of a grass lawn. You may still want to retain a grass lawn for practical purposes, but parts of it can be allowed to "go wild", especially parts that are well screened. If your lawn doesn't already contain plenty of wild flowers (or weeds), you can sow a seed mixture, or for a small area you can plant them as wild-flower plants.

PLANTING

SOWING AND PLANTING WILD FLOWERS

1 The most satisfactory way to create a wildflower lawn is to sow a special wildflower mixture instead of lawn seed. Be careful to clear the ground of problem perennial weeds before you start.

2 To bury the seeds, simply rake first in one direction and then in the other. It does not matter if some seeds remain on the surface. Keep the area well watered until the seeds germinate. Protect from birds if necessary.

3 For a very small area, you may prefer to buy wild-flower plants. You can raise your own from seed or buy them. They are available from specialist nurseries and some garden centres.

4 You can plant into bare ground or put them in an existing lawn left to grow long. Remember to keep them well watered until established.

Choosing Plants

Plants for Wildlife

Most plants help to attract wildlife in some form, but some are especially good at enticing particular types. *Buddleia davidii*, for example, is also called the butterfly bush because these creatures find it so irresistible. Nepetas are usually buzzing with bees.

SHRUBS FOR BUTTERFLIES

The butterfly bush (*Buddleia davidii*) has to be high on the list, but remember the other buddleias, such as *B. alternifolia* and *B. globosa*. Other shrubs popular with butterflies include ceanothus, heathers, many hebes, lavender, and *Spiraea* x *bumalda* (now more correctly *S. japonica*).

Buddleia davidii is sometimes called the butterfly bush, because butterflies are so strongly attracted by it. It's very easy to grow, even on poor soils, but regular pruning is necessary to keep the plant compact. There are varieties in shades of blue, purple, pink and white.

BORDER PLANTS FOR BUTTERFLIES

These border plants are as irresistible to butterflies as the best of the shrubs. Some of these flower late, which is a bonus in the garden, among them most of the perennial asters, such as *A. amellus*, *A.* x *frikartii*, *A. novae-angliae*, *A. novi-belgii* and *Sedum spectabile* and its hybrids.

Sedum spectabile will bring a border to life in autumn, and be the centre of attraction among the local population of bees and butterflies. There are several good varieties. This one is 'Meteor'.

ANNUALS FOR BUTTERFLIES

Many summer annuals, such as pansies and French marigolds, will also attract butterflies. Others that are particularly popular with them include ageratum, candytuft and *Alyssum maritimum* (now more correctly *Lobularia maritima*).

French marigolds are excellent garden plants, flowering from early summer until the first frost if dead-headed, and attract butterflies throughout the season. This variety is 'Red Cherry'.

PLANTS FOR CATERPILLARS

Caterpillars sometimes require totally different plants from butterflies for their food, and the availability of these significantly determines the local population. The fact that butterflies usually lay their eggs on different plants (and often weeds) from the plants they feed on for nectar is a great consolation for the gardener, otherwise they would not be so welcome in the garden. Stinging nettles (*Urtica dioica*) are popular with many species, and some feed on thistles. Among the ornamental garden plants that are eaten by caterpillars of some species are nasturtiums (*Tropaeolum majus*) and canary creeper (*Tropaeolum peregrinum*).

Nasturtiums (*Tropaeolum majus*) are cheerful and easy-to-grow hardy annuals, but some butterfly species lay their eggs on the leaves. For that reason this is a mixed-blessings plant, as the caterpillars could become a pest that you then have to control.

Butterflies are sometimes very specific about the plants on which they lay their eggs, however, so in some countries other plants may be preferred to suit local species. If you are keen to encourage butterflies, consult books on the subject that give advice on which food plants to provide.

MOTHS IN THE NIGHT

Night-flying moths, and other night-flying insects, are not everyone's idea of creatures that will beautify the garden, but for anyone interested in wildlife of all kinds, insects that come out at dusk can be equally exciting. These are generally attracted by night-scented plants such as some of the nicotianas and night-scented stocks (*Matthiola bicornis*, now more correctly *M. longipetala*).

Evening-flowering nicotianas will attract insects such as night-flying moths. They are usually very fragrant too, which is a bonus for us. Many of the modern hybrids have been bred to open during the day, so check in the catalogue or on the packet if you want one that flowers in the evening.

FOR THE BIRDS

Birds are attracted by nesting sites and food plants. Dense climbers and evergreen hedges provide nesting sites for many species. Birds that eat mainly seeds are likely to be enticed by plants such as teasels (*Dipsacus fullonum* and *D. sativus*), which have large seed heads, while birds that enjoy berries will be encouraged into the garden by many *Sorbus* species as well as pyracanthas.

Pyracanthas are grown primarily for their berries. The birds will leave them alone at first, but they often provide a useful meal when severe weather arrives.

GOOD BEE PLANTS

If you're a bee-keeper, or are simply fascinated by these industrious insects, plants that attract bees will be high on your planting list. On the other hand, if you regard them as unpleasant insects with a nasty sting, you may prefer to avoid such plants.

Catmint (*Nepeta racemosa*, still widely sold under its older name of *N. mussinii*, and *N.* x *faassenii*) and marjorams are among the plants especially attractive to bees, but so are many other summer border flowers, such as the hardy geraniums. For spring, include brooms (cytisus), aubrietia and crocuses, and for autumn the perennial asters listed for butterflies and *Sedum spectabile*.

Nepeta x *faassenii* is a lovely summer border plant, much-loved by bees. It may be best to avoid planting it where it will overhang a narrow path, to reduce the risk of being stung.

FOR BENEFICIAL INSECTS

A diversity of flowers is the best way to attract beneficial insects (predators) to the garden, and annuals are especially useful. One of the best is the poached-egg plant (*Limnanthes douglasii*), with its pretty carpet of yellow and white flowers. Although an annual, it self-seeds readily.

Limnanthes douglasii is a bright and cheerful little annual that will usually self-seed itself to provide more plants the following year.

Small Gardens

Size is relative when it comes to gardens, but most of us have a smaller one than we'd like. Not only do small gardens make it difficult to grow all the plants that tempt us, lack of space also tends to cramp our style when it comes to design. Even those fortunate enough to have a large back garden sometimes have a small front garden, and such restraints can seem limiting – especially if space for a drive has to be found.

There are as many solutions as there are gardens, but the illustrations and ideas that follow show that a small garden does not necessarily mean small impact. Even an unpromising, tiny, town front garden can be transformed with a little imagination. And, of course, some of the ideas shown for small gardens can be adapted for corners of a large one.

Boundaries also assume greater importance with a small garden. The fence, hedge or wall can dominate the view, whatever you do within the central planting area. It may be necessary to turn these to advantage, perhaps by erecting a decorative fence, such as a painted picket style, planting a dwarf flowering hedge or painting an existing wall a pale colour to reflect light and to act as a pleasing backdrop for wall shrubs and other plants.

■ ABOVE
A cottage-style front garden bursting with colour and fragrance.

■ OPPOSITE
Clever planting and design of this small town garden has created the illusion of space.

INSPIRATIONAL IDEAS

A small garden can have just as striking an impact as a large expanse. Try to resist the temptation to overlook dramatic features or large plants. Bold statements are often most effective in small spaces, and a lot of small plants can draw attention to limited space.

■ OPPOSITE ABOVE
If a very small garden seems hemmed in by fences, turning the eye inwards towards the centre of the garden can be a good idea. The raised bed becomes the focal point from all parts of this tiny garden, drawing the eye inwards and away from the limitations of the boundary. Sufficient space was left at the end for a small sitting and barbecue area.

■ OPPOSITE BELOW
If your front garden is small, this example should convince you that there is plenty of scope for impact no matter how small the area. The Japanese-style entrance demonstrates effectively that shape and structure, together with colour, can be more important than the number of plants.

■ BELOW
A small back garden can have all the charm and elegance of a traditional garden more often associated with grand country houses. It's not only the formal structure of the garden but the strong white-and-silver theme that makes the whole design look well thought out and integrated. Picking up the colour in the paintwork of the gazebo and painting the central plinth white not only echoes the theme but ensures there is relief to the green of the surrounding trees and the box (*Buxus sempervirens*) hedges when the flowers have finished.

INSPIRATIONAL IDEAS

The vertical plane should be considered when making the most of small spaces. Tall features, such as birdbaths, can be useful to draw the eye upwards, as can vertical features such as high walls decorated with pots, or trellises clothed with climbers or painted brightly.

■ ABOVE
This narrow plot is typical of many small back gardens, and the straight path to the gate limits the scope without major reconstruction. It benefits greatly from having a gravel path instead of concrete slabs, which would have emphasized the rigidity of the path, and by training the hedge into an arch over the gate. The gate alone would not have been an attractive focal point, but the arch transforms it into an acceptable feature. Having the lawn at the top half of the garden and dense planting at the end, rather than running the lawn along the whole length of the garden, ensures the eye does not take in everything at once. Despite the limitation of size and shape, there is plenty to discover in this garden. The dense planting helps to overcome the lack of structural features.

■ OPPOSITE BELOW
Where space is very sparse, it's a good idea to extend a garden vertically. Although the ground area occupied by this garden is severely limited, the way it has been clothed from ground almost to first floor level has ensured that it is packed with colour and interest. Good use has been made of foliage plants so the display looks well clothed throughout the summer months.

■ ABOVE

Small country cottages and town houses with only a narrow strip of land between house and pavement (footway) or road can cramp the style of even the most enthusiastic garden designer. It may be best to abandon attempts at clever designs and concentrate on a mass of colourful annuals in summer and bulbs in spring. Window boxes and hanging baskets provide additional planting space and give the garden a vertical element, and with such a small garden the regular watering they require should not be an onerous chore.

Painting the wall almost always improves a small garden like this, and helps to show hanging baskets to maximum advantage.

Know-how

BEAUTIFUL BOUNDARIES

Unattractive walls and fences can be clothed with climbers and wall shrubs, but these may make a small area seem even more enclosed. If the view beyond the garden is an attractive one, it may be worth making a feature of the boundary itself.

■ RIGHT

PICKET FENCES Picket fences are always more attractive than a filled-in panel or closeboard fence. Normally they are left a natural wood colour or painted white, but why not be bold and splash out with the colours? One of these fences has been painted pastel pink to match the roses, the other sugar-almond blue to differentiate between the two properties.

DESIGN TIP *Bear in mind the colours of the flowers in adjoining borders, not only at the time of year when you paint the fence but throughout the rest of the year.*

■ ABOVE

FEATURE FENCE If you get on well with your neighbours, and you want to let in a little light, a fence with "windows" is one solution. Although you may want to modify the style to suit your own taste, the principle of making a feature of your fence is a useful one to bear in mind for a small garden.

DESIGN TIP *Fences look best if they are maintained at least annually with a fresh coat of preservative or paint. If you want to make a feature of your fence rather than mask it with climbers, be sure to allow for easy access for painting or preserving in your design, not obscuring it with large trees or shrubs.*

■ RIGHT

LIVING FENCE An existing solid fence can be improved by erecting a trellis in front of it and planting climbers such as clematis and roses. Here, a figure has been sited to bring a sense of summer enchantment, and also to provide a focal point in winter when the foliage cover has gone.

DESIGN TIP *If you find an exposed trellis unattractive in winter, include an evergreen such as ivy. But bear in mind that evergreens that twine through their support make maintenance of the trellis and fence difficult.*

■ BELOW

CAVITY WALLS Low walls are often better than tall ones for a small front garden, but plain single-skin walls can look drab and uninspiring. Building one with a cavity like this not only provides more planting space but also helps to bridge and link both sides of the garden boundary.

DESIGN TIP *Unless the boundary has to deter animals, a low wall or even a small-post-and-chain-link fence is effective. It is also possible to mark the boundary by planting up to the edge of a bed, which can be viewed from both sides.*

Know-how

INTEGRATING THE PRACTICALITIES

Planning should also involve practical essentials like somewhere to dry the washing and a hide for the dustbin (trashcan), as well as more stimulating features like a built-in barbecue. The most attractive garden can become an irritation if there's nowhere to dry the clothes or there's an inconvenient walk to put out the household refuse.

■ LEFT

CLOTHES DRIER The only space for a clothes drier in this small garden was in the paved area shown. A rotary drier was chosen with the socket well hidden by beach pebbles where one of the paving slabs had been removed. This makes it possible to remove the drier when it is not in use, leaving the garden relatively unaffected by this necessity.
DESIGN TIP *Try to avoid a clothes line that runs straight down the garden, or across it at a conspicuous spot. Unless removed after use each time, it will visually divide the garden. Rotary driers can sometimes be masked completely by screen block walling in a convenient corner.*

■ LEFT

BARBECUES Even if your use of the barbecue is infrequent, having one built in gives the impression of a garden well thought out and cleverly designed. All the racks and basic equipment can be bought as kits, so usually you only have to build the walls.
DESIGN TIP *Obtain specifications from kit manufacturers at the design stage. Armed with the dimensions of your preferred kit, it will be easier to integrate it into the brickwork or ensure that it's a good fit with the particular walling block that you are planning to use.*

■ BELOW

REFUSE This corner of a small garden can double as a built-in patio, barbecue or a refuse hide, depending on what's most applicable.
DESIGN TIP *Keep as many utilities as possible together in a small area if possible. This will minimize their impact on the rest of the garden.*

■ ABOVE

DRAINS Drain inspection covers sound mundane, but they are important where they occur in the middle of a crucial part of the garden, such as a patio or in the lawn. These metal covers immediately attract the eye, rather like an unattractive focal point, detracting from the more desirable elements. Special replacement covers that have a planting cavity or a shallow tray to hold paving are available. It is important to cut the paving accurately to ensure a neat appearance.
DESIGN TIP *Don't simply place a container over an inspection cover: it will almost certainly draw attention to the cover, which will probably project beneath the base of the container.*

Know-how

CREATING ILLUSIONS

Illusions are useful design devices, whatever the size of garden, but they are especially valuable in small ones. Mostly they are used to suggest that the garden is larger or more densely planted that it is in reality.

■ ABOVE

BEYOND THE DOOR Doors and gates suggest that it's possible to explore more of the garden. This large gate is clearly part of a garden on a grand scale, but you might be able to come to an arrangement with a neighbour to set a decorative gate between your two properties. If you are on friendly terms you can actually use it, otherwise agree to keep it locked. Both will benefit from the impression that the garden extends beyond its real limits.
DESIGN TIP *If using this kind of device, it's best if both gardens have a path leading to the gate, so that it really does look as though there's more garden to explore.*

■ LEFT

PAINTED ILLUSIONS If you are artistically talented, or can draw upon the services of someone who is, painting a false perspective into a scene that suggests a path or border continues can be surprisingly convincing. Here the path turns to the left immediately beyond the gate, but at first glance it appears as though it continues beyond.
DESIGN TIP *This kind of design device works most convincingly where the scene appears to continue beyond a door or gate.*

■ LEFT

ENDLESS PATHS Dense planting with tall shrubs or trees at the end of a garden can suggest that the property goes further, even though the path turns or leads nowhere in particular. The effect works best in summer, when plants are in full leaf.

DESIGN TIP *A path will give the illusion of being longer if it tapers towards the far end. Dense planting at the perimeter of the garden also helps to imply there's more garden beyond.*

■ BELOW

DECEPTIVE TRELLIS Decorative trellis is usually more pleasing than a plain wall, and hints at things beyond.

DESIGN TIP *If using trellis ornamentally, do not over-plant and avoid covering it with climbers.*

Know-how

USING VERTICALS

In a large garden, the verticals are usually provided by trees, but in small gardens it is often the boundaries and house walls that obtrusively provide the vertical element. Arches, pergolas and trellises are useful for adding height within the garden, especially before newly planted small trees can play a useful role, but much can be achieved by covering existing walls and fences with climbers and wall shrubs.

■ LEFT

BUILT-UP BORDERS A small town or courtyard garden can appear almost claustrophobic, but it's possible to make a virtue of its enclosed nature by surrounding yourself with lush growth. Build up the borders all around to create a secret hideaway.

DESIGN TIP

This kind of planting works best if the borders have irregular outlines extending towards the centre, rather than straight, narrow borders. Use tubs to draw the eye into the centre. Use plenty of evergreens and variegated plants, and medium-sized with small plants towards the front of the border and climbers and tall plants at the back.

■ OPPOSITE ABOVE

STYLISH SUPPORTS Climbing and rambling roses require a suitable support, and although wires can be stretched at intervals along the wall, a trellis is more decorative. This is especially useful if the wall itself is not particularly attractive as the trellis remains a feature even when the rose is bare.

DESIGN TIP *Try extending the trellis beyond the height of the wall or fence. This will produce a better display of roses and also ensure fewer thorny stems hanging where they could be a hazard.*

■ RIGHT

AVENUE OF ARCHES As most of the height was provided by the boundary and house walls, with a void in the centre, an ornate avenue of arches has been used to take the eye to the centre of the garden. It also creates a corridor linking two distinct areas of the garden. When the climbers have covered the frame, the tunnel effect will be emphasized.

DESIGN TIP *If the garden is small, it may be best to angle a pergola or arch to take the eye at an angle. This prevents the whole garden being absorbed at a glance.*

■ ABOVE

CLIMBERS AS CLOTHING Clothe the house wall whenever possible. Although the temptation is to use evergreens such as ivies, if the property is attractive in its own right, make use of seasonal flowering climbers such as roses and wisterias.

DESIGN TIP *Deciduous climbers such as roses are shown to advantage against a painted wall. Only those plants that can be lowered easily from the wall for periodic painting of the house are practical choices, however.*

■ ABOVE

COVERED IN CLIMBERS Clothing the lower level of a house will make the most of vertical space in a tiny garden. Here a colourful, evergreen *Euonymus fortunei* variety has been used beneath the window, and pyracanthas for greater height either side.

DESIGN TIP *Evergreens are a good choice for this kind of position, but use bright flowers near the base to pack a punch and give the garden colour.*

Planning and Planting

BEAUTIFUL BASEMENT

A small basement garden can be transformed into a delightful outdoor room like this, with a little planning and some clever planting. An advantage of a small space is the low cost: the expense is limited by the small amount you can pack in.

PLANNING

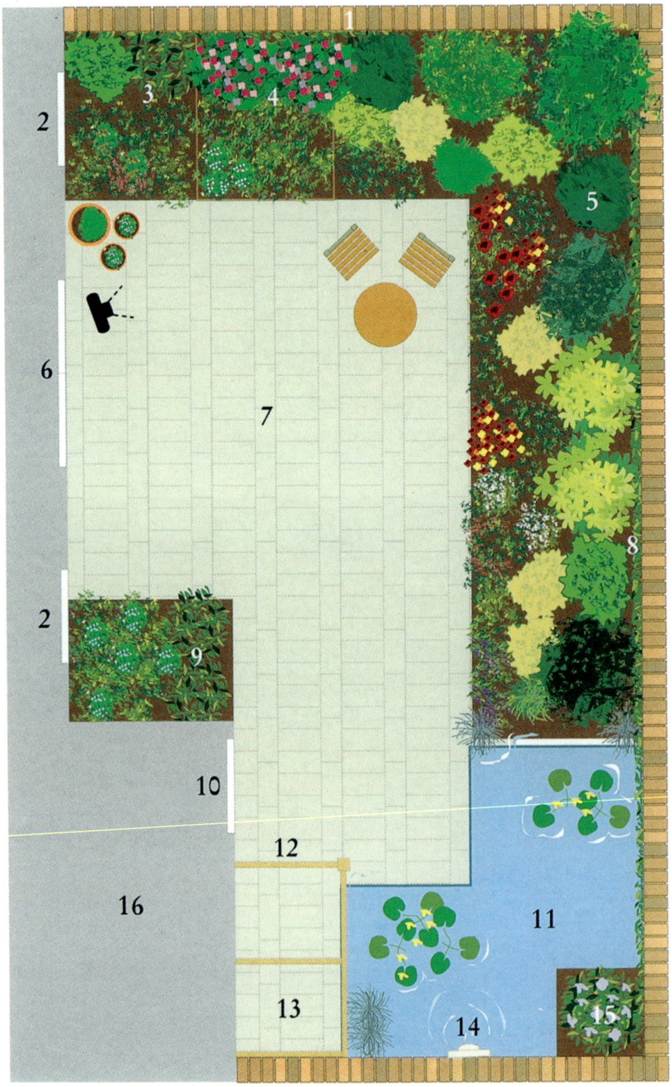

KEY TO PLAN

1 Wall
2 Window
3 Ground-level bed with mixed planting
4 Low-level raised bed with mixed planting
5 High-level raised bed with mixed planting
6 French window or patio door
7 Patio paved with slabs
8 Climbers on wall
9 Dwarf shrubs
10 Back door
11 Pond
12 Pergola
13 Space for dustbin (trashcan)
14 Wall fountain
15 Small bed with specimen shrub
16 House

Viewpoint on photograph

Basement gardens often seem unpromising at first – dark and uninteresting with little to bring cheer or admiration. But if you paint the walls white to reflect as much light as possible, add some raised beds to provide more impressive planting areas, install a pond with wall fountain, and buy some stylish garden furniture, then you have a garden packed with interest and impact.

In a small garden like this, accommodating practicalities such as the dustbin (trashcan) is always a problem. The best solution is to tuck the unsightly necessities away at the back where they will not be visible from seating areas. Washing lines can be replaced with a rotary drier, which can be stored when not in use. Dustbins can be tucked away in the alcove formed by the pergola.

PLANTING

RAISED BEDS

Bricks are a better choice than walling blocks for raised beds built close to the house. Even if a different kind of brick is used, it is likely to blend more harmoniously with the building than concrete or reconstituted stone blocks.

Bricklaying low walls is not a difficult skill to acquire, and the wall will go up surprisingly quickly once the footing has been prepared. You can always hire a professional if you don't have the time to build a wall yourself.

HOW TO BUILD A RAISED BED

1 All walls require a footing. For a low wall, the thickness of a single row of bricks is required. A double row of bricks is required for a taller wall. Excavate a trench about 30cm (1ft) deep, and place about 13cm (5in) of consolidated hardcore in the bottom. Drive pegs in so the tops are at the final height of the base. Use a spirit level to check levels.

2 Fill with a concrete mix of 1 part cement, 2 parts sharp sand, and 3 parts aggregate, and level it off with the peg tops. After the concrete has hardened (1–2 days) lay the bricks on a bed of mortar. Place a wedge of mortar at one end of each brick to be laid. For stability, make a pier at each end, and at intervals of 1.8–2.4m (6–8ft) if the wall is long.

3 For subsequent courses, lay a ribbon or mortar on top of the previous row, then "butter" one end of the brick to be laid. Tap level, checking constantly with a spirit level. The wall must be finished off with a coping of suitable bricks or with special coping sold for the purpose.

Planning and Planting

A Private Garden

Privacy can be important in a small garden, especially if it is overlooked by neighbouring properties. If you want seclusion, then planting plenty of tall evergreens around the perimeter will provide a sense of enclosure and privacy. Most of the design elements are then thrown towards the centre of the garden, so that the eye is taken inwards and the garden does not seem claustrophobic.

KEY TO PLAN

1 Conifer
2 Specimen evergreen shrub
3 Ground cover
4 Evergreen shrub
5 Gravel
6 Planted container and ornaments
7 Feature slab
8 Seasonal plants
9 Plants in pots
10 Patio
11 Seating area
12 Crazy-paved patio
13 House
Viewpoint on photograph

This garden looks in on itself, with all the colour and bright plants running along the centre of the garden. The dense evergreen planting around the boundary and the use of conifers and other tall evergreens ensure a feeling of seclusion and privacy.

It is important to avoid a ribbon effect when a main path runs the length of the garden, so the path here has been broken up with decorative feature slabs, and patches of gravel take the eye outwards to the flowerbeds on either side. By mixing paving materials and taking the path out to the sides in an irregular manner, the eye is drawn to the planted areas and not just along the path.

TUBS AND POTS

The larger the pot or container, the more plants you can pack in and the more they are likely to thrive in the generous amount of potting soil.

PLANNING

PLANTING TUBS AND PATIO POTS

1 Filled tubs and pots can be heavy to move, so plant them up in their final positions if possible. Cover the drainage holes with a layer of broken pots, large gravel or chipped bark.

2 A loam-based potting mixture is best for most plants, but if the pot is to be used where weight is a consideration, such as on a balcony, use a peat-based or peat-substitute mixture.

3 Choose a tall or bold plant for the centre, such as *Cordyline australis* or a fuchsia, or one with large flowers such as the osteospermum that has been used here.

4 Fill in around the base with some bushier but lower-growing plants. Choose bright flowers if the centrepiece is a foliage plant, but place the emphasis on foliage effect if the focal point is a flowering plant.

5 Cover the surface with a decorative mulch such as chipped bark or cocoa shells if much of the surface is visible (this is worth doing anyway to conserve moisture). Water thoroughly.

PLANTING

Planning and Planting

WAYS WITH WALLS

The walls of a small enclosed garden can be oppressive, yet masking them with evergreen shrubs and conifers may emphasize the smallness. This design opens up the centre and uses decorative trellis to make a feature of the walls.

PLANNING

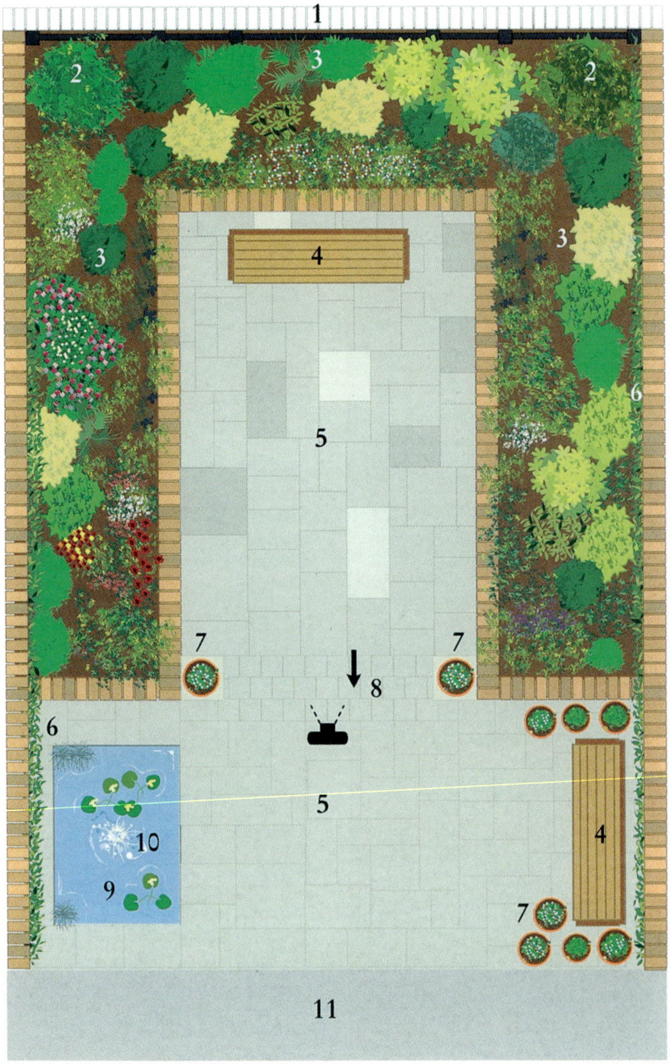

KEY TO PLAN

1 White painted wall with trellis
2 Small tree
3 Raised bed with mixed planting
4 Garden bench
5 Paved area using random slabs
6 Climber growing against wall
7 Containers with seasonal planting
8 Steps
9 Formal pond
10 Fountain
11 House

↓ Direction of steps down

Viewpoint on photograph

Decorative trellises ensure instant impact and will in time be covered with plants, preventing walls looking dull or oppressive. A white trellis looks good against a green backdrop of foliage, but don't be afraid to use a dark colour against a wall, especially if the wall is white or a light colour.

The raised beds in this design elevate the plants, so the boundary walls behind do not appear quite so high. Similarly, a change of level adds interest, but to relieve the possible dominance of the paving in the lower area a formal pond complete with fountain provides a focal point, especially when viewed from the garden seat on the opposite side.

WATER LILIES

Plant water lilies in spring, before the leaves have fully expanded. They can be planted in special planting baskets or in a container with solid sides, such as an old washing-up bowl.

PLANTING

HOW TO PLANT A WATER LILY

1 Use a heavy soil that is not too rich in nutrients. Aquatic planting soil is available from aquatic specialists.

2 Don't add ordinary fertilizers to the soil, as they may cause a proliferation of algae. Use a slow-release fertilizer.

3 Remove the water lily from its container, and plant it in the new container at its original depth.

4 Add a layer of gravel to reduce the chance of fish disturbing the soil. It also helps to keep the soil in place when the container is lowered into the water.

5 Flood the container with water and let it stand for a while. This reduces the chance of the water becoming muddy when you lower it into the pond.

6 Place the container in a shallow part of the pond initially, especially if new leaves are about to develop. Move it into deeper water a week or two later.

Planning and Planting

SIMPLE SHAPES

Tiny gardens benefit from simple designs, so that they remain uncluttered and any geometric shapes are obvious and easy to see. In this garden it is the choice of plants that will transform it from a simple plan to a striking and well-designed garden with plenty of impact despite its small size. The design pivots around a tiny diamond-shaped lawn, set on the angle of the brick pathway.

PLANNING

KEY TO PLAN

1 Metal fence
2 Gate
3 Specimen shrub
4 Dwarf shrubs and evergreen border plants
5 Path of clay pavers with "rope" edging
6 Corsican mint (*Mentha requienii*) lawn edged with brick
7 Bay window
8 House

Viewpoint on photograph

It's never a good idea to divide a tiny garden with a straight path from door to gate, which has the effect of slicing it into two smaller pieces, but don't be afraid to keep the design simple. Here, by positioning the gate towards the centre of the boundary it has been possible to introduce a strong line, while varying the depths of the beds allows for more interesting planting. Even so, this arrangement could have still been dull without the extra dimension created by the Corsican mint lawn. This can be used as an intimate sitting area, but its role as a textural feature is equally important.

In the photograph opposite, the plants are still small; after a season or two little of the soil or mulch would be visible.

CHOOSING A NON-GRASS LAWN

Corsican mint and thyme lawns can be planted in the same way – in the photographs opposite, thyme is being used.

PLANTING

HOW TO PLANT NON-LAWN GRASS

1 Thoroughly dig over the area and clear the ground of weeds at least a month before planting. Hoe off any seedlings that appear in the mean time. Rake the ground level before planting.

2 Water the plants in their pots, then set them out about 15–20cm (6–8in) apart, in staggered rows to work out the position and how many plants you need.

3 Knock a plant from its pot and carefully tease out a few of the roots if they are running tightly around the edge of the pot.

4 Plant to the original depth, and firm the soil around the roots before knocking out and planting the next plant. Water thoroughly and keep well watered for the first season.

Planning and Planting

CREATING FOCAL POINTS

Drawing the eye inwards helps to overcome some of the shortcomings of a garden as tiny as this. Focal points like the chimney pot and containers take the eye to individual elements within the design rather than passing straight over the garden from gate to door in a single glance.

PLANNING

KEY TO PLAN

1 Metal fence
2 Gate
3 Mixed planting
4 Path of paving setts, with "rope" edging
5 Container on gravel base
6 Herbs
7 Chimney-pot feature
8 Climber
9 Bay window
10 House

Viewpoint on photograph

Here containers of various kinds have been used as focal points, and they are especially useful at those times of the year when there is little colour and plants in the borders have died back. Like the previous design, the path has a diversion, which avoids a straight walk from gate to door.

Although modern paving setts have been used for the path, a "rope" edging has been used to reflect the style associated with the period in which the house was built. With a small garden like this, where the house forms a dominant backdrop, it's important that home and garden look well integrated and harmonize as much as possible.

A NEAT EDGE

Emphasize the profile of your beds and borders, as well as your paths, by giving them a crisp or interesting edge. Select an edging that suits the style of your garden. If you prefer an old-fashioned look, reproduction edgings are now readily available.

OTHER IDEAS

Try using empty wine bottles, neck-down, for an unusual edging – leave just a couple of centimetres (an inch) or so of bottle showing.

If you live in a coastal area, consider using large seashells for an edging.

PLANTING

NEAT EDGING

1 For a period garden, Victorian-style rope edging looks appropriate. You can use it to retain a gravel path or as an edging to a paved path.

2 Wavy-edged edgings like this are also reminiscent of some of the older styles of garden, but they can also be used to advantage in a modern setting to give a formal effect.

3 Sawn log rolls make a strong and attractive edging where you want a flowerbed to be raised slightly above a lawn, but remember it may be difficult to mow right up to the edge.

Planning and Planting

NEAT CORNERING

Corner sites can present special problems, but this design has unusually managed to marry straight lines and curves in a successful and distinctive way. It sometimes pays to be bold and imaginative when the site is a difficult one.

PLANNING

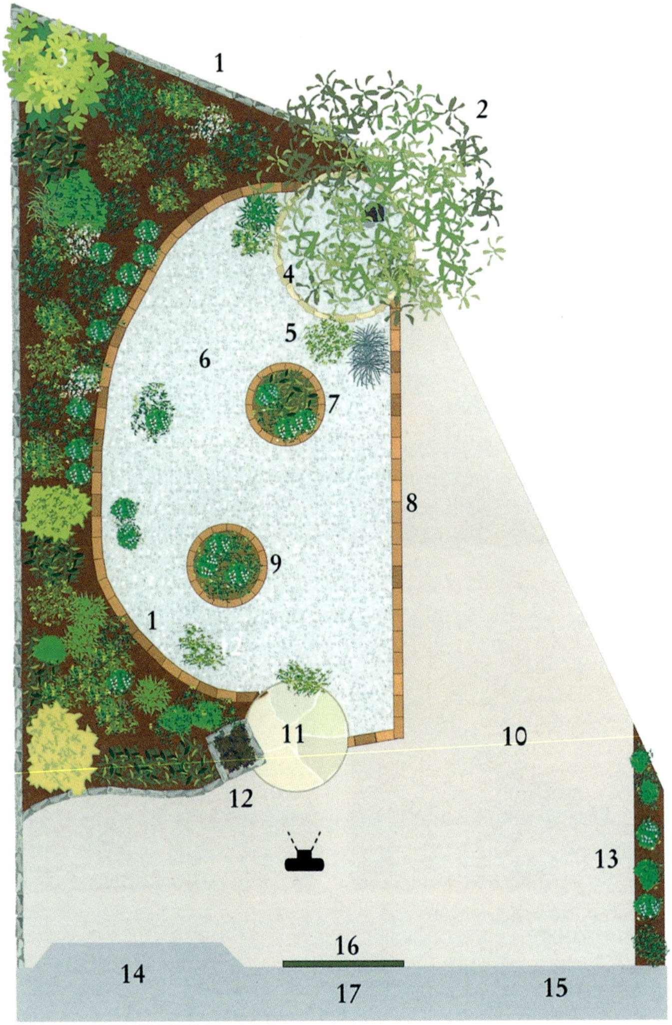

KEY TO PLAN

1 Low wall
2 Birch tree
3 Mixed planting
4 Raised circular bed
5 Plants in gravel
6 Gravel
7 Brick-edged bed with perennials
8 Brick edge
9 Brick-edged bed with seasonal plants
10 Drive
11 Circular stone area
12 Stone pillar with planting area
13 Dwarf shrubs
14 Bay window
15 Garage
16 Door
17 House
Viewpoint on photograph

Awkward corner sites can be especially difficult to design, and if they also have to accommodate a driveway too, the problem is further compounded.

Maximum use has been made of the existing birch tree in this plan, as it takes the eye from the bleakness of the drive. Creating a circular bed around it emphasizes it as a focal point, and to give the garden a sense of unity, the circular theme has been repeated with a couple of round raised beds and an interesting circular stone feature, linking the drive and gravel area.

USING GRAVEL

Gravel is best laid over a weed-suppressing base, but it's still possible to plant through both materials if necessary.

PLANTING

HOW TO LAY AND PLANT THROUGH GRAVEL

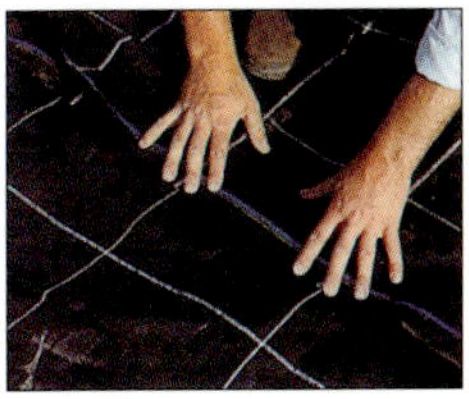

1 Dig the area to hold 5cm (2in) of gravel. Level the ground, then lay heavy-duty black plastic or a mulching sheet over the area. Overlap strips by about 5cm (2in).

2 Tip gravel on to the sheet, then rake it level. To plant through the gravel, draw back an area of gravel from where you plan to plant and make a slit in the plastic.

3 Plant normally through the slit, enriching the soil beneath if necessary with fertilizer or garden compost.

4 Firm in the plant with your hand and water thoroughly, then smooth the plastic back and re-cover the area with gravel.

Choosing Plants

PLANTS FOR SMALL GARDENS

Almost any plant other than medium-sized or tall trees or very large shrubs and rampant ground cover can be grown in a small garden. Often quite large plants are used, but they need to be pruned back regularly to maintain a compact size. Whenever possible, it's best to choose naturally compact plants that won't become a nuisance.

EVERGREEN TREES

If conifers are excluded, there are few evergreen trees suitable for a small garden. Few broad-leaved trees are evergreen in temperate climates, and unfortunately many of those that are, such as the evergreen oak (*Quercus ilex*), grow far too large for most gardens. There are some worth searching out, such as *Drimys winteri*, which is too large for a tiny garden, but is not a fast grower. It's not a good choice for cold areas, however. Hollies (ilex) are really tough, and can be trained into a conical or standard tree with a clear trunk.

Drimys winteri is an uncommon plant, especially where winters are cold, but it makes an interesting large shrub or small tree with large, leathery evergreen leaves and fragrant white flowers in late spring.

DECIDUOUS TREES

It's a pity to exclude trees from a small garden, but choose those that remain small and have more than one season of interest. *Acer griseum*, for example, has a lovely cinnamon bark which looks

Crataegus oxyacantha (now more correctly *C. laevigata*) 'Rosea Flore Pleno' is a pretty hawthorn with double pink flowers in late spring. These trees never become very large.

wonderful in winter sunlight as well as fantastic in autumn colour. Many hawthorns (crataegus) make pleasing compact trees for a small garden. For flowering trees, look for those with columnar growth, such as *Prunus* 'Amanogawa'.

CONIFERS

Conifers come in many shades of gold and green (some with a hint of blue), as well as various shapes and sizes. The vast majority are evergreen. Unfortunately, most of them grow far too tall for a small garden. Select those with narrow, columnar growth that will not ultimately become too tall. Some to look for are *Juniperus scopulorum* 'Skyrocket', *Juniperus communis* 'Hibernica' and *Taxus baccata* 'Fastigiata Aurea'. *Cupressus macrocarpa* 'Goldcrest' also has a pleasing upright profile as well as a bright colour.

DWARF CONIFERS

A visit to any garden centre will reveal a bewildering choice of dwarf conifers, but always check on likely size after say 10 or 15 years of growth. Some will remain dwarf and may even be at home in

Cupressus macrocarpa 'Goldcrest' eventually makes a medium-sized tree, but has a narrow growth that means it does not take up excessive ground space. Young foliage is a beautiful yellow

a rock garden; others may grow surprisingly large. Among those that grow shrub-size are *Thuja orientalis* 'Aurea Nana', *Thuja occidentalis* 'Rheingold' and *Chamaecyparis pisifera* 'Filifera Aurea'. *Juniperus squamata* 'Blue Star' remains low-growing, and there are many other ground-hugging conifers.

EVERGREEN SHRUBS

You will be spoilt for choice with evergreen shrubs, so decide how large or small you want the plant

Thuja occidentalis 'Rheingold' is slow-growing and forms an oval to conical bush that always looks neat. The colour is old gold, and is especially pleasing in winter.

to grow to reduce your short list. If you have an acid soil, rhododendrons are a likely choice, but some can grow huge while others are suitable for a rock garden. There are bound to be varieties of appropriate size for your needs. Hebes are also available in many shapes and sizes, but always check that the ones you like are winter-hardy in your area. Heathers are evergreen and they are bound to be compact enough for your garden. The winter-flowering *Erica carnea* varieties are especially useful.

Hebe x *franciscana* 'Variegata' is delightfully bright and compact dwarf shrub, but it may suffer – or even be killed – where winters are cold.

DECIDUOUS SHRUBS

The problem with many deciduous shrubs is their short period of interest: flowering sometimes lasting no more than a couple of weeks. To make the best use of space, choose some that have golden or variegated foliage for a longer period of interest, or select those that have early colour, like chaenomeles, which bloom in spring, or that have late-season interest, like *Cotoneaster horizontalis* with its bright berries and vivid autumn foliage colour. Some, such as hydrangeas, also retain their flowers for a long period, and the dead heads also make an interesting winter feature.

The flower colour of *Hydrangea macrophylla* is often affected by the acidity or alkalinity of the soil.

BORDER PLANTS

All but the largest and tallest or most rampant herbaceous plants are suitable for a small garden, but where space is limited it's best to concentrate on those that flower early or late, or that look good over a long period and don't only look good for a week or two in summer. Lupins look fantastic for a couple of weeks, but for the rest of the season offer little interest.

Doronicums have nothing to offer by the time summer arrives, but they make an eye-catching display in spring.

Select summer flowers that bloom over a long period, or that have attractive foliage. For early border flowers, doronicums, with their yellow daisy-type flowers, look good, while at the end of the season schizostylis and varieties and hybrids of *Sedum spectabile* will sustain the colour.

EVERGREEN BORDER PLANTS

Make a point of visiting gardens in winter, and note which border plants remain evergreen. There are not many of them, but they are invaluable for sustaining interest during the bleak months. They include bergenias, ajugas and *Stachys byzantina*.

Ajuga reptans 'Atropurpurea' is one of several attractive bugles that make an attractive edging. They are almost evergreen and grow in sun and shade.

Family Gardens

Some gardens are designed primarily to be admired, others to be lived in – a place where children can play and adults can relax and perhaps enjoy a meal with friends. With careful thought, however, it's possible to design a garden that's both good to look at and comfortable to live in.

Children make the most demands on a garden, not least because they require a play area, which may not always be compatible with the kind of flower garden you have in mind, but also because the plants near play areas have to be that much tougher to withstand the occasional ball or rowdy play. It's a good idea to ban thorny or prickly plants, such as roses, in this area, to avoid unnecessary injuries.

Where there are very small children, ponds are not a good idea unless they are well protected. Some people fence them off or install protective metal covers for them, but such devices will not enhance the visual appeal of your pond and can be decidedly off-putting. It may be better to choose a water feature without standing water while the children are young.

■ ABOVE
Somewhere to entertain and relax is an essential ingredient of a family garden.

■ OPPOSITE
A place for the family to play and a desirable garden don't have to be an impossible mix. Turn a swing into a feature, rather than hiding it away.

INSPIRATIONAL IDEAS

Children can enjoy "adult" gardens, too, especially if there are lots of interesting shrubs and plants. Plants with big or bold leaves, or insectivorous plants, will stimulate their imagination and encourage interest as they grow older.

■ BELOW
A play area can be incorporated into the garden plan as easily as any other feature. Here, the sandpit has been positioned between two wooden walkways, with another small play area beyond the flowerbed. Using the small bed to divide up the play zone like this ensures it forms part of the garden and is not perceived as an appendage divorced from the garden proper.

■ ABOVE
Children would love this walkway along the back of a border and the climbing mesh against the other wall. And when they have outgrown such fun things, they can be removed, and the garden is left without any redesigning to be done.

■ RIGHT
This is unashamedly a garden for grown-ups to enjoy in the evening, but children will be fascinated by its magical grotto-like enchantment.

Illuminating part of your garden will enable you to derive many more hours of pleasure from it, and it will be a marvellous place to entertain your friends on a summer evening.

Inspirational Ideas

It is possible to create a stylish design that will appeal to parents and children in equal measure. A well-designed garden should be flexible enough to accommodate a safe play area for children and an entertainment and dining area for the whole family to enjoy.

■ ABOVE
Older children, able to use a trampoline unattended for example, do not usually have to be supervised so closely. As equipment like this is not an attractive feature in design terms, it's best to tuck it away out of sight, but not on a hard paved surface. This one has been positioned in a large bay of the lawn screened from the house by shrub borders.

■ OPPOSITE
A lawn for play is an essential part of a garden that young children can enjoy, but it can be a challenge to accommodate larger toys such as swings or see-saws. In this garden, the swing has been positioned in an area of the lawn that is clearly visible for supervision, but an "adult" space can easily be reinstated when the swing is no longer required.

Know-how

EATING OUT

Family gardens have to be multi-purpose, but, unless the garden is large, it may be necessary to place the design emphasis on one or two particular needs. If you do lots of entertaining, then a barbecue and seating area is likely to be a priority; if you seldom ask people around for outdoor meals but have young children who need somewhere safe and secure to play, a lawn and play area may be more important to you.

Eating out in the garden is so much more relaxing than meals around the dining table. Children love the fun of a barbecue, but there's a lot to be said for the convenience of preparing the food indoors and simply taking it outside to eat. A barbecue can be a colourful and cheerful occasion, and a time when your labours in the garden will be appreciated by all the family.

■ BELOW

ADDING COLOUR A bright or colourful tablecloth will transform a drab table in an instant. Add a few pots of seasonal plants, or a simple flower arrangement, for that finishing touch.
DESIGN TIP *Be prepared to move the table around the garden on different occasions, to take advantage of seasonal plants. Use a variety of bright tablecloths to keep each occasion special.*

■ BELOW

GARDEN LIGHTS Even the simplest meal becomes an adventure for children if it's eaten outdoors after dark. Patio lights that you can fix to a sunshade are simple to install and provide all the light you need for a simple occasion like this. DESIGN TIP *Garden lights can transform your garden after dusk, but be careful with the use of spotlights – wherever possible make sure they point down rather than up if there is a risk of their shining into your neighbour's house. Patio lights cast a glow rather than a strong beam so should not be annoying to neighbours, and the parasol helps to confine the light and cast it downwards.*

■ ABOVE

KEEP IT SIMPLE A few flowers and foliage picked from the garden, a simple salad seasoned with fresh herbs and a bowl of strawberries, will provide all the ingredients for a relaxing meal in the garden. For a quick meal, keep it simple: you'll enjoy it as much as something more lavish in this relaxing environment. DESIGN TIP *Don't be content with a natural wood finish. Be prepared to paint the table and chairs if this creates an interesting focal point, or helps to express your creative sense of design.*

■ RIGHT

PORTABLE TABLES This small garden has all the essential elements for outdoor living: a built-in barbecue, a pretty setting and a bottle of wine at the ready. You don't need to set aside a large area for this kind of outdoor living. DESIGN TIP *If the garden or sitting area is very small, a lightweight and easily portable table that can be brought out for the occasion might make better use of the available space than heavy, fixed or less mobile furniture.*

Know-how

Sitting Pretty

Seating is an integral part of most gardens, but in a family garden it can be used to suggest a place for everyone – children and parents – to sit and enjoy the pleasures that outdoor living and a well-planned garden can bring.

■ RIGHT

DESIGNING WITH CHAIRS A seat that has its own space built into the design will always make the garden look well planned and structured.

DESIGN TIP *It's important to have the exact seat in mind at the design stage, as the recess must look made-to-measure.*

■ BELOW

BENCH SEATS Children will probably be as happy sitting on a seat made from old railway sleepers (railroad ties) as on stylish manufactured furniture.

DESIGN TIP *A seat like this is best positioned in an informal part of the garden, perhaps near or among trees, where it will blend in with the background and look more sympathetic with the surroundings than more traditional seats.*

■ LEFT

FEATURE SEATS Improvised seats can be a test of initiative, but are great fun to make. Children will find them exciting to sit on, and they often make decorative focal points. This one is made from an old garden roller, with a clipped dwarf hedge for the surround.

DESIGN TIP *Try to position a seat like this where it also makes a focal point when viewed across the garden.*

■ RIGHT

USING TREES

Tree seats always attract admiring comments, and they appeal to children as much as parents. A seat like this can make a feature in an area of the garden that might otherwise lack interest. White paint helps to bring light to what can be a gloomy position, and attracts the eye from across the garden.

DESIGN TIP

Choose a tree with a large trunk, if possible. If you build a seat around a fairly slim tree, the proportions will look wrong and the impact will be less effective.

Know-how

A RELAXING TIME

Family gardens should look lived-in, and loungers and hammocks will create this relaxed and friendly atmosphere. There are many types to choose from – select seating that will match the style of your garden, whether it be formal or country cottage.

■ LEFT

HAMMOCK If you have a stately tree, it can become a support for a hammock and a swing seat for the children or grandchildren. A corner of the garden like this can be shared by all generations of the family.

DESIGN TIP *A shady tree is the best location for a hammock.*

■ BELOW

SUN LOUNGERS Loungers can be moved around the garden with ease. If you choose a bold colour, they will act as a focal point.

DESIGN TIP *Placing two or more loungers together gives the impression of shared pleasure. Placing a small table between them with a collection of cool drinks will look even more tempting.*

■ LEFT

WOODEN FURNITURE

Even wooden garden furniture can be made comfortable with a few cushions, and a feature like this can be easily incorporated into almost any plan.

DESIGN TIP

Wherever possible, position your furniture as near as you can to fragrant plants.

■ RIGHT

POOLSIDE LOUNGERS

Sometimes a quiet place to lounge in tranquil isolation, perhaps to read a book or have a nap, is more appealing than a spot on a sunny lawn with the rest of the family.

DESIGN TIP

A simple piece of garden furniture like this pool lounger can serve as a useful focal point in an otherwise flat area.

Know-how

FAMILY LAWNS

A family lawn creates a wonderful area for children to play in, but with a young, active family it can be the hardest part of the garden to keep in good repair.

With just a little thought and know-how, you can keep the lawn green and growing by mowing and feeding, and by carrying out the occasional repair job.

■ BELOW

Lawns or flat, grassy areas are suitable for many children's games, but they do need a durable surface. Ball games in an unsuitable garden can create havoc. Keep your lawn as uncluttered as possible and minimize your flower beds. They can always be developed more intricately as the children get older. For maximum play efficiency, the ideal lawn for games should be sited against a garden or garage wall which can easily take the brunt of hit and kicked balls.

SEED MIXTURES

A seed mixture for a family lawn should contain the following grasses in approximate proportions.

3 PARTS DWARF PERENNIAL RYE GRASS (*Lolium perenne*)
Hardwearing and quick to establish.

4 PARTS FINE FESCUE (*Festuca*)
These grasses that make up a luxury lawn are quick to establish, but are rather delicate and easily pushed out by stronger grasses.

1 PART BROWNTOP BENT (*Agrostis canina*)
A fine-leaved grass that is slow to establish but eventually forms a neat, dense turf.

2 PARTS SMOOTH-STALKED MEADOW GRASS (*Poa*)
A creeping grass that, once established, is hardwearing and resistant to dry weather.

■ LEFT
In a medium-sized garden a circular or central lawn area will provide space for many different ball games. Any plants sited near these areas should be chosen for their ability to withstand damage from flying balls, and children searching for lost balls. Avoid plants with spines or thorns which will inevitably result in nasty cuts and scratches. Deciduous plants are usually better able to recover from damage as scarred leaves will be shed each year.

■ BELOW
All lawns must be cut regularly to look good and stay healthy. If there is an asthmatic in the family a grass lawn should pose no problem because the grasses will not get a chance to flower. Areas of long grass, such as in a wildlife garden, should be avoided.

Planning and Planting

URBAN ELEGANCE

This town garden is the perfect place to relax in, to unwind from the stresses of a busy life. The dominance of greens and whites in the planting plan gives the garden a sense of unity and subtlety, as well as a sense of cool tranquillity.

PLANNING

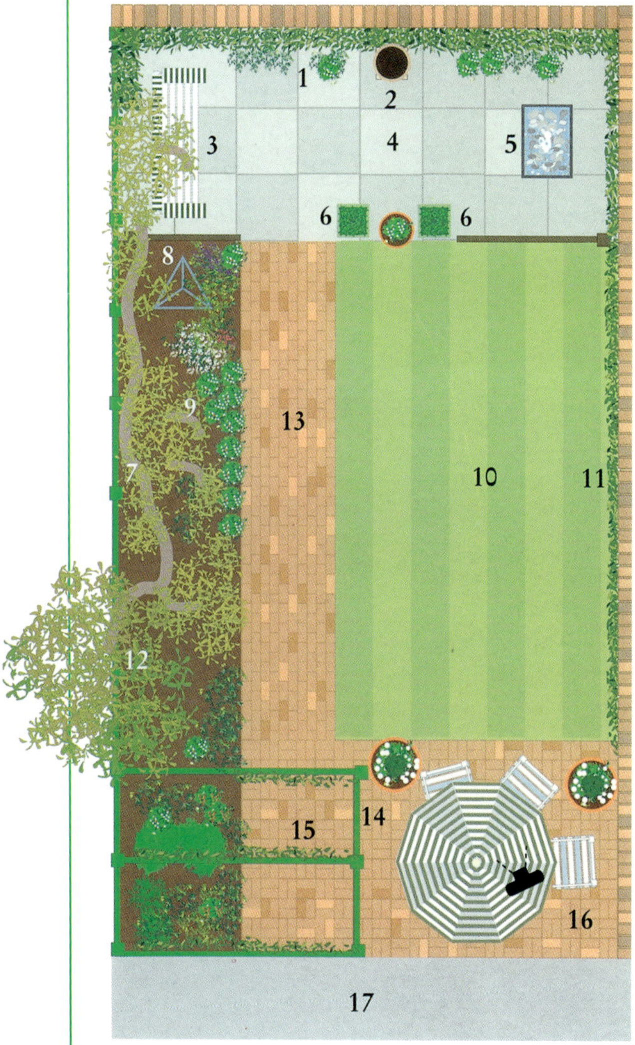

KEY TO PLAN

1 Hedge
2 Urn
3 Garden swing seat
4 Paved area
5 Pebble fountain
6 Clipped box
7 Trellis
8 Tripod for climbers
9 Low raised bed with mixed planting
10 Lawn
11 Wall climbers
12 Specimen tree, pruned and trained to grow along boundary
13 Brick path
14 Patio overhead (beams above window level)
15 Climber over patio overhead
16 Patio
17 House

Viewpoint on photograph

This is primarily the kind of garden that would appeal to adults, but there is a large lawn for anyone who needs to let off steam. However, a high-quality lawn like this is too good for rough play: a paved area is more suitable for ball games or frequent use. The lawn is an important and dominant design feature of this plan, creating a sense of open space that lets the garden "breathe".

The tree on the left-hand side of the garden is unusual as it has been persuaded to grow along the edge of the garden rather than over it, so avoiding a potential shade problem. A small tree, left to grow naturally, would be just as effective in this situation.

As planting space is limited, the bed along the side of the garden accommodates seasonal plants and permanent evergreen plants, to pack in colour where it's needed, and to introduce an element of variety from season to season.

■ RIGHT
HOW TO BUILD PATIO OVERHEADS
Patio overheads are a kind of pergola with one end of the overhead beams fixed to the house or garden wall. These are particularly effective for linking the home and garden visually, and of course they provide a useful support for climbers as well as a degree of shade. If you want a more enclosed structure, with permanent shading and a greater degree of privacy, it's possible to fix reed mats over the top, although additional battens, laid at right angles to the overhead beams, will be required to support them.

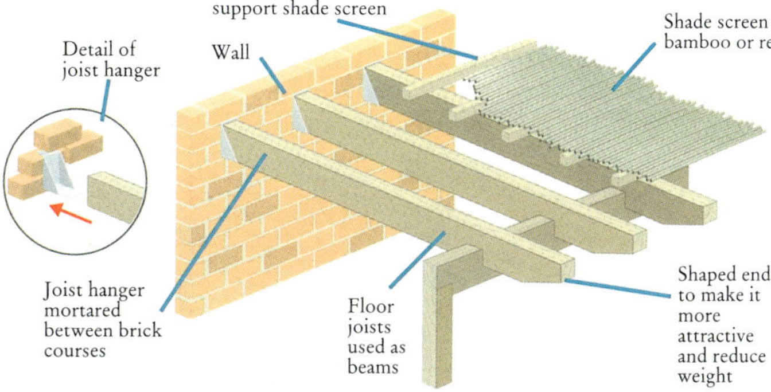

PLANNING

Remember that patio overheads that join the house should always be high enough to clear the window and not block out the view if vigorous climbers cascade from the beams.

Use floor joists for the overhead beams, and secure them to the wall with joist hangers (see illustration). These are designed with a lip to be mortared into the brickwork, so on an existing wall it will be necessary to chisel out sufficient mortar to accommodate the hanger. Once the joist hanger has been mortared into position and the mortar has set, the beam can be inserted and secured by nailing through the fixing holes in the hanger. The hangers are available from builders' merchants and large do-it-yourself stores.

If the span is short, the beams may only require the support of one cross-beam supported on posts, as shown. Wider spans will need intermediate post and beam supports.

If you wish to add shading for summer, nail battens parallel to the wall to support a reed or bamboo screen (these usually come in rolls), as shown in the illustration. If you wish to have the shading in position only for the summer, it should be possible to tie it in position, but do this securely.

Be sure that the posts are strong enough for the structure and that they are well concreted into the ground or fixed in special post supports.

PLANTING

PLAY HOUSES

You should be able to add a few finishing touches to the basic structure of a store-bought, manufactured play house, and if your children are involved in choosing the embellishments and colour schemes, they'll find it that much more exciting.

If you do decide to go along the DIY route, it is a good idea to make solid structures to be adapted for use after the children have finished with them. Ensure that home–made equipment is strong, sturdy and steady, that all wood is sanded down and coated in exterior grade varnish and that nails and screws are safely sunk below the surface. Any ready–made play equipment that you buy should have been made to approved standards and you should check over and maintain it regularly.

The cheapest play–houses are made from materials such as cloth and PVC, and have a tough, tubular support frame. These are available in a range of bright colours. More expensive but much more durable and equally colourful are those made from rigid plastic.

Using a tent as a temporary camp can satisfy almost the same needs as a playhouse. The advantages are that a tent is generally cheaper than a wooden play house and if well looked after, it will survive longer than cloth or plastic ones.

Planning and Planting

A House of Their Own

Children's needs often have to be accommodated within an existing garden, or designed into a new one in a way that, when the facilities have been outgrown, they can be removed without leaving an obtrusive space or in need of re-designing. Here, the children's area has been created in a part of the garden separate from the main ornamental area.

PLANNING

KEY TO PLAN

1 Tree house in large tree
2 Rough grass
3 Den created from horseshoe of shrubs
4 Play house
5 Sandpit
6 Hedge
7 Flowerbed
8 Lawn
9 Herbaceous border
10 House

Viewpoint on photograph

An area for children should reflect their ages, and of course with a growing family there may be a spread of ages to accommodate, all needing different kinds of stimulation. This plan shows features that will appeal to young children and older ones.

In a garden like this, younger children will have to be supervised carefully, for there are hard surfaces. Thorny plants like roses are a potential hazard, and a tree house will definitely be out of bounds for the very young. Older children will love the tree house and the den, however, and a garden with hiding places and secret corners will feed their imagination.

Depending on the age of the youngest child, it may be necessary to fence off the area beyond the play house, with a gate to the adventure area beyond.

Most families inevitably end up acquiring one or more pieces of play equipment for their children. Portable sandpits can be great fun for toddlers, whilst play equipment that will be used for several years, such as a swing, should be carefully sited, and then can be softened or disguised to become a permanent garden feature.

Planning and Planting

OUTDOOR ENTERTAINING

This garden is clearly designed for the whole family to enjoy the great outdoors in the garden. There are plenty of seats for family and friends, a built-in barbecue, and a sand pit for youngsters. There's also plenty of space to play in this safe and enclosed environment.

PLANNING

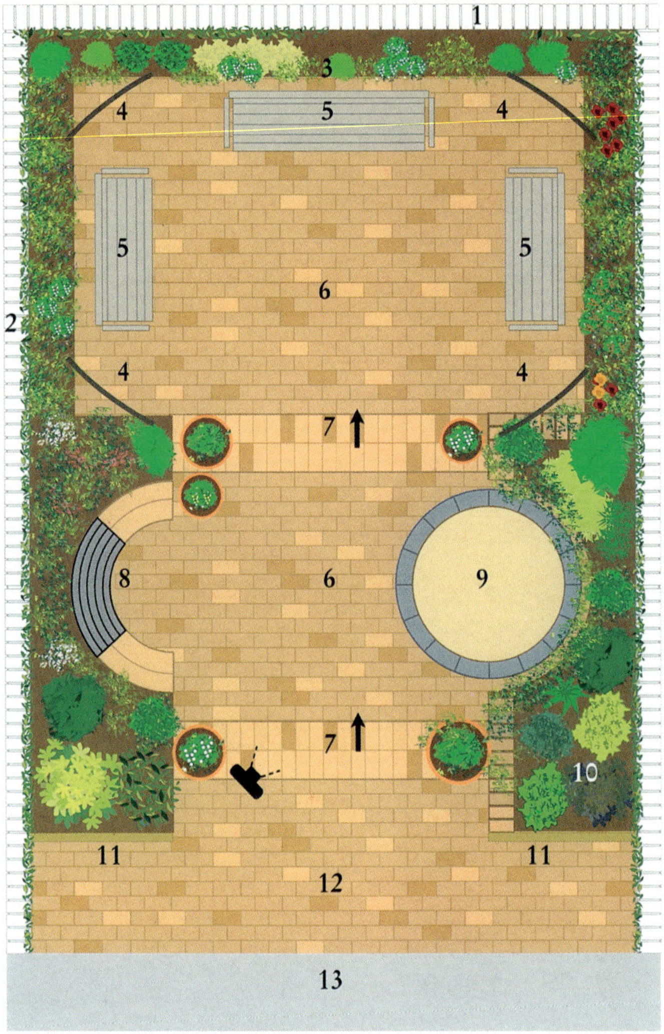

KEY TO PLAN

1 Wall, painted white
2 Wall, with climbers
3 Dwarf shrubs
4 Metal arch for climbers
5 Garden bench
6 Brick paving
7 Steps
8 Barbecue with brick shelves on each side
9 Sandpit
10 Shrubs
11 Timber rail
12 Brick terrace
13 House

↑ Direction of steps up

Viewpoint on photograph

This garden shows many design elements that guarantee impact: changes of level, a choice of areas for sitting and relaxing, attractive paving that harmonizes with the walls, some strong focal points, and a symmetry of construction that suggests good design.

It may seem strange that a sandpit should become a focal point, but when its usefulness as a sandpit is over, and young children have grown up, it can be turned into an attractive circular pond, perhaps with a fountain to bring movement and relaxing sounds to the scene.

LIGHTING UP

Garden lighting can be enchanting and atmospheric, and it can even make your garden a safer place if potentially hazardous steps are illuminated. If you are considering installing a high-voltage system, you should always consult a qualified electrician. A low-voltage system, however, is a relatively simple do-it-yourself job, but take professional advice, if in doubt.

PLANTING

GARDEN LIGHTING

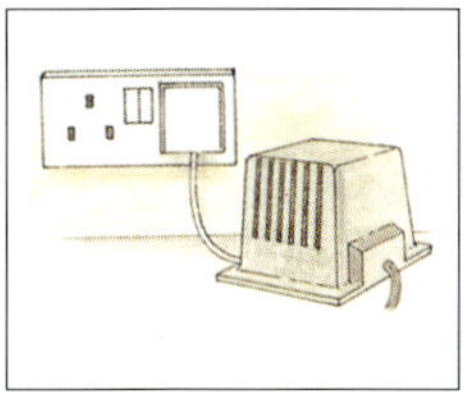

1 A low-voltage lighting kit will come with a transformer. This must always be protected from the weather, positioned in a dry place indoors or in a garage or outbuilding.

2 Using an electric drill, make a hole through the window frame or wall, just wide enough to take the cable. Fill in any gaps afterwards, using a mastic or other waterproof filler.

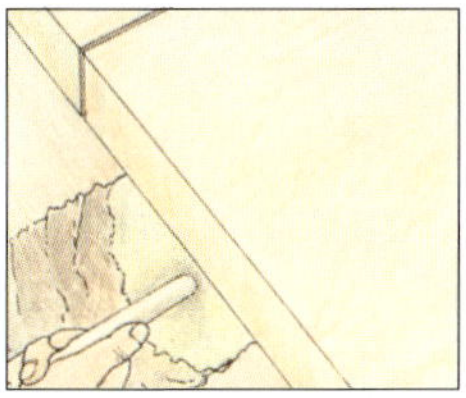

3 Although the cable carries a low voltage, it is still a potential hazard if left uncovered. Unless the lights are positioned close to where the cable emerges, run it underground in a conduit.

4 Most low-voltage lighting systems are designed to be moved around. Many of them can be pushed conveniently into the ground wherever you choose to use them.

Planning and Planting

LINE AND COLOUR

The planting in this garden is secondary to the impact of strong lines and colours, and it is clearly designed primarily as an outdoor room for eating and entertainment.

PLANNING

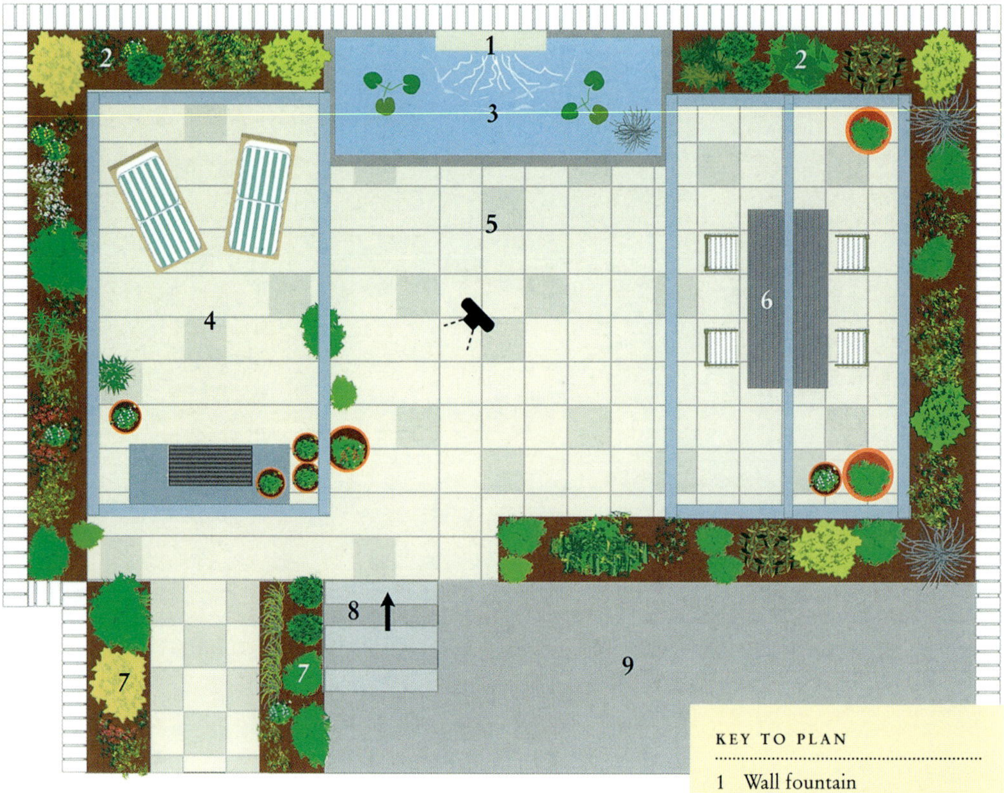

KEY TO PLAN

1 Wall fountain
2 Low-growing mixed plants
3 Pond
4 Barbecue and relaxing area
5 Tile paving
6 Eating area with patio overhead
7 Low-growing shrubs
8 Steps
9 House

↑ Direction of steps down

Viewpoint on photograph

Many garden designs place the emphasis on plants, but if your interests lie in relaxation and outdoor living rather than in gardening as a hobby, it's a good idea to confine the planting to a few beds as a backdrop or to soften the harsh effect of walls or fences. A garden like this, designed for lots of outdoor eating and entertaining, may be used much more intensively for relaxation than designs intended primarily to show off the plants.

SUN SHADES

Sunny summer days are what we all dream of, but there are times when we all need to retreat to some shade. Parasols and awnings can be pretty as well as practical, and they can make striking focal points.

■ ABOVE
Parasols like this can have as much impact as a flowerbed, and they make stylish focal points.

PLANTING

■ ABOVE MIDDLE
An awning is a useful windbreak for a breezy day as well as a practical sunshade for when you need to retreat to somewhere cool. This one comes with a lightweight metal frame that is easily erected, and the awning is simply slipped over it.

■ ABOVE RIGHT
You couldn't help but feel grand sheltering from the blistering sun in this elegant structure, which would bring colour to your garden even if the flowers were not performing. A teepee structure like this helps to create a feeling of cosy intimacy as you share a meal beneath it.

Planning and Planting

AN ENCHANTED JUNGLE

This dense, lush garden has both sophistication for grown-ups and drama and adventure for children, with changes of level and lots of tall, leafy plants, including a banana plant, bedded out for the summer. This plan is perfect for dining and playing.

KEY TO PLAN

1 Shrubs
2 Decking with table and chairs
3 Decking at higher level
4 Steps
5 A focal-point foliage plant (here a banana plant)
6 Barbecue
7 Group of containers
8 Patio
9 Door
10 House

↓ Direction of steps down

Viewpoint on photograph

PLANNING

Even a small area can look densely planted if you envelop your sitting area with a living screen of well-chosen plants. Changing levels and using shrubs to obscure the various sections of the garden also help to make it an exciting garden to explore and play in.

The choice of decking in this design helps to create a jungle-like atmosphere as it blends in perfectly with the plants, having a natural affinity with them.

The lower paved area acts as a practical bridge between home and the plant-filled area, and it is here that the barbecue has been situated, leaving the eating area free of anything that would detract from its natural-looking setting.

GIANT FOLIAGE PLANTS

An impressive banana plant has been used as a focal-point foliage plant in the garden photographed opposite, but such exotic plants need to be over-wintered in a conservatory or a large greenhouse if you live where temperatures drop to freezing. There are many hardy foliage plants with big or

PLANNING

bold leaves, however, and a clump of them can create the impression of lush, tropical growth.

The plants in the illustration all prefer moist soil, such as that found in a bog garden, but you can grow them in a normal bed or border if you use a trickle irrigation hose to ensure adequate moisture. Where conditions suit, the gunnera leaves can grow to 1.8m (6ft) across on stems up to 3m (10ft) tall, though in dry conditions they will be probably be smaller.

GIANT FOLIAGE PLANTS

KEY TO PLANTS

1 *Gunnera manicata*
2 *Petasites japonicus giganteus*
3 *Rheum undulatum*
4 *Rheum palmatum tanguticum*

Planning and Planting

A Secret Garden

This garden has lots of features packed into a modest-sized plot, happily marrying an open area of lawn for relaxation and play with plenty of screening and a sense of seclusion.

PLANNING

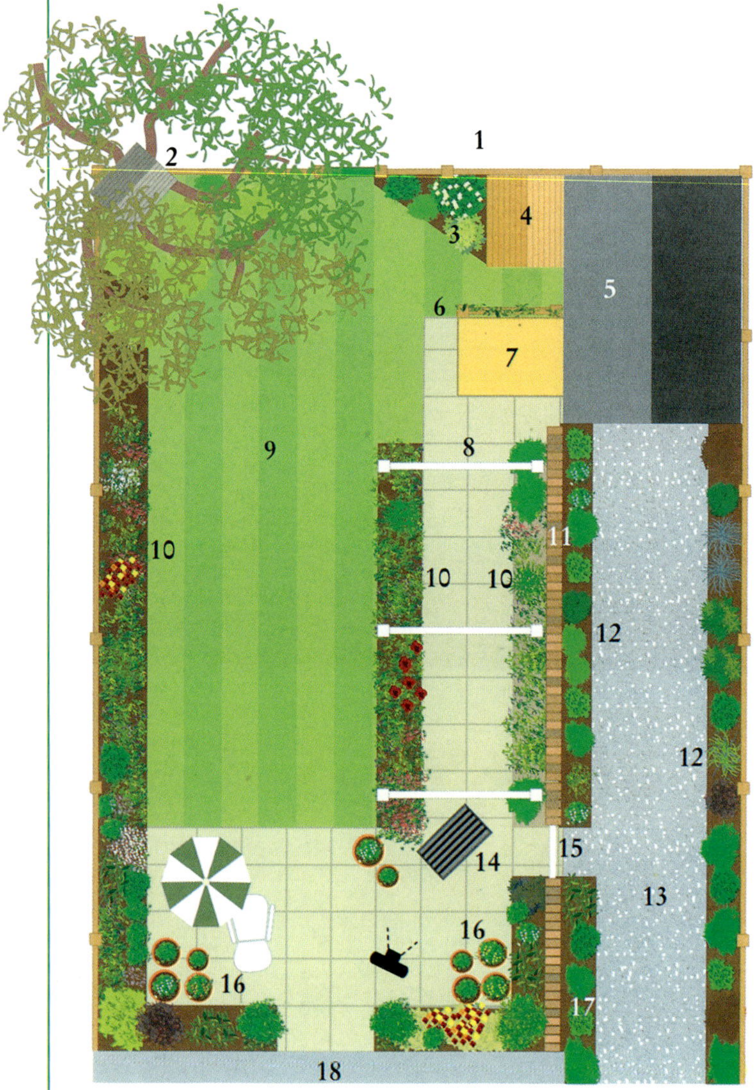

KEY TO PLAN

1 Woodland
2 Tree house
3 Shrubs
4 Shed
5 Garage
6 Climber-covered trellis
7 Sandpit
8 Pergola
9 Lawn
10 Mixed border
11 Wall
12 Ground-cover shrubs
13 Drive
14 Barbecue
15 Door to drive
16 Group of containers
17 Dwarf shrubs
18 House

Viewpoint in photograph

Children have been well catered for in this garden, with a sandpit and a tree house, together with a lawn where the whole family can play and relax. The pergola gives shade and a sense of seclusion, and it ensures that the garden has height and a sense of structure. A trellis positioned behind the sandpit helps to screen the garden shed from view.

A garage and drive can dominate a garden if not screened. Here a dividing wall solves the problem by disguising the drive. If building a brick wall seems a daunting job, screen (pierced) walling blocks are easy to lay and will still act as a screen, especially if climbers or shrubs are used to clothe them.

LIGHTWEIGHT PERGOLAS

The strongest pergolas are made from sawn wood (lumber), but a lightweight structure can be easily constructed from rustic poles and will blend in with the surroundings effectively.

PLANTING

HOW TO JOIN RUSTIC POLES

1 Using a handsaw, saw a notch of suitable size at the top of the upright post to take a horizontal piece of wood snugly.

2 Where two rails have to be joined, do this over an upright. Cut matching notches so that one piece sits directly over the other.

3 To fix cross-pieces to horizontals, cut a V-shaped notch into the crosspiece, using a chisel if necessary, then nail into place.

4 Use halving joints where two pieces cross. Make two saw cuts halfway through the pole, then chisel out the waste. Use a wood adhesive and secure a halving joint with a nail for extra strength.

5 Bird's-mouth joints are useful for connecting horizontal and diagonal pieces to uprights. Remove a V-shaped notch about 2.5cm (1in) deep, then saw the other piece to match. Use a chisel to achieve a good fit.

Choosing Plants

PLANTS FOR FAMILY GARDENS

Most plants have a place in the family garden, and the best plants are simply those that you like, provided they are not harmful. It is easier to suggest plants to avoid rather than specific plants to grow. However, plants with large, unusual or dramatic foliage will be popular.

PLANTS TO AVOID

Avoid very spiky plants, but take care: the leaf tips of Spanish bayonet (*Yucca gloriosa*) look no more hazardous than other yuccas, but this one has treacherous leaf tips that arch out and can cause a painful stab. Roses with many or large thorns are also best avoided.

Potentially poisonous or irritant plants should also be avoided. Some have poisonous roots or leaves, but berries are the greatest hazard as they look tempting. Some plants cause dermatitis and other skin irritations. A few are potentially very hazardous, however, a common one being rue (*Ruta graveolens*), the sap of which can cause a very severe allergic reaction on bare skin in sunlight.

FASCINATING ARUMS

Aroids, plants of the arum family, are strange plants that children will find fascinating. The arum lily (*Zantedeschia aethiopica*) is often grown as a cut flower and as a pot plant in conservatories, but where winters are not severe it can be grown as a garden plant, too. Arums have their true flowers clustered inconspicously on a club-like or poker-shaped spadix, which is surrounded by the showy coloured spath. For children, try the mouse plant (*Arisarum proboscideum*) or the voodoo lily (*Sauromatum venosum*). The latter can be flowered out of soil or water indoors, then planted in the garden to produce its impressive foliage. The smell of the flowers can literally make you want to vomit, something children can find amusing. For the garden try the dragon arum (*Dracunculus vulgaris*), which has huge velvety-crimson spathes 30–60cm (1–2ft) long and flowers that smell of rotting meat, which attract flies. Other arums have flowers that look like cobra heads.

Dracunculus vulgaris is not a plant you could pass by without noticing – at least not when it is in full flower. Their eye-catching crimson flowers have a very unpleasant smell.

QUICK AND EASY ANNUALS

Plants that grow quickly, especially from seed to flower in a matter of months, are more likely to hold the interest of youngsters. Small-growers like the poached-egg plant (*Limnanthes douglasii*) are easy for a child to sow and flower, and are worth growing as good garden plants anyway. But it's the tall sunflowers that will probably encourage children to get involved in regular watering and feeding.

Limnanthes douglasii, sometimes known as the poached-egg plant, is a really easy hardy annual to grow. Although the parent plant dies at the end of the season, self-sown seedlings usually appear.

FRUITS FOR FUN

Things that can be safely eaten hold their own special attraction, and apples and pears can make decorative garden features if grown as a cordon or espalier against the garden fence or up a wall. A family apple tree, with several different varieties grafted on to the same plant, is sure to create interest and is an ideal way of growing several varieties in the space of one.

Pears trained as espaliers can, with patience, look much more attractive than those grown in tree form. The fruit will also be very much easier to reach when it comes to harvesting.

BORDER PLANTS

It's a good idea to concentrate on those almost indestructible herbaceous perennials such as day lilies (hemerocallis), red-hot-pokers (kniphofias) and hostas. If you have young children, it may be best to avoid plants that attract bees, such as catmints (nepetas).

Hemerocallis are sometimes called day lilies because individual blooms are so short-lived. Fortunately, a succession of them is produced over a long period.

SHRUBS

For backbone planting, tough variegated evergreens that stand up to occasional rough play yet still look good through the year are difficult to beat. You will also need plenty of deciduous flowering shrubs, but as core plants, use shrubs such as *Aucuba japonica* in one of it many variegated forms, *Elaeagnus pungens* 'Maculata' and phormiums (these may be vulnerable where winters are cold).

Aucuba japonica 'Variegata' is a really tough shrub, for sun or shade, and a useful evergreen for those difficult spots that every garden has. There are other variegated varieties to choose from.

Elaeagnus pungens 'Maculata' is an outstanding evergreen that looks especially good positioned where winter sunshine can highlight the gold in the variegated leaves.

HERBS

Many of us grow a few herbs for the kitchen, but some of the more interesting ones can get children interested in the different aromas as well as possibly their use at table. A collection of mints with all their various smells, from spearmint to apple, thymes and the tall, aniseed-flavoured fennel (*Foeniculum vulgare*) are good multi-purpose herbs to start with. Herbs in containers, or grown in a herb "wheel" will also keep children involved.

Fennel *(Foeniculum vulgare)* has feathery foliage that makes it an attractive ornamental as well as a culinary herb. There is a bronze form as well as the more common green one.

BULBS

Children enjoy planting bulbs and corms, from which some of our best and brightest flowers come. Get them to plant spring crocuses and autumn-flowering colchicums in borders or a corner of the lawn if it's suitable. Colchicums are especially rewarding as they can flower within weeks of planting. Choose big and spectacular plants for summer bulbs, such as *Allium giganteum* or one of the foxtail lilies (eremurus).

Colchicum autumnale is sometimes called an autumn crocus. Colchicums usually bloom in early autumn, when colour in the garden is becoming scarce.

Kitchen Gardens

While some gardeners are uninspired by the concept of kitchen gardens, others are happy to devote much of their free time and all available space to growing vegetables and fruit. Most of us, however, would probably prefer to combine the edible with the ornamental, whether they grow side by side as in a potager or in separate parts of the garden.

It's unreasonable to expect self-sufficiency in produce from all but the largest gardens, and even then few are prepared to devote the time and effort required. Most of us aspire to be good gardeners, not smallholders, so the ability to harvest our own new potatoes while they are still expensive in the shops, pick an apple from the tree and take a bite, or perhaps have a constant supply of salad crops and herbs during the summer, is all we ask. It is the satisfaction of having grown your own, and the knowledge that they are fresh and free from pesticides (assuming you've been careful on this point), that's the special reward.

■ ABOVE
Every garden has space for fruits and vegetables, and the benefits are great.

■ OPPOSITE
Red cabbages, contained by a dwarf box (*Buxus sempervirens* 'Suffruticosa') hedge, look highly ornamental.

Inspirational Ideas

Growing plants that you can eat as well as admire is a bonus. Some vegetables, such as ruby chard and beetroot, even cut-leaved lettuce, are pretty as ornamental plants in beds and borders. Try planting vegetables and fruit in beds and borders, with flowers.

■ BELOW
A kitchen garden is likely to be visually more acceptable if it is broken up into small beds, here with a decorative "rope" edging. The crops are easy to cultivate without having to walk on the soil, as all parts can be reached with a hoe from the paths. It's possible to arrange the beds in a geometrical pattern to emphasize the sense of design. The paths between them can also be made interesting, depending on the materials used and how they are laid. Here light-coloured bricks complement the rope edging, unifying the design.

■ OPPOSITE ABOVE
In a cottage garden, it's perfectly natural to see a corner given over to growing vegetables. Provided it is a weed-free and neat area, it should not look unattractive. Adding a few bright flowers around the edge, like these French marigolds, will make it look more ornamental – and it is thought that these plants can help to deter pests.

■ OPPOSITE BELOW
Old-fashioned cottage gardens often used to have vegetables in the front garden, and crops like pumpkins and squashes were very decorative towards the end of the season. Don't be afraid to use a few flowers alongside the vegetables. This practice used to be quite common and, as this picture shows, makes a far more pleasing garden than vegetables alone. The white picket fence also makes this a lively garden to look at and shows that the kitchen garden does not have to be tucked away in a utilitarian part of the entire garden.

Inspirational Ideas

You don't need space for an orchard to grow your own fruit. Apples, pears and peaches are among the fruits easily trained against a wall or fence as a fan, espalier or cordon. Soft fruit such as strawberries can be grown in pots or in small beds in sunny positions.

■ OPPOSITE
Herb gardens are sometimes created more for their ornamental effect than for culinary benefits. There's lots of scope for geometric designs, and focal-point features such as birdbaths and sundials.

■ RIGHT
If you garden on a patio or balcony, your herbs may have to be confined to containers. This is not always a bad thing: the mints in this growing bag will remain confined and the spreading roots will not be able to invade surrounding territory. Next to the mints is a collection of three attractive ornamental sages, and the remaining pot holds a small collection of various herbs.

These practical herbs have been placed unashamedly against a raised bed with flowers as a backdrop: petunias and the yellow trailing *Lysimachia nummularia*.

■ ABOVE
Kitchen gardens can make charming decorative features. In this walled garden, the design has been marked out by edgings of box or rue, but the contents of each bed are surprisingly diverse. Some contain potatoes or tomatoes, in others ornamental plants such as dahlias are growing. There are also beds with herbs, and beds containing soft fruits such as gooseberries.

Despite the diversity of plants being grown within the beds – vegetables, herbs, fruit, and flowers – the design looks unified and well planned because the area has been laid out to a recognizable pattern.

Know-how

KITCHEN CONTAINERS

If you don't have space for a large kitchen garden, think creatively. It may be possible to grow a small selection that combines the ornamental with the tasty.

Salad crops such as tomatoes and lettuces are especially good for growing in containers, as they respond well to confinement, they are easy to grow, and you don't need many plants for a small family. They can be grown in window boxes or patio pots. Be prepared to stretch your horizons, however, as most vegetables can be grown successfully in containers with a little determination.

■ BELOW LEFT

LETTUCES Lettuces are really easy to grow, and small varieties don't require much space. Sow a pinch of seeds each week from spring onwards for a succession of hearted lettuce, or choose loose-leaf types such as 'Salad Bowl' so that you can harvest individual leaves over a long period. This does not leave such obvious gaps when you harvest, in comparison with a hearty variety where you use the whole head.

Choose different types of lettuce with a variety of leaf shape and colour, to make attractive displays in troughs, containers or window boxes.

DESIGN TIP *If growing in window boxes, use two or three liner boxes (cheap plastic troughs) to fit inside a more attractive outer box. Sow in succession in the various boxes, and move those at their most attractive stage into the decorative outer box. When harvesting is over, replace the inner trough with one containing maturing lettuces and resow the one removed.*

■ RIGHT

POTATOES Maincrop potatoes are not a practical proposition for containers, but it's worth planting a few tubers of an early variety to bring on and harvest while the tubers are still small and especially tasty. This is the time when potatoes are also at their most expensive in the shops. Start them off in a frost-free greenhouse or conservatory, in large pots or growing bags, and move them outdoors as soon as it's reasonably safe to do so. If frost is forecast, bring them in until it's safe to place them outside again. A pot is easy to move, but a growing bag is best placed on a board that two people can easily lift to move in if frost threatens. This sounds a lot of effort when you can pop around to the local shop for them, but a meal or two of freshly harvested young new potatoes really is a treat.

DESIGN TIP *Potatoes are for eating, not admiring, so place the containers where they will not be conspicuous, but make sure they receive plenty of light.*

■ LEFT

OTHER VEGETABLES Marrows, courgettes (zucchini) and cucumbers can all be grown successfully in growing bags or large containers such as half-barrels. This courgette (zucchini) in a half-barrel is beginning to crop.

DESIGN TIP *Marrows and courgettes (zucchini) are decorative, with large yellow flowers. Some varieties have yellow fruit.*

■ BELOW

CONTAINER VEGETABLES If you don't mind giving over a substantial part of your patio to vegetables you can pack in many different kinds. Use large containers that hold plenty of potting soil, and don't neglect the watering.

DESIGN TIP *Large tubs like this are not particularly attractive. You could try decorating them with acrylic paints, or building a low screen tall enough to hide the containers.*

■ RIGHT

USING GROWING BAGS It's surprising what you can raise in a few growing bags. These two contain early potatoes, spinach, lettuce, and salad onions. Choose small varieties or those that can be harvested early.

DESIGN TIP *It may be better to concentrate all your vegetables in one part of the patio, especially if they are in growing bags, otherwise they may begin to detract from the ornamentals.*

Know-how

FRUIT IN FOCUS

Orchards are attractive features in their own right, but they demand considerable space. In small gardens, fruit such as apples, pears and peaches are best grown as cordons, espaliers or fans. These are plants grafted on to a dwarfing rootstock and trained to crop on heavily pruned shoots. Cordons usually have one main stem trained at an angle of about 45°, espaliers have a central upright stem with horizontal tiered branches, and fans have their shoots trained fan-like against a wall or fence. Apples can also be grown in large pots, and some modern varieties have narrow pole-like growth that makes them suitable for a confined space, so they are suitable for even a tiny garden.

■ RIGHT
FLAGPOLE APPLES "Flagpole" apples, of which there are several good varieties available, grow naturally on an upright stem with no branches, but plenty of fruiting spurs. These are ideal trees for a confined space, and you can have a whole collection of them in a small garden.
DESIGN TIP *Try planting a row of different varieties along one boundary of the kitchen garden. They will form a productive screen and boundary marker.*

■ LEFT
STEP-OVER APPLES "Step-over" apples are single espaliers that make a neat edging. They are pretty in flower and attractive in fruit, while taking up the minimum of space. Like all espaliers, they will require annual pruning to maintain their trained shape.
DESIGN TIP *These make a neat and productive edging for a kitchen garden, and would even look attractive at the edge of a flower border.*

■ LEFT

POTTED PEACHES Peaches make attractive fan-trained fruits for a warm position, but this one, known as 'Garden Silver', is growing in bush form in a 30cm (1ft) patio pot. Not all peaches will perform like this in a small pot, however.

DESIGN TIP *Peaches make good patio plants as they are highly ornamental in spring when covered with pink blossom.*

■ ABOVE

CONTAINER APPLES Apples can be grown in large pots, provided they have been grafted on to a very dwarfing rootstock. The crop will be limited but acceptable, and a pot-grown apple always makes a good talking point.

DESIGN TIP *Don't grow apples in containers where you have the choice of planting in the ground – those in the ground don't demand frequent care such as watering. Container-grown apples are best used in paved gardens or on balconies where the options are limited.*

■ ABOVE RIGHT

ESPALIER PEARS This is what is called a productive fence. The espalier 'Conference' pear is laden with fruit and looks highly decorative too.

DESIGN TIP *Try training espalier fruit trees along fences bounding your kitchen garden. They'll look good and release valuable space within the vegetable and fruit bed for planting other fruits.*

■ RIGHT

FAN PEACHES The most decorative way to grow peaches and nectarines, if you want a heavy crop on an ornamental plant, is to grow them as a fan trained against a wall or fence.

DESIGN TIP *Grow a peach against a warm, sunny wall, but don't expect a heavy crop if you live in a cold area.*

Know-how

HERBS

Many herbs are highly ornamental, with pretty flowers and sweet scents, and do not look amiss in flower borders, but herb gardens and herb features make pleasing designs that many people try to incorporate even when the herbs have little culinary attraction.

■ ABOVE

PATIO HERBS Herbs are most likely to be used when planted conveniently for the kitchen rather than tucked away at the end of the garden. The herbs shown are growing in a bed next to the patio, and when you sit on the built-in seat and brush against them, the aromas of the herbs are released.

DESIGN TIP *Place the most ornamental herbs, such as the coloured and variegated sages and chives, towards the front of the bed, with the less attractive kinds such as tarragon and lovage behind. Herb beds can look uninspiring in winter, so try to create a positive setting for them. The garden will then remain attractive long after most of the herbs have died back.*

■ ABOVE

CONTAINER HERBS If space is really tight, a small collection of herbs can be grown in a container like the one shown. Herbs can also be grown in window boxes, but it's probably best to use such valuable space for flowers.

DESIGN TIP *Plant your herbs in an impressive container if it's to be placed in a prominent position. This imitation lead container is made from glass fibre.*

■ ABOVE

HERB BEDS Instead of growing your herbs in rectangular beds, try growing them in beds that form a geometrical pattern. Even when the herbs have died back, this part of the garden will remain interesting due to its strong design.

DESIGN TIP *Give the beds a definite edge to help pick out the shapes and patterns. Here, granite setts have been used to edge the beds and form a contrast with the gravel paths.*

■ ABOVE

HERB WHEEL No matter how small your garden is, it should always be possible to introduce a herb feature. The herb wheel is an old design, especially popular during the nineteenth century. The centrepoint of this design is a variation on the traditional herb wheel.

DESIGN TIP *Introduce this kind of very formal and symmetrical feature only if you have the time to spend keeping the herbs trimmed. While the shape remains well defined, a herb wheel makes an excellent focal point, but if the plants are allowed to become overgrown and mask the outline of the rim and spokes, much of the effect is lost.*

Know-how

AN INTEGRATED APPROACH

If you can't bring yourself to devote part of your garden to vegetables and herbs alone, consider integrating as many as possible with the ornamentals. Many are quite pretty in their own right, and when merged with other ornamentals they can work surprisingly well.

■ LEFT
POTAGER In a potager, flowers and vegetables are grown together without strict demarcation lines. You will probably either love this effect or find it disconcerting – it's not the kind of feature many find visually neutral.
DESIGN TIP *A potager is best given its own area of the garden, perhaps separated from the purely ornamental part of the garden by a dwarf hedge or perhaps a picket fence.*

■ RIGHT
FORMAL VEGETABLE GARDEN Try creating a formal garden with beds edged by dwarf box (*Buxus sempervirens* 'Suffruticosa'), and planting ornamental plants in some and vegetables in others. It will make an unusual and surprisingly interesting garden.
DESIGN TIP *Plant the beds that had vegetables in summer with winter-flowering bulbs and spring bedding. That way you'll gain more ornamental value without sacrificing much in terms of crops.*

■ ABOVE

ORNAMENTAL VEGETABLES Rhubarb chard is a spectacular plant whether grown in rows in the vegetable garden, or used with summer bedding plants. Here it has been used as a centrepiece of the bed with lobelia around the edge.

DESIGN TIP *Rhubarb chard makes a pleasing "dot" plant to bring height to summer bedding schemes. Even if you don't like the taste and have no desire to harvest it, consider using this plant as an arresting ornamental foliage plant.*

■ ABOVE

MIXED GARDENS In this cottage garden blue cornflowers (*Centaurea cyanus*) rub shoulders with blue borage, while all around is a wide range of vegetables. Anyone who likes a neat and tidy garden with plants in distinct "compartments" will find this kind of garden disturbing, but it has a special charm and has the benefit of deterring pests and diseases because of the diversity of plants grown.

DESIGN TIP *If the rest of the garden is formal in style, separate this kind of feature with a hedge or screen, otherwise the apparent chaos of this style of vegetable growing will be emphasized. It doesn't matter in a cottage garden, where plants often merge into one another.*

■ RIGHT

PLANTING FOR HARVESTING Beetroot has beautiful foliage that we often take for granted. Here it is being grown as an ornamental, but you could clear it to harvest then replant the vacated space with something else.

DESIGN TIP *If you want to harvest a crop, it's best to plant in separate blocks where the space can easily be replanted, rather than interplanting with flowers, which can make harvesting difficult and leave unattractive gaps afterwards.*

Planning and Planting

KITCHEN CORNER

Where there's space, it's a good idea to position the kitchen garden to one side of the house, perhaps partitioned by a hedge. Here a warm corner has been put to good use as an attractive herb garden.

PLANNING

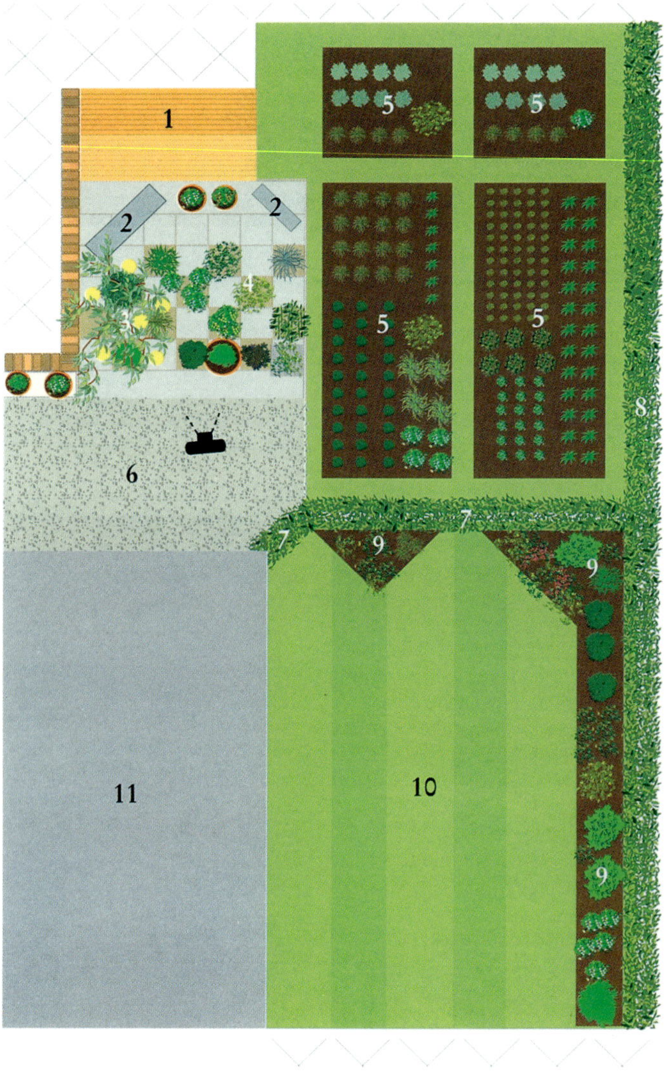

KEY TO PLAN

1 Shed
2 Stone seat
3 Small specimen tree
4 Chequerboard herb garden
5 Vegetables
6 Gravel
7 Archway through yew hedge
8 Yew hedge
9 Dwarf shrubs
10 Lawn
11 House

Viewpoint on photograph

× Garden continues

HERB WHEELS

Herb wheels are charming and popular features that display herbs to their best advantage. They are sometimes made out of old cart or wagon wheels, but these are not easy to obtain. It's far easier to adapt the concept and make a brick "wheel". The larger the "wheel" the more "spokes" you can introduce.

Allocate a contrasting colour, scent or leaf shape to each bed within the spokes to give definition to the wheel.

MAKING A HERB WHEEL

1 Mark a circle about 1.5–1.8m (5–6ft) across, using a line fixed to a peg to ensure an even shape. If it helps, use a wine bottle filled with dry sand instead of a stick to mark out the perimeter. Excavate the ground to a depth of about 15cm (6in).

PLANTING

2 Place bricks on end, or at an angle, around the edge. If you place them at a 45° angle it will create a dog-tooth effect; bricks placed on end will look more formal. Either lay them loose in compacted earth, or bed them on mortar.

3 Lay rows of brick, cross-fashion, as shown. If the diameter does not allow for them to be laid without gaps in the centre, stand an ornament or pot in the middle if you are not planting directly into the soil in that position.

4 Top up the areas between the "spokes" with good garden or potting soil. Add fertilizer at this point, if necessary.

5 Plant up each section, using plants that will balance each other in size of growth if possible. You could, for instance, grow a collection of different thymes. For a smart finish, carefully cover the soil with fine gravel.

Planning and Planting

ORNAMENTAL KITCHEN GARDEN

The vegetables don't have to be tucked away out of sight. You can mix them with flowers, and enclose both in formal dwarf box hedges to create a wonderful ornamental kitchen garden with lots of style.

This plan shows a kitchen garden laid out in formal style, where there is space to make a long-term feature of it. Although box hedges grow reasonably rapidly, it will take perhaps four or five years to form neatly clipped hedges like those shown in the photograph.

Growing vegetables in an ornamental setting like this, and being prepared to plant and sow flowers among them, makes a kitchen garden to be admired and not just used.

PLANNING

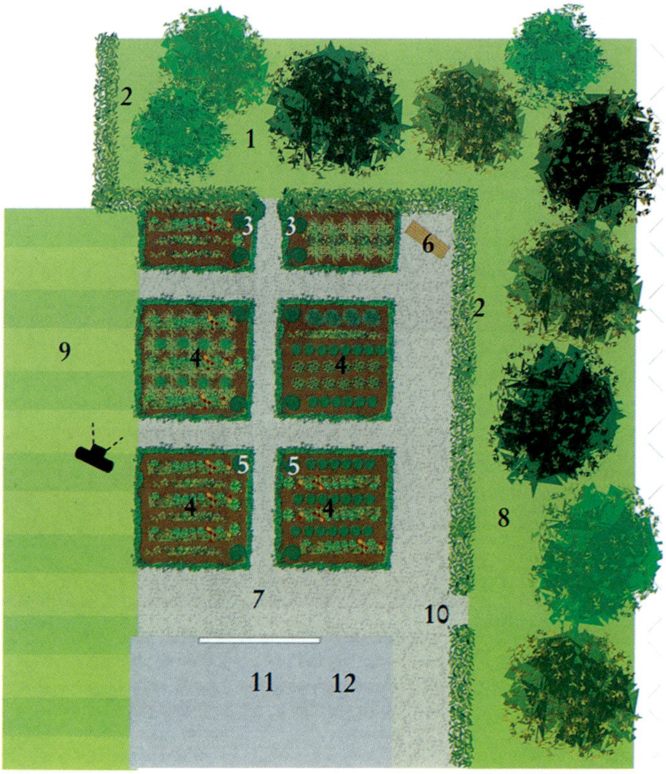

KEY TO PLAN

1 Informal garden and woodland
2 Hedge
3 Specimen conifer
4 Flowers and vegetables enclosed in dwarf box hedge
5 Topiary
6 Garden bench
7 Gravel
8 Woodland garden
9 Lawn and ornamental garden
10 Path to woodland garden
11 Main bedroom overlooking the vegetable garden
12 House

× Garden continues

Viewpoint on photograph

PRUNING CORDON AND ESPALIER APPLES

Cordons and espaliers are frequently used in small gardens because they are more decorative than bush forms, and they save space. The drawback is that they require regular pruning – once in summer and again in winter on old plants that have become congested. This winter pruning is only to thin out the number of spurs (short, stubby shoots) when they have become so congested that there is insufficient space for the fruits to develop properly.

A single-tiered espalier – sometimes called step-over training – can be used for a fruitful edging to the beds instead of, say, a dwarf box edging.

PLANTING

HOW TO PRUNE ESPALIERS

1 Shorten new leafy shoots that have grown directly from the main branches back to three leaves above the basal cluster of leaves. This should only be done once the shoots have dark green leaves and the bark has started to turn brown and is woody at the base. In cold areas it may be early autumn before the shoots are mature enough.

2 If the shoot is growing from a stub left by previous pruning – and not directly from one of the main stems – cut back to one leaf above the basal cluster of leaves.

HOW TO PRUNE CORDONS

1 Cut back shoots growing from stubs left by earlier pruning to one leaf above the basal cluster.

2 A cordon is pruned in the same way as an espalier, though the basic shape of the plant is different. Cut back shoots growing directly from the main branch to three leaves above the basal cluster of leaves.

Planning and Planting

Pivoting on Circles

This plan shows what can be achieved in a relatively small garden only 11m x 9m (36ft x 30ft), and should be an inspiration for all who think that you need a large garden to come up with an imaginative design that's packed with innovative features.

KEY TO PLAN

1 Trellis
2 Gazebo
3 Mixed border
4 Large rock
5 Fence
6 Raised circular patio
7 Pots on rustic pine poles
8 Bricks set into lawn
9 Bubble pool
10 Lawn
11 Low wall
12 Mixed planting
13 Split-level brick steps
14 Herb wheel
15 Border of aromatic herbs
16 House
Viewpoint on photograph

PLANNING

As this plan shows, herbs can be worked into a highly ornamental garden without sacrificing anything in terms of beauty or impact. This garden was initially designed with a shallow circular pool where the herb wheel is positioned now, but to demonstrate how easy it is to modify an existing plan to suit a particular need, we've made this area into an attractive herb garden.

The number of herbs you can grow in even a large herb wheel is limited, and tall ones such as fennel are unsuitable. To accommodate the larger types and increase the range of herbs available, the border closest to the house and herb wheel has also been planted with various aromatic herbs. By including plenty of shrubby ones, such as coloured and variegated sages, this kind of border can look highly attractive and scent the air near the house.

PATIO HERB FEATURES

If your patio is looking drab and in need of colour, lift a few of the paving slabs to plant patches of brightly coloured or scented herbs. Try to remove the slabs without breaking them, and save them for another purpose. Remember that many herbs will look effective for only part of the year, so choose your plants carefully.

PLANTING

HOW TO PLANT A PATIO HERB FEATURE

1 Lift the paving slabs using a cold chisel and club hammer. They will come up fairly easily if bedded on sand or blobs of mortar, but if laid over a concrete base it will be necessary to break up the concrete. In which case it may be preferable to build a small raised bed for your herbs instead.

2 The ground will have become compacted and may be composed of impoverished sub soil. Start by breaking it up with a fork, then add a generous amount of planting mixture or rotted garden compost. Dig it in thoroughly.

3 It is important to give the feature some height, so plant a large herb in the centre. This is a bay (*Laurus nobilis*), but you could use rosemary (*Rosmarinus officinalis*).

4 Plant up with herbs of your choice. Here golden marjorams are being planted in one corner.

Planning and Planting

FOCUS ON HERBS

A geometric herb garden makes a super feature whether or not you have a culinary need, and is often planted with medicinal and cosmetic herbs purely for their decorative and historic interest. A feature like this is sometimes more decorative than useful, in which case the emphasis should be on aesthetically pleasing planting rather than only herbs that you hope to harvest.

PLANNING

KEY TO PLAN

1 Fence covered with climbers, ground-cover plants beneath
2 Path (paving slabs)
3 Pergola, covered with golden hop (*Humulus lupulus* 'Aureus')
4 Dwarf shrubs
5 Broad path (paving slabs) beneath pergola
6 Herbs
7 Sundial
8 Birdbath
9 Trellis screen
10 Gravel
11 Dustbins (trashcans)
12 House

Viewpoint on photograph

Herb gardens are popular features, but they require structure and year-round focal points such as a sundial or birdbath to retain interest, when they have died back for winter. In a formal herb garden like this, paths play an important role – they mark out the beds but also form the main structural element during the winter months. It is important that these are attractive and well laid. Brick is a popular choice, but clay pavers are a good alternative. To break up the ground textures, paving slabs have also been used in this design.

WHAT TYPE OF SOIL?

Whether planting ornamentals or edibles, it's a good idea to test your soil. It will tell you which plants will thrive, and whether to improve your soil to grow particular plants.

Some kits test only for pH (which tells you how acid or alkaline your soil is). The test opposite is for nitrogen, but the same instructions will apply to most other kits.

PLANTING

HOW TO TEST YO

1 Collect a soil sample from about 5–8cm (2–3in) below the surface. Take a number of samples from around the garden and either test each of them separately or mix them in one test.

2 With this kit one part of soil is mixed with five parts of water. Shake vigorously in a clean jar, then allow the soil particles to settle – this could take half an hour to a day, depending on the soil.

3 Using the pipette provided in the kit, draw off some of the liquid from the top few centimetres (about an inch) when the mixture has settled.

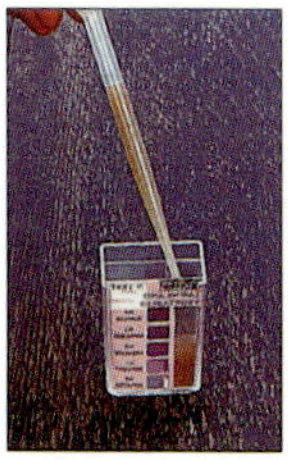

4 Transfer the solution to the test and reference chambers in the plastic container, using the pipette.

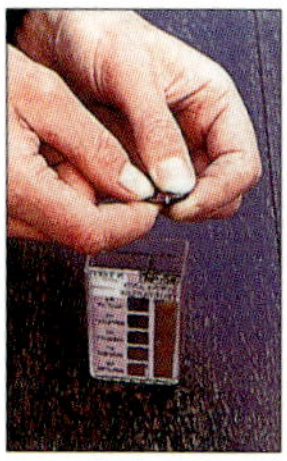

5 Select the appropriate test capsule, and empty the powder into the test chamber. Replace the cap, then shake vigorously.

6 After a few minutes, compare the colour of the liquid with the shade panel that forms part of the container. The kit will explain the meaning of each reading, and what – if anything – needs to be done.

Planning and Planting

FORMAL BUT DECORATIVE

Celebrate the tasty delights of the kitchen garden with a formal but decorative design that makes even the humble cabbage look ornamental, and provides space for cut flowers, too. This style of kitchen garden may be less practical than a rectangular plot where the crops are grown in long rows, but it's far more decorative.

PLANNING

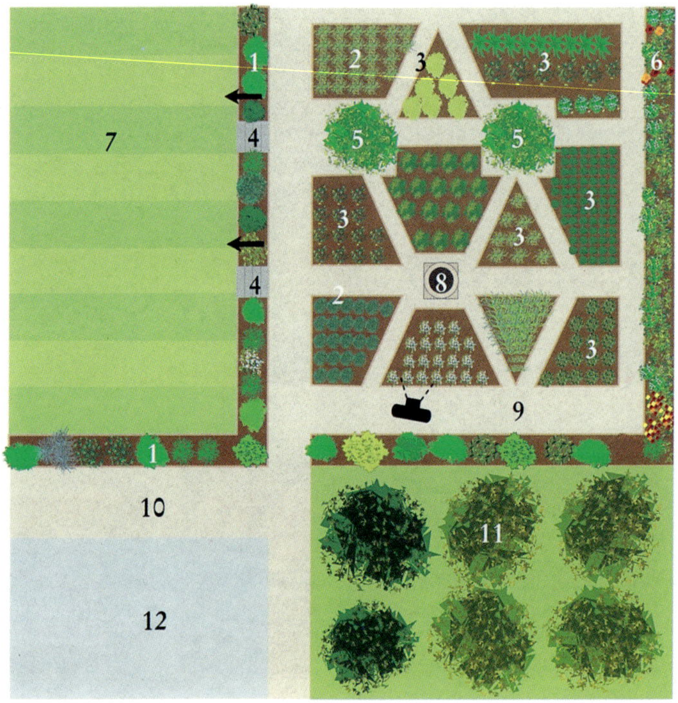

As this kitchen garden is quite close to the house, a formal design with a patchwork of small beds has been chosen to make a decorative contribution to the garden as well as a culinary one.

Starting with clear ground it would have been possible to devise a more traditional and strictly symmetrical design, but the presence of a couple of old pear trees dictated a more flexible approach. Although the beds do not create a symmetrical design, there is the suggestion of a regular pattern, and the idiosyncratic shapes add to the charm of this interesting kitchen garden.

KEY TO PLAN

1 Dwarf shrubs on bank
2 Sweet-pea teepee surrounded by vegetables
3 Vegetables
4 Steps to lower lawn
5 Pear tree
6 Annual cut-flower border
7 Lawn on lower level
8 Urn on plinth
9 Stone and earth path
10 Gravel
11 Orchard
12 House

× Garden continues
← Direction of steps down
Viewpoint on photograph

GROWING VEGETABLES IN SMALL BEDS

There are many advantages to growing vegetables in small beds. You can do all the cultivation without walking on the soil and compacting it, so no-dig systems are a practical option. With these techniques, the only digging to be done is that needed to clear the ground of weeds initially and to incorporate lots of organic material such as rotted manure or garden compost at the same time. Subsequently, more organic material is added to the surface as a mulch, and this is worked into the soil by worms and other creatures. If lots of organic material is added regularly, the soil fertility and structure will be improved each year, and crop yield will certainly benefit.

PLANTING

■ ABOVE
These beds are of irregular size because they form part of a larger pattern of beds, but even the larger ones are not difficult to cultivate from the surrounding pathways.

■ ABOVE
A traditional vegetable plot can be converted into a 1.2m (4ft) bed system simply by sowing in short rows and doing all the cultivation from the paths between them.

Some gardeners using this system use only organic manures and fertilizers and achieve wonderful crops without manufactured fertilizers. Small beds help because the lack of soil compaction means the soil structure is not harmed, and it's easier for worms and insects to work the manures and composts into the soil.

No-dig systems can be achieved on a traditional vegetable plot by dividing the area into 1.2m (4ft) strips, which makes cultivation from the paths practical without standing on the soil.

■ LEFT
A potager is an area where vegetables and flowers are grown together. The flowers are often cut for floral decoration, and in this garden each bed has a teepee of sweet peas to provide a supply of cut flowers for the home.

Planning and Planting

Creating a Herb Garden

Herbs are the most attractive of all plants grown in the kitchen garden, and for that reason decorative herb gardens are popular features. In a large garden, it's worth setting aside a separate, enclosed area in which a herb garden like this can be created. It will be a place in which to sit and relax, and if you plant whole beds of one kind of herb, you'll be able to harvest plenty without spoiling the decorative effect.

PLANNING

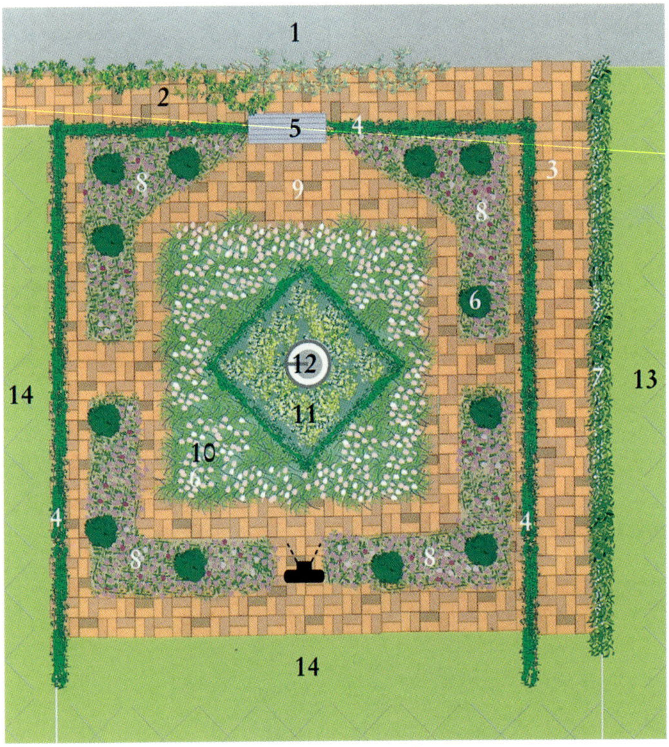

KEY TO PLAN

1 Garage
2 Climbers against garage wall
3 Path
4 Dwarf box (*Buxus sempervirens* 'Suffruticosa') hedge
5 Garden bench
6 Clipped box (*Buxus sempervirens*)
7 Yew hedge
8 Thyme
9 Brick paving
10 Chives
11 Golden marjoram
12 Sundial
13 To orchard
14 To house
× Garden continues
Viewpoint on photograph

A herb garden like this will make a culinary contribution, but it should really be viewed primarily as a decorative feature. Instead of growing a few plants of many different kinds of herbs, which might be more practical for kitchen use, making a bold splash with a few of the most decorative herbs creates a more striking visual feature and imparts a stronger sense of design.

Herb gardens like this depend on a symmetrical design, but they require a strong centrepiece around which the garden hangs – here an attractive sundial. An edging of box helps to hold the design together when it forms part of a larger garden.

GROWING HERBS IN CONTAINERS

Even if you have a large herb garden like the one shown in the plan and photograph here, a small container packed with a collection of herbs would be useful close to the kitchen door.

If you simply don't have space for a proper herb garden, a feature like the wine-case herb box shown opposite, will provide the occasional picking of fresh leaves and it looks good too.

PLANTING

HOW TO MAKE A WINE-CASE HERB FEATURE

1 Remove any wire staples from around the edges of an old wine case, and sand down rough edges. Apply two coats of exterior varnish, inside and out. Allow the varnish to dry thoroughly between coats.

2 Place broken pots or similar drainage material in the bottom of the box, then stand the pots of herbs in the container to work out the best arrangement.

3 Fill the box with a gritty potting soil, then start planting. Loosen a few of the roots from the rootball before planting to encourage the plant to root. Finish planting, then sprinkle a slow-release fertilizer over the surface. Water well, then cover the surface with a mulch such as finely chipped bark.

4 Stand the finished container within ready reach of the kitchen, and remember to keep it well watered. Harvest only a small amount of leaves each time if you want it to remain an ornamental feature.

Choosing Plants

Plants For Kitchen Gardens

When it comes to edible crops, you'll grow what you like and not what necessarily gives the heaviest crops or looks the most pleasing. Flavour is everything when growing for your own consumption. Our suggestions here are for crops that are likely to give a good yield for the space and effort, or that are interesting and deserve to be better known. In the case of herbs, our suggestions are for those that are decorative as well as of culinary merit – if space for a kitchen garden is limited, you can grow these in flower and shrub borders, or in window boxes, containers, planting spaces on patios or between paving slabs.

EASY SALADS

A collection of salad crops must surely include lettuce or endive, and of course tomatoes. If you consider these uninteresting, try red lettuce and perhaps yellow tomatoes. Sow lettuces little and often for succession. Tomatoes crop best under glass in cooler climates, but they are less trouble to look after outdoors, especially if you choose a bush type that does not require the removal of sideshoots. Radishes are ready within weeks when growing conditions are good, but they'll disappoint if not sown little and often as they deteriorate rapidly if not harvested regularly.

For out-of-season salads, consider some of the less common leafy vegetables such as corn salad.

Lettuce 'Lolla Rossa' forms a loose ball-shaped head, but you can pick individual leaves if you don't need the whole head at once. The crisp and tangy, frilly leaves add a touch of colour to a summer salad.

Endive makes a refreshing change from lettuce, but it tastes better if blanched for a few days before harvesting. Unlike lettuce, it will also tolerate a few degrees of frost. This variety is 'Green Curled'.

UNUSUAL OR INTERESTING VEGETABLES

Growing ordinary vegetables may become inspiring, and most of them you can buy readily in your local supermarket. Growing your own provides an opportunity to experiment with some of the more

Rhubarb chard is one of the few vegetables that most of us would be happy to include in the flower garden. Sometimes it is even used in summer bedding displays.

This strange-looking and decorative vegetable is called a custard marrow or patty pan squash.

interesting kinds, or varieties that may not be profitable commercial crops but have a good flavour, such as the 'Pink Fir Apple' potato, with its knobbly tubers. Asparagus peas are quite decorative with their red flowers and angular seed pods, while Swiss chard and rhubarb chard are leafy plants that are highly ornamental. Instead of the ordinary marrow (squash), try the custard marrow (patty pan squash) with its distinctive flattish fruits with scalloped edges.

DECORATIVE HERBS

Many herbs can be grown as ornamentals in the shrub border: rosemary, sage, and bay, for example. Others, such as marjorams, chives, golden lemon balm and borage, are ideal for a

Sage is a compact shrub that looks good towards the front of a shrub border. *Salvia officinalis* itself is green, but there are varieties with attractive variegation in gold or shades of pink and purple, which are often grown as ornamentals.

Chives are deservedly one of the most widely grown herbs. Their grass-like leaves and pretty pink flowers in summer make them very ornamental, and they are sometimes planted as an edging.

mixed or herbaceous border. Thymes are happy in a rock garden. All of those mentioned, with the exception of borage, also make pleasing container plants.

PICK OF THE FRUITS

Tree fruits are particularly rewarding to grow, as the crop is often heavy for a given area, and the cropping lasts for many weeks, usually months if fruits such as apples and pears are stored. Apples and pears can also be bought trained as fans, cordons and espaliers, which are ideal for a small garden.

If growing soft fruit, make sure you grow for flavour to make the effort worthwhile (and be sure to protect them from birds). You can buy huge and luscious-looking strawberries in shops or markets, but some of the varieties with smaller fruits may have a better, often sweeter, flavour.

'Waltz', one of the apple varieties that grows like a pole without normal side branches, the fruit being produced on spurs close to the main stem. These are ideal for a tiny garden where you also require a vertical tree.

Pears don't have to be grown as large trees. This 'Beurre Hardy' is growing as a decorative fan, and picking is easy.

DECORATING YOUR GARDEN

■ ABOVE:
Even a pair of beehives situated beneath an apple tree in the corner of this garden can create a charming decorative effect.

■ OPPOSITE:
This formal bedding scheme full of colourful annuals is perfectly complemented by the addition of an elegant urn on a plinth.

Introduction

If you long to relax in a garden with just as much style as your home, but your plant knowledge is elementary and you don't have any enthusiasm for double digging, then it's time to think of your garden in a new way. We're all quite happy to use decoration to give personality to our homes, but traditionally, lovely gardens seem to depend on a grounding in horticulture and lots of hard work. Since a lot of us don't have the time or the knowledge to make a great traditional garden, it's easy to be put off and just make do with a patch of lawn and a few hardy plants. But gardens don't have to be all hard work. There's a lot you can do with very little effort to create great impact in the garden, and then you can sit back and enjoy relaxing outside in your own private plot.

■ ABOVE
A well-thought-out garden will bring you many, many happy hours.

■ OPPOSITE
A half-concealed entrance to a secret place adds a delightful air of mystery.

INTRODUCTION

The key is to take your interior decorating ideas and skills and to adapt them for the outside of your home. A splash of paint outside can have just the same impact as it does inside. "Flooring" outside doesn't have to be limited to the ubiquitous green carpet of grass. There are plenty of other choices: flagstones, pavers, cobbles, wooden decking or brick. You can add fixtures and fittings, furniture and decorative touches such as pictures, sculpture, ornaments, lighting and painted pots, in just the same way as you would indoors.

■ ABOVE
Pots of leafy evergreens always look charming on a flight of old steps.

This is just a taste of the many ideas packed into the pages of this book, which, I hope, will inspire you to think of your garden in a new way so that you can really make the most of your outdoor space, even if your plant knowledge is all but non-existent.

And don't be put off if you think your garden is either too small to bother with, or so large that gardening has become an elephantine task. The smallest garden can become the most successful decorated garden room for all the family if it is well-planned to include eating and play areas. If your garden is large, you could just decorate the patio area for entertaining to begin with and

■ BELOW
Carefully trained trees form a cool and shady canopy for hot summer days.

work round to other areas when you have the time and the funds. Large or small, the best way to get the most from any garden is to set up a comfortable seating and/or eating area, so it's always ready for relaxing and entertaining. No need to wait for high summer before you sit outside: if everything is at hand, it's easy to carry out food or drinks, even on fine spring days.

STARTING FROM SCRATCH

There are lots of ideas in the pages of this book that can be introduced into an established garden. It's when you have a "blank canvas" that the whole operation becomes somewhat daunting.

Although the idea of decorating the garden in the same way as you would a house, taking away the need for a wealth of horticultural knowledge, makes the whole project a little more attainable, there are extra dimensions to gardens that need to be addressed.

The most obvious one is that every garden has some planting, and even the most hardy slow-growing plants will grow, altering the structure of the garden as they go. The other big difference between indoors and outdoors is the levels. Inside, floors are flat. Outside, the ground may not be, and, if it is, you may want to alter the levels to add interest. A step up or a step down can completely change the space.

You may also want to divide the garden into different areas, which also adds interest. You can do this with levels, or with low walls or trellis screens. If you want to add such elements to the garden, and you don't feel confident about planning hard landscape yourself, you may want to bring in the help of a garden designer. Whatever your decision, the key is not to be fazed by this basic planning.

■ ABOVE
Colourful plants spill over exuberantly on to a path of brick, their sharp pinks and purples enhancing its roseate tones.

Start by making a list of your needs and wants. Where would you like the patio area? It is usually situated right next to the house, but it doesn't have to be if there's another part of the garden that gets more sun. Do you want a water feature? Do you need a play area? Is there room for ball games, or is your backyard too small? Would a sandpit, play house or climbing frame, which all use up less space, be more suitable? How much planting area do you want? Is space more important to you, or do you find tending plants relaxing? Do you want a lawn, or, especially if space is limited, would it be better to pave the area? Where will you store lawnmowers, tools, pots and compost (soil mix)?

Such a list will help you to work out the areas you need, whether you decide to plan out the space yourself or you get someone else to do it for you. The ground planning is key because once the levels, patio and planting areas are sorted, the garden has a structure you can build on.

FIXTURES AND FITTINGS

Permanent structures lend personality to a home. They're not part of the architecture, so they reflect the style of the current owner, yet they have an air of permanence that furnishings and accessories could never give. Fixtures and fittings are the easiest way to impress your personality on the garden. Fit a small garden building, an arbour, an arch or pergola, some trellis or simply some shelves for general storage or displays of potted plants, and you'll see an immediate change. These may seem like big projects, but with garden buildings in kit form and a variety of trellis panels available from most garden centres, there's a lot you can do in a weekend. Once built, structures can be customized with MDF (medium-density fiberboard), fretwork and paints or stains for an easy-to-build but highly individual finished effect.

THE BASIC DECORATING

The quickest way to introduce all-year colour into the garden is to paint it on. No worrying about what will flower when, or how to keep the colour going through the winter – it's there for keeps. Adding colour in the garden with paint and stain has become easier in recent years as there's a much wider choice of exterior paints and stains. Where once we were limited to pine green or various shades of brown, now turquoise greens, pinks, blues and lilacs are being added to the repertoire available to the general public. Use it to paint fences, trellis work and garden buildings, then, to add to the impact, you can plan the planting to complement the colour scheme. Quite apart from the finished effect, one advantage of painting the fences is that even while the plants are immature the garden doesn't look quite so naked.

SOFT FURNISHINGS

Once the basic decorating is done, you can begin to choose the soft furnishings, which, in the garden, is the planting. If you're a novice, and you don't want to spend hours nurturing plants, the best solution is to choose traditional favourite evergreens, shrubs, climbers and perennials. These have become popular because they almost always grow successfully. Evergreens and trees are all hardy provided they are given plenty of water during their first year. They can be used to provide structure to the planting, and can be supplemented by easy-to-grow shrubs that show plenty of colour, such as fuchsia, hebe, pyracantha, hydrangea, weigela and shrub roses. Hardy climbers that can be used to furnish fences include climbing roses, honeysuckle, clematis and jasmine. Easy-to-grow herbaceous plants that die down in winter but return year after year include *Alchemilla mollis*, *euphorbia* and border *Geranium* (Cranesbill). If in doubt, buy plants that are in plentiful supply in the garden centre since these are usually the popular easy-to-grow varieties. Check the flowering or berrying period to make sure they weren't put on show in the only week they bloom, and check the height and spread they will reach

■ LEFT
Loose hedging, tied in an arch over a pathway and studded with flowers, divides a garden into areas of interest.

■ LEFT
Setting out one or two seats in a sunny corner of the garden and adding potfuls of plant colour will give you an instant and irresistible al fresco room.

when mature. All this information should be on the plant label.

For instant colour, which you can use to supplement the planting, pot seasonal bedding plants into containers. These can be used to decorate the patio, as a focal point in the garden, or even placed in the borders to boost the colour between seasons.

Buy young plants from the garden centre that are already showing colour and plant them in pots, adding fertilizer to be sure of a splashy show. Keep them moist and deadhead them regularly for a long flowering season. The advantage of containers is that once they have finished flowering they can be moved to a more secluded part of the garden, while others, coming into bloom, can be moved to centre stage.

DECORATIVE FEATURES

Inside, you probably have paintings, lighting, ornaments and sculpture, vases of flowers and potted plants, which all add decorative personality to the home. With a little thought, it's easy to see how you can decorate the garden with the outdoor equivalents.

Mosaics make perfect all-weather outdoor art, and can be used as pictures, sculptures or even to decorate furniture. Scarecrows can be outdoor sculpture, as can piles of pots, groups of watering cans and old tools or the more obvious fountains and wall masks. Bird-feeding tables, bird baths and birdhouses become ornaments, as do painted pots and wind chimes. Stamp your style on your garden using all of these, perhaps keeping to a colour theme for continuity.

FURNISHING THE GARDEN

Although the garden furniture is really the finishing touch to the garden, it can also be the very first thing you do. Even if you don't have the time or the budget to make over the garden, if you do nothing else, it's worth making a comfortable seating area so that everything is in place for relaxing in the garden – be it reading a book on your own or inviting friends over for a meal. If you're planning the garden from scratch, you may like to think about built-in furniture – a bench under a pergola, for example. If not, invest in all-weather furniture that doesn't have to be dragged in and out every day. It doesn't have to be expensive, though it does need to be comfortable. Add cushions and throws to any that falls short of the mark.

You can give the seating area a relaxing ambience by aiming to stimulate all the senses. Glean visual inspiration from the pages of this book and add perfume by choosing scented varieties of plant, such as honeysuckle, old-fashioned roses, summer jasmine and tobacco plants. Smell stimulates the tastebuds, too, so add in some sweet-smelling herbs such as marjoram, sage or rosemary and potted summer fruits, such as strawberries. Bring on the music with wind chimes or a water feature, and add soft feathery foliage such as love-in-a-mist for that touchy-feely element.

IN A NUTSHELL

Think of your garden as a place to relax: plan it to suit you and your lifestyle; decorate it as boldly as you would your home using paint, stain, flowers and foliage for your favourite colour palette; furnish it for comfort; add finishing touches, scents and sound for ambience; then sit back and enjoy.

DECORATING A GARDEN TO LIVE IN

The first step to decorating your garden is the planning. Take time to think about what you want from your space, and remember that the smallest plot merits as much thought as the most sprawling of areas.

Decide what is important to you, whether it is an array of brightly-coloured flowers, a shady arbour for quiet contemplation, or a fun play area for energetic children. Whatever you want from your garden, there are three main elements to consider: privacy, atmosphere and the plantings. Setting the right mood in your garden can be easily achieved through the careful placing of an ornament here or a scented plant there. Throughout these pages you will find many, many ideas for a perfect garden retreat that has year-round appeal in colour, texture and fragrance.

■ ABOVE
A garden can be many things, but ultimately it is a place for relaxation.

■ OPPOSITE
The finer points of an ornamental bird bath may be lost on birds, but they will still return to your garden again and again for drinking water and bathing.

Inspirational Ideas

The most relaxing and visually pleasing gardens are usually the result of careful planning. You will need to consider how best to use the available space, the vistas you can create and the ambience of the garden, to prepare the "canvas" for your decorative touches. Once you begin to reap the rewards of such forethought, you will certainly feel it was all worthwhile.

■ OPPOSITE
Delicate ornamentation can be inappropriate for utilitarian areas of the garden, such as vegetable patches, which need to withstand heavy-duty usage. However, these plots will blend nicely with the garden if well laid out and decorated simply with splashes of colour.

A good place to start is to consider what you want from your garden. You will probably want somewhere to sit and, perhaps, eat. If you have children, you will want space for them to play, and you will also need to provide some kind of storage area for tools, pots and other garden paraphernalia. All this is perfectly possible, even in a tiny garden. An area 2m/6½ft square is sufficient space in which to sit and eat. Children would be thrilled with a sandpit, even one of just 90cm/3ft square and, if there is just a little more space, there will be room for a small play house.

Plan out in your mind the best place for each of these activities in much the same way as you might plan your kitchen, where you also need to allocate space for working, eating and leisure. Once these priorities are fixed, it will be much easier to work out the layout of the garden. This is important, even if you won't have the resources for new paving and landscaping in the foreseeable future. For example, there may be a flower bed just where you feel it would be best to create a seating area. With the garden layout left as it is, you will continually have to bring furniture in and out when you need it. That is tiresome and no more convenient than a sitting room would be if you had to bring in a chair every time you wanted to relax. However, with a few little changes, such as turfing over a surplus flower bed, you can organize the garden so it is ready for relaxation any time you want.

Once the main areas are worked out, it is much easier to decide where you want to have planting areas, and within this framework you will be able to transform the space into a decorative outdoor room that you will want to use for much more of the year than just the few months of summer.

■ LEFT
Dividing up the space in your garden creates visual depth. Here, box orbs help to define a vista of the arbour at the end.

■ ABOVE
Garden paraphernalia displayed on a wire shelf transforms the functional into the decorative.

■ BELOW
Low hedging is cleverly used here for a rich and interesting design, to form visual divides and create several rooms within one garden.

Planning for Privacy

You will only be able to relax in the garden once you have organized the basic needs: privacy and shelter. Without the benefit of enclosed spaces, especially in built-up areas, these considerations can be problematic. However, there are ways of achieving them. Trellises can be fixed on top of walls and fences to create extra height: cover them with decorative climbers. You could plant fast-growing conifers, such as thuja, but check their potential height when mature or you could end up not so much overlooked as overshadowed.

Privacy is particular important for seating areas. Even if you live in the middle of the country and have a huge garden, you will feel much more comfortable if you site seating where, at least on one side, there is the protection of a screen of some sort. This could be the garden boundary wall, a hedge or even trellis arranged to lend a more intimate feel.

PRIVACY FROM ABOVE

If you are closely overlooked, you may also want to create privacy from above. One of the most successful ways of doing this is to create a pergola and encourage it to become entwined with vines or other climbers. That way, you have a "roof", which filters the natural light and allows a free flow of fresh air underneath.

PLANTS FOR SCREENING

Buxus sempervirens
Carpinus betulus
Chamaecyparis lawsoniana 'Green Hedger'
Crataegus monogyna
Elaeagnus ebbingei
Escallonia 'Iveyi'
Fagus sylvatica
Fargesia nitida
Griselinia littoralis
Ilex aquifolium
Ligustrum ovalifolium
Osmanthus delavayi
Prunus cerasifera
Prunus laurocerasus
Pyracantha 'Mohave'
Taxus baccata
Thuja orientalis
Ulmus parvifolia
Viburnum rhytidophyllum

■ RIGHT
Let the scent of verbena and honeysuckle perfume this outdoor room. Edwardian ironwork lends an air of bygone elegance to this brick bay.

■ LEFT
The sense of privacy offered by an enclosed space lends a romantic touch to any garden. Here, a combination of trees, shrubs and potted plants has created an intimate patio area at one side of the garden lawn.

■ OPPOSITE
A combination of trees and plants of different heights is used in this flower-bed to screen one part of the garden from the next.

■ LEFT
Secret places can be created in even the smallest of spaces. This pathway winds through plantings in a tiny 3m/10ft plot.

■ BELOW
Even in a large garden that is not overlooked, a seating area is more comfortable if it is sheltered and secluded. Here, two rustic wattle hurdles have been used to create an informal outdoor "room".

Atmosphere and Romance

Once space in the garden has been defined, you can begin to set the mood. Creating ambience relies on stimulating the senses, and sight, sound, touch, taste and smell are all supplied free of charge by nature. Simply by being outside, you are closer to nature, so it should be easier to bring atmosphere and romance into your garden than anywhere else in your home. Finding ways to stimulate each of the senses is what this book is all about, and these pages are packed with decorative ideas to enhance the garden.

A SENSUOUS GARDEN

Combined with the visual delights offered by the plants, a garden planned for the senses will produce inspired results. In addition to the sound of birdsong and the buzzing of insects, you can add the music of wind chimes or the evocative trickling of water in even the smallest plot. The garden also provides the most glorious fragrances, both sweet – from flowers such as roses, honeysuckle and jasmine – and aromatic – from lavender and piquant herbs. Touch, too, can be stimulated as it is impossible to walk through a garden without being touched by – or reaching out to touch – some of the plants; this is especially pleasing if they have interesting textures: try to include a range of fleshy, frondy and feathery plants. Finally, eating out in the garden contributes taste to complete the sensory picture.

OUTDOOR INTIMACY

The most romantic gardens always give a hint of intimacy. They could literally be enclosed outdoor rooms, such as courtyards, balconies or roof gardens, which automatically offer a private area. If your space is larger, you can add romantic interest by building separations in to the garden to create hidden places. This isn't as difficult as it sounds, and can be made a highly successful feature of even the smallest gardens. You can put a door in a fence or wall to hint at another space; add dividers to give the feeling of moving from one area to another, or provide screening for an eating area.

These dividing tactics also create the illusion of space. Adding a separation means you are able to see beyond one area into another, which lends perspective to the whole space, giving it structure and shape. However light the screening, it hints at secret places and romance.

■ LEFT
Springtime blossom flutters to the ground through this delicate ogee archway, which gives the feeling that one is moving out of one area of the garden into another.

■ ABOVE
Colourful mosaic tiles add tactile interest and visual appeal to a shady area of the garden.

■ ABOVE
Dining al fresco means seasonal food and delightfully simple table decorations.

■ ABOVE
Seedheads and Chinese lanterns hung up to dry supply bright colour.

■ LEFT
It is impossible to wander down this path without reaching out to touch the exuberant bushes of scented lavender.

■ RIGHT
A very modern mosaic, in the style of a Mexican ceramic sun, set against a brick wall, adds immeasurably to the atmosphere of the garden.

■ BELOW
Water flows elegantly over this exquisite, wall-mounted, cast-iron lily pad. The sound of trickling water enhances any outdoor area, and a water feature such as this, attached to a wall, need not take up an inordinate amount of space.

■ RIGHT
A miniature courtyard is set out as an enchanting outdoor room. The cherry tree suggests pretty "wallpaper", while the fallen blossom forms a natural carpet. There is even a "coffee table" positioned in front of the bench, and an alcove is set in the wall.

Finding the Levels

Whereas indoors you would prefer your floor to be level, outside the opposite is true. This is probably because inside the various heights of furniture automatically give you interesting levels and furniture tends to occupy a greater proportion of the floor space. Outside, even a furnished garden has greater expanses of floor space, which could result in monotony. Unless you are considering a very tiny garden space, similar in size to a room indoors, or you have decided to have a particularly formal design, such as a knot garden or parterre, you will probably want to create some change in level.

Adding a split-level dimension to your garden can be as simple as raising one area above another by the height of just one single step. If you are not in a position to re-landscape your garden for the sake of a change of level, there is still a lot you can do. Add staging at one side and use it to display potted plants; use a plant stand to lend height; make a feature of garden buildings to give architectural interest; or use plants of various heights to create changes of level.

■ OPPOSITE
A pretty Victorian wire plant stand, filled with flowering plants, brings flashes of white high up in the middle of a largely green planting area.

■ ABOVE
Flowering climbers, such as clematis, don't have to be restricted to walls and fences. By training them up obelisks, you can take the colour even higher.

■ LEFT
Even in a tiny patio area, there is room to create levels. Here, raised beds are built in white-painted brick to match the garden floor.

Planning the Planting

Herbaceous borders provide wonderful colour in summer but die down to next to nothing in winter, so it is good to provide an evergreen structure of plants to see you through the seasons. These will contribute to the "architecture" of the garden, creating levels, screens and sculpture, and a backdrop of deep colour to offset the plants and flowers.

The arrangement of shrubs in the garden can introduce all manner of interesting design features. Plan to have taller shrubs at the back of the borders, slowly graduating towards the front, or you can make more structured steps. You can arrange rows of small, lightly screening plants across the garden to create a living screen, and you can use specimen trees or trimmed topiary as living sculpture.

The colour scheme for the rest of the planting can be planned around this basic structure, but the structural shrubs and trees can also be chosen to ensure some colour all year round: include fruit trees for blossom in early spring, shrub roses for summer colour, late-flowering clematis and wonderful berries, such as those of pyracantha in autumn and holly in winter. This display of year-round colour can be added to and complemented with a collection of carefully-chosen autumn-flowering bulbs such as colchicum, schizostylus and cyclamen.

Container Choices

The most flexible colour is added with pots and containers. By planting up moveable pots you can put the colour where you want it, and re-plant with new seasonal colour as the old blooms die down. Pot up bulbs in the autumn in anticipation of spring colour and, as they die down, put them in a secluded part of the garden for their leaves to soak up the light, ensuring a better show next year.

Colour creates far more impact if you keep it to a theme – blues and pinks, perhaps, or oranges and yellows – and this theme can be strengthened with the use of paint and wood stain on nearby fences, garden buildings, furniture or on the pots themselves.

With the introduction of comfortable furniture, and with the finishing touches of accessories and decorations, a garden quickly becomes an outdoor room ready for entertaining and relaxation.

■ ABOVE
A beautiful specimen plant, such as this standard rose, makes a delightful feature in an unusual container.

■ ABOVE RIGHT
A well-established honeysuckle will form a living scented screen in the garden, gathering to it all forms of butterflies and bees.

■ RIGHT
Seasonal flowers look lovely potted up and grouped for massed colour. Containers allow you to move the colour around the garden to create focal points wherever you want them.

■ LEFT
You can use garden flowers outside in the same way as you might use potted plants inside. Here, spring flowers make a charming window sill display.

■ LEFT
Erect an evergreen archway to create an illusion of space. The glimpse of another area leads perspective to the whole garden, adding structure and depth.

■ RIGHT
Glorious roses 'Marigold' are the focus of attention in this garden, supported by plain brick pillars.

■ ABOVE
After the springtime glory of its blossom, this small apple tree once more takes the centre stage in the garden as the beautiful white clematis 'Marie Boisselot' grows up through the branches.

Decorative Garden Floors and Walls

The floor and walls offer the basic structure to the garden room, setting the tone in stone or brick, wood, gravel or grass. And even though these elements may seem fixed, there is still scope for decoration with imagination and flair.

For visual impact, you can combine hard and soft textures, setting a Victorian rope-effect edging next to an emerald lawn, for example, or you can vary the levels. A floor patterned with tiles can have an instant decorative effect, while planting a lawn with chamomile in place of grass will provide a beautifully subtle fragrance when walked on.

Gardens walls can provide interest at different levels. Don't be afraid of using indoor effects such as shelving or pictures for an eye-level display.

■ ABOVE
Old stone steps provide the backdrop for a wealth of summer colour.

■ OPPOSITE
Vertical lines on this path draw the eye to a distant vista and a welcome garden seat.

Floors: The Place to Start

Outside, even more than in, the "floor" has a huge impact on the overall effect, and decorating your garden has to start with the groundwork. Perversely, the smaller the area, the harder the floor has to work. Where there is plenty of space, sweeping lawns are fine. Where space is at a premium, it may hardly seem worth getting the mower out, and a combination of hard and soft surfaces becomes more sensible and visually pleasing.

Just as inside the house, the basic choice outside comes down to one between hard and soft flooring – the hard being patios and paths, the soft being planting. But while a single floor surface running seamlessly from wall to wall looks wonderful inside, outside, in anything but the smallest patio, it is likely to look flat and dull. Introduce variation, texture and a change of levels to create a much more interesting vista.

If you can afford it, and you want to start from scratch, it really is worth getting the floor right, as that offers the best basic structure to the garden. Even the most charming planting, pots and decorative details are diminished when set against the tedium of uniform concrete slabs, while a well-thought-out floor looks elegant even before you add a single plant. And in later years, it will be much easier to make a complete change in the planting, the pots, even the boundaries, in order to create a new look, rather than structuring the ground.

Even if it really isn't feasible to make a major change, there are ways to improve the situation – perhaps by removing some of the paving slabs to increase planting space, both around the perimeters and within the main paved areas. Or you could use decorative detailing to disguise parts of a less-than-pretty surface.

■ BELOW
A small paved patio teeming with plants and pots of different heights.

■ LEFT
The clay-tiled floor and brick retaining walls of an old, demolished greenhouse make an evocative setting for a herb garden and a focal point within the whole context of this established garden. A similar effect could be achieved using new tiles designed for outside use, laid diagonally in alternating colours.

■ LEFT
A soft green lawn creates a smooth carpet along the length of this shady walkway.

■ BELOW
A raised bed of brick set on gravel provides easy access for the gardener, and the geometric design mimics the formality of classical gardens.

■ RIGHT
This tapestry of purple and lilac planting, bordering a herringbone-patterned brick path, is reminiscent of a soft carpet laid on parquet flooring. Mosses, alpines and other low-growing plants have been allowed to take up residence on the curved English York stone steps.

Surface Choices

Flooring occupies the greatest area of the garden, and as such it will have a huge impact on both the visual aspect of your outdoor space and the practicalities required for its upkeep. The choice of flooring will depend partly on budget and the availability of materials in your locality, and partly on the look you set out to achieve. The most successful choice of surfacing will finally be a compromise between function and appearance.

■ OPPOSITE
A sweeping lawn makes an enviable natural emerald carpet, perfect for wetter climates. An expanse of cool, green grass punctuates the visually busy areas of planting, inducing a sense of calm in the garden.

Choosing your hard surface material can be difficult. Outdoors, little surpasses the beauty of natural stone, especially a local stone, which will harmonize with its surroundings. Another good material to use is frostproof flat-surfaced brick; specially made brick pavers are the ideal choice for patios and paths. Aggregates, in the form or gravel or shingle, are another form of natural stone. Other decorative hard surfaces can be achieved with a clever use of pebbles, slate or ceramics.

If such materials exceed your budget, there is a wide choice of concrete pavers. Not all are uniform, uninspired slabs: many have subtle variations of tone to give a naturally aged look; some come in the form of ready-to-split blocks of cobbles, each of which comes away slightly differently for a more natural effect.

Not-so-hard underfoot floorings can be made of wood: this may be custom-made timber decking or reclaimed materials such as railway sleepers (ties). When it comes to soft flooring, the obvious solution is a lawn; bear it in mind that herbs such as chamomile or thyme can make interesting alternatives to grass. Planting also offers a soft floor, though this will only be suitable for a look-but-don't-walk area.

The choice of material is one thing, deciding on its best form for your garden is another. Stone is available in rectangular slabs, squares, cobbles or crazy paving; concrete comes in any number of shapes. The form you choose and the way in which the material is laid can affect the whole look of the garden. Smaller units can make a tiny plot seem larger. Bricks laid widthways across a path give a tranquil look; laid lengthways they lend dynamism. A herringbone arrangement looks both attractive and established. Using differently sized units of the same material offers variety, while laying materials diagonally can visually enlarge a tiny area.

The surface you choose should always fulfil its function. Wooden decking laid under overhanging trees will quickly become covered with slippery algae. If children are going to play daily on a patio, you may find that flat slabs are more useful than characterful old bricks.

■ LEFT
Small pavers laid end-to-end visually elongate the curved path in this small garden, leading the eye through the planting, which is contained by the well-defined path edge.

Stepping Up

Changing the level in a garden immediately adds an extra dimension. Even a single step gives the feeling of moving from one area to another, while lending visual depth to the whole garden. Flights of more than two steps need plenty of space and can quickly eat into a small garden, as each one needs to be at least 30cm/12in deep, and shallow enough to make them easy and safe to negotiate, especially in wet or frosty weather.

Flights of stairs leading down to the garden can be a real bonus, because it doesn't take much effort to make a feature of them. Pots of plants on each step always look charming, especially if they end in a flourish at the bottom with a carefully arranged group.

■ ABOVE
Steps leading from the courtyard are framed with a mass of exuberantly flowering plants, which soften the harsh line of the stair rail.

■ ABOVE
Miniature violas, one plant to a pot, make an enchanting decoration for weathered old stone steps.

■ LEFT
A few small steps leading to a doorway form the perfect stage for a cluster of containers. This group of evergreens is augmented for the festive season by a potted topiary tree of blue spruce and fir cones.

■ RIGHT
Changes of texture as well as levels give definition to garden spaces. Here, a feature has been made of little-used weathered wooden steps, which rise from a cobblestone courtyard.

■ BELOW
Risers of plain stone steps make the perfect setting for a charming decorative detail, like this line of mosaic flowers.

Floor Edgings

The way a path or patio is edged plays an important part in the design of the flooring. Many well-designed pavers and setts (small cobble-like pavers) have complementary kerb edging.

One idea is to make edgings by laying pavers in a different direction to the rest of the path or patio, or setting them on their sides to create a ridge. Bricks can be set at an angle to make a zigzag edge. Specially designed edges in stone, brick, concrete and metal are also available. Alternatively, you can create your own border in, say, shells or corks "planted" upright at the edge of a flower bed. You could also grow a neat miniature hedge of box or lavender, but this would need trimming or pruning from time to time.

■ ABOVE
Original Victorian rope edgings are enjoying renewed popularity, and are particularly suited to the gardens of older houses and cottages. Many new variations of rope edging are now available for a more contemporary look.

■ ABOVE
These antique, charcoal-coloured clay edging tiles aligned in a row would provide a neat finish to a pathway or terrace in a formal town garden.

■ LEFT
Scallop shells left over from the dinner table or cajoled from the fishmonger make a delightful edging in shades of soft coral that co-ordinate well with terracotta paving. Because edging materials do not need to be particularly durable, they offer an almost limitless number of decorative possibilities.

Making Patterns

There is a great tradition of elaborate "floors" for outside use. The Romans created intricate mosaics on courtyard floors, a skill that reached its zenith in richly decorated Islamic outdoor pavements. In the Middle East and India, decorative walkways were composed of ceramic tiles laid in geometric patterns.

Echoes of highly intricate and decorative floor styles can be seen in Victorian English architecture: many terraced houses are approached by "tessellated" pathways, with square, rectangular and triangular tiles laid in formal patterns of contrasting colours – black and white, or cream, chocolate and terracotta.

Pebbles are another traditional mosaic material, and their natural colours and smoothly rounded forms can be used to make exquisite textural panels or complete garden floors. Simple geometric shapes are traditional, though in the hands of an artist they can become elaborate, figurative works of art.

■ ABOVE
Even old hub caps from agricultural machinery can be used to add texture to an ordinary gravel pathway.

■ ABOVE
Pieces of water-worn slate collected from the beach and set edge on in mortar make an elegant textural plaque. In spring, forget-me-nots can be planted round it to create a vibrant azure border.

■ ABOVE
Tessellated tiles, rescued from a crumbling city pathway and destined for a builder's skip, make an enchanting detail in a flower bed.

■ ABOVE
Even artefacts as unprepossessing as old drain covers look good when grouped together, creating a pleasing effect with their simple geometry.

Floor Plantings

Outdoor flooring looks more established if small mosses, plants and lichens are allowed to grow between the pavers – though the effect can be enhanced by a little judicious weeding: self-seeded violas look enchanting, but thistles are less appealing.

Floor patterns using plants rather than hard materials have been created throughout the ages. The most obvious examples of these are Elizabethan knot gardens and baroque parterres. In these, an outline shape is formed using hedging in straight lines, geometric patterns or curves to create, in the case of a knot garden, an elaborate knot effect. Traditionally, different plants are then grown within each section of the knot. Parterres can be on a much grander scale, and often incorporate topiary, lawns and highly formalized plantings. At a more affordable level, you can cultivate mini-gardens or "lawns" by removing a paver and introducing low-growing plants in its place. This is a particularly effective way of softening uninspiring areas of large concrete slabs. Try planting a miniature herb lawn that releases its aroma as you brush past. Chamomile (the non-flowering variety 'Treneague') and thyme are particularly effective. Or you can plant larger herbs, such as lavender and sage. Low-growing flowers, such as alyssum, violets, violas, pinks or any of the alpines, will provide a subtle but telling splash of floor-level colour.

■ ABOVE
A carpet of leafy green foliage sprouting up between the cracks in the concrete gives this garden corner an appealing summer look.

■ ABOVE
An alpine garden planted into an old millstone gives this floor an extra dimension.

■ ABOVE
This fascinating three-dimensional, ceramic sun makes an original floor feature. Planted with low-growing plants, such as "mind-your-own-business" (*Soleirolia soleirolii*), it takes on the appearance of a rich green tapestry that enhances the sun motif.

Herb Wheel

If you have an old cartwheel, why not paint or varnish it and set it into the ground ready to plant? Few of us have access to cartwheels, but an acceptable second best can be made from bricks. Adjust the size of your wheel to suit your garden. Bricks offer a convenient way to make "spokes", but you could use dwarf dividing "hedges" of hyssop or thyme. Place an attractive terracota pot in the centre as the hub of the wheel, and plant with herbs, or place an upright rosemary in the centre. A rosemary may become too large after a few years, so either keep it clipped to shape and size or replace it every second or third year.

1 Mark a circle about 1.5–1.8m (5–6ft) across, using a line fixed to a peg to ensure an even shape. If it helps, use a wine bottle filled with dry sand instead of a stick to mark out the perimeter. Excavate the ground to a depth of about 15cm (6in).

2 Place the bricks on end or at an angle around the edge. If you place them at a 45 degree angle it will create a dog-tooth effect; bricks placed on end will look more formal. Lay them loose in compacted earth, or bed them on mortar.

3 Lay rows of brick, cross-fashion, as shown. If the diameter does not allow for them to be laid without a gap in the centre, stand an ornament or pot in the middle – if you are not planting directly into the soil in that position.

4 Top up the areas between the spokes with a good garden or potting soil.

5 Plant up each section, using plants that will balance each other in size of growth if possible. You could, for instance, grow different types of thymes.

6 For a smart finish, carefully cover the soil with fine gravel.

Pretty Pebble Rug

Create an outdoor "fireside rug" from pebbles, broken garden pots and old china ginger-jar tops. Choose a simple design that is not difficult to achieve: you can always add to it as your confidence grows. The "rug" will make an appealing, witty motif in any paved patio or terrace.

■ RIGHT
The subtle colour variations of natural stones, slate and terracotta harmonize beautifully in this decorative panel.

Preparation

The bed on which the "rug" is to be set should be prepared to a depth of about 10cm/4in, allowing a 5cm/2in clearance below the level of the rest of the paving. Dig out the area to the dimensions of the panel and to a depth of 15cm/6in. Mix equal parts of fine aggregate and cement. Then, using a watering can, dribble in water a little at a time until you have a dry, crumbly mix. Use this mix to fill the area, leaving a 5cm/2in clearance. Level and allow the mix to dry. Gather together plenty of materials for the design and lay them out for size on the dry bed before you begin. Using tile nippers, cut off the bottoms of at least six terracotta pots and snip off the rims in sections. Choose pebbles and slates that are long enough to be wedged in at least 2.5cm/1in below the surface of the "rug".

Aftercare

Protect the "rug" for three days by covering it with a board raised on bricks then overlaid by plastic sheeting. Avoid walking on the "rug" for at least a month to allow the mortar to cure fully.

Tools and Materials

- spade
- fine aggregate to fill the area to a depth of 10cm/4in
- cement
- watering can
- selection of pebbles, pieces of slate, terracotta pots, china ginger-jar pot lids
- tile nippers
- sharp sand
- mortar colour
- straight edge
- hammer
- soft brush
- board to cover rug area
- 4 bricks
- plastic sheeting

1 Prepare the mortar bedding by mixing equal quantities of sharp sand and cement. Add the mortar colour and mix in well. The design is worked while the mortar mix is dry, to enable you to change it if necessary. But the whole design must be completed in a day because moisture from the atmosphere will begin to set the mortar.

2 Pour the dry mix on to the flat bed and, using a straight edge, smooth it out until it is level with the rest of the paving. Then remove a small quantity of the mix from the centre so that it does not overflow as you work. This extracted mix can be put back at a later stage as required, as the design begins to take shape.

3 Plan the border design by arranging the pebbles, slates and the rim sections from the terracotta pots around the outside edge of the "rug" until you have a level, decorative border design. Working inwards, gently hammer the pieces into place.

4 Brush the mortar over the worked areas to make sure any gaps are filled. To build up the border design, continue working towards the centre, carefully hammering in the pebbles, slates and terracotta. Use china pot lids to add splashes of colour to the four corners.

5 Plan the design using the terracotta bases, pebbles and slate. Make sure the central area of mortar is level. Using tile nippers, cut the pieces of terracotta to size, then gently hammer everything into position. When the pattern is complete, brush the mortar around the decoration and use a watering can to dampen the surface. As the mortar absorbs the moisture, it will set hard.

Miniature Pebble Circle

Here is a very simple mosaic made from pieces of slate and old flower pots, plus a few beach pebbles, which can be used as a decorative detail anywhere in the garden.

Tools and Materials

- spade
- 16 brick pavers
- 5kg/11lb bag ready-mixed sand and cement
- mortar trowel
- slates
- terracotta crocks
- pebbles

1 Prepare a smooth circular area in the garden. Lay the pavers so that they radiate outwards, leaving the central area free. How far you extend the pavers will depend on the size of your prepared area.

2 Add sufficient water to the sand and cement mix to achieve a crumbly consistency. Using a mortar trowel, smooth the cement into the circle.

3 Working quickly before the cement sets, press in a border of slates, setting them on edge.

4 Working in concentric rings, add a circle of terracotta crocks and another of slates, then add a "wheel" of pebbles and terracotta.

■ OPPOSITE
Include this pebble circle as a decorative panel in a paved or gravelled area of the garden, or include it in a herb bed.

■ RIGHT
Try to include at least three different materials in the circle, as contrasting colours add interest to the design.

Mosaic Slabs

These large-scale pebble mosaics are very hardwearing and can be repeated as many times as necessary to lay as part of a path or patio. The square slab measures 36cm/14in across – anything larger becomes too unwieldy and will be more likely to break.

■ RIGHT
Sort your collection of pebbles by colour and shape to make decorative slabs with regular patterns. Using smaller frames, you can also create little pebble pictures to set in a floor or wall.

Tools and Materials

- selection of pebbles
- large sheet of paper
- hammer
- nails
- 4 38cm/15in lengths of 5 x 2.5cm/2 x 1in wood
- plastic sheet
- rubber gloves
- cement
- large bucket

1 Lay out the design first on a piece of paper the same size as the finished slab. Nail together the four pieces of wood to make a square frame.

2 Cover with a plastic sheet and put the frame in the centre. Wearing rubber gloves, mix the cement in a bucket and fill the frame.

3 Use your hands to press the cement down firmly, especially into the corners. Smooth the surface just below the top of the frame.

4 Transfer the pebbles from the paper on to the cement, pressing each firmly in place. Leave for several days to allow the cement to set.

5 Remove the slab from the frame by banging the edge of the frame firmly on a hard surface. Repeat to make as many slabs as you need.

DECKING

Timber decking is a flexible material to work with, both in terms of actual installation and in how it is treated afterwards, as its appearance can be varied with wood stains or paint. It can also be used with other materials such as paving and gravel to give interesting textural variations.

Decking is a surface associated with hot, dry climates, and it will give your garden a warm, sunny feel. In fact, it can also be used in wetter, colder areas as long as the timber is pressure-treated first.

On level or gently sloping ground, decking is not difficult to construct. Begin by mortaring rows of bricks on to a concrete

■ ABOVE
Whitening wood, whether with bleach or a pale woodwash, accentuates the natural grain and gives it a lovely weathered, seaside look, as if it has been exposed to years of sunshine.

■ RIGHT
Timber decking and a metal rail are the perfect choice for a raised patio overlooking a marine view, giving the terrace a nautical feel. Laying the timbers diagonally, as here, has the effect of visually enlarging a small area.

foundation at right-angles to the intended direction of the decking and about 40cm/16in apart. Lay wooden joists along the rows of bricks, including a waterproof membrane such as plastic sheeting between the bricks and the joists. Screw the planks to the joists, and face the edges of the deck with lengths of timber. Allow narrow gaps between the boards to give free drainage and to allow for expansion in the wood.

Small, slatted panels are available ready-made from timber merchants and can be laid on compacted soil or gravel to make paths as well as patios. Lay them in alternate directions to give a checkerboard effect over a large area.

Reclaimed wood in the form of disused railway sleepers (ties) is very stable and will make a secure timber surface simply laid on compacted gravel. Sleepers have many uses in the garden: use them for edging borders and making raised flower beds, as well as for edging pathways and steps, to give the garden a unified appearance.

Walls: The Garden Framework

It is the garden walls – and the plants and decorations you dress them with – that welcome visitors at eye level. So make your boundaries a vibrant part of your garden design, using colour, texture, pictures and decorations.

Garden walls and fences are essentially functional. They are there to define the boundaries, to keep children and pets safely within and intruders out. Nevertheless, they also fulfil a design function, affording the garden its main vertical structure. Depending on the circumstances, this can be emphasized or played down. The obvious example for most houses is the contrast between the front and back gardens. At the front, fences are usually low or visually lightweight, creating a boundary without obscuring the house to provide an open, welcoming look. At the back, however, the boundaries are more likely to be solid walls or fences to provide privacy from neighbouring gardens. They also form the background against which the garden can be planned. For this reason, the walls shouldn't be too dominant in themselves.

■ BELOW
An arched rose garland and mature border shrubs have created natural walls down the length of this garden path.

■ BELOW
Slow-growing topiary hedges lend an air of solid formality and neatness to any garden scene.

■ ABOVE
Well-established borders and hedges can be trained to form archways, framing paths and providing superb impact.

■ RIGHT
Foxgloves and trailing leaves cloak an old bent brick wall, lending it an informal and welcoming look.

■ BELOW
Climbing honeysuckle helps make a feature of this tumbling-down wall.

Boundary Choices

The most appealing garden walls are those of well-seasoned brick, evocative as they are of the walled gardens that are integral to large country houses. They lend an air of permanence, have a pleasing crumbly texture and, because they retain and reflect heat, they can create a protected micro-climate within the garden. Garden walls look best built with local materials – stone, flint or local stock brick. If you are building or repairing a wall, seek out these local materials, as they will blend perfectly with the wall's setting.

■ OPPOSITE
Clambering yellow roses make a summer decoration, taking over from a spring flowering of wisteria.

■ BELOW
Crossed rustic poles bring decorous restraint to unruly rose shrubs.

PLANTED WALLS

As an alternative to hard materials, the plants themselves will also make effective garden "walls". Box and privet offer classic hedging that is very appealing and provides a rich green boundary all the year round. Hedges can be clipped into simple topiary shapes, which look just as good in small urban gardens as they do in larger rural ones. The trick is to keep them to the scale of the garden and its surroundings. Elaborate peacocks look fantastic in the country but, in urban situations, a neat orb or stately obelisk is more appropriate.

Larger conifers, such as thuja, can also provide lofty verdant hedging, which is perfect for protecting your privacy in built-up areas. However, some conifers will eventually grow very tall – up to 15m/50ft – so make sure you buy one of the more manageable varieties, such as *Thuja* 'Lutea nana', which stops at a modest height of about 1.8m/6ft, or 'Rheingold', which reaches 3–3.5m/10–12ft.

Another way of creating a living wall is to fix a trellis on which to grow climbers and ramblers. The classic choices are roses, honeysuckle, jasmine, clematis and the potato vine, *Solanum crispum*

or *S. jasminoides*, all of which produce flowers, for a fabulous floral wall. Cleverly painted, they can be combined to provide colour interest all year round. If your horticultural knowledge stops short of the encyclopaedic, plan your planting the easy way, by buying a new climber in flower every two or three months. They will all come up again the following year, ensuring another lovely display of seasonal colour.

More open plan screening can be provided by low walls teamed with low hedging. Again, the traditional box or privet will work well, or you can plant a pretty floral hedge, such as lavender or fuchsia – both of which will impart a beautiful fragrance over the garden.

WOOD AND METAL

As a non-planting option, wood is an ever-popular boundary choice, and will require very little upkeep once it is in place. Traditional picket fencing looks wonderful in classic clean white, or it can be painted to complement the plants. In country districts, rustic poles look good, especially if you don't want to obscure a wonderful view. Position them either upright in lines or arranged in a series of long, low crosses to create a loose trellis.

Metal is another hardwearing material for boundary dividers. Railings, marching regimentally across the front garden, look very smart in a city, while ornamental metal lattice or trellis produce a decorative effect almost anywhere.

■ BELOW

Metal railings are the classic smart answer for front gardens in town, but they are just as pleasing when used to enclose a rambling country plot. Their appeal is the precise, military line they draw that unequivocally says "no entry" without obstructing the view.

■ LEFT
This living wall of roses makes a delightful garden boundary. Even grown over quite a flimsy framework of trellis or chain link, roses soon thicken into dense cover, which protects your privacy as much as any more solid planting.

■ BELOW
A high brick wall is effective at keeping out visitors but can be monotonous on the eye. Growing reliable climbers, such as clematis and rose, will help minimize the repetition of the brickwork.

■ ABOVE
This white climbing rose overhangs the roof of an outbuilding and acts as a natural barrier, preventing intruders and protecting the privacy of the garden. Blooming foliage always looks magnificent, especially when it is used to enhance an existing garden structure.

FENCES

Fencing, wooden or otherwise, makes the ideal boundary choice when privacy is not the priority – such as at the front of the house, where you may prefer to be a little more open and welcoming while still needing a clear definition of your boundary.

The most common garden boundaries consist of wooden lapped fencing, which is relatively inexpensive to buy and very quick and easy to put up. Wooden fencing can be bought in panels, ready-treated against rot, and is nailed or screwed to posts, which can be fixed into "collars" of long metal spikes, firmly driven into the ground. A similarly solid-looking boundary is wattle fencing. Woven from young willow branches, this traditional fencing dates back to the Bronze Age in Britain. With its bark intact, the wattle provides a very attractive fine texture against which plants can grow and clamber. Wattle fencing is available as "hurdles" (panels) of various widths and heights, and it is erected in much the same way as more commonplace wooden fencing.

■ BELOW
Picket fencing makes for a simple but efficient boundary, which can be left plain or painted to match a colour scheme.

■ ABOVE
White-painted picket fencing provides a classic boundary marker that is perenially pleasing. The crisp, uniform line of wooden posts, with its picot edging at the top, provides a framework to the garden that looks smart wherever you live.

Entrances and Exits

■ RIGHT
Even the entrance at the back of the house can be embellished with some well-chosen containers.

■ BELOW
A discreet basket in full bloom hangs beside an old garden storeroom door, and acts as an enticement to visitors passing through the garden.

Depending on where they are, garden gates and doors have different functions and a different decorative appeal. Front gates welcome visitors, directing them towards the front door, and like front fences are generally lower and more screen-like in appearance. Gates and doors at the side of the garden and leading into the back serve quite the opposite purpose, that of protecting against intruders, and are generally more solid.

The entrance and exit each have their own role in the visual design of the garden. They offer a break in the possible monotony of a wall and, since their presence suggests that they lead somewhere, they can also lend an intriguing extra dimension to the garden. Even if it doesn't actually go anywhere, a door in a wall or fence gives the romantic impression of leading to a hidden garden or unknown space. A solid back gate also allows a feeling of privacy: in the garden, you are in a secret place, accessible only to those you allow in.

■ ABOVE
This tall, metal gate leads from one part of the garden to another, lending intrigue to a space that would have offered less interest had it been one large open area.

■ ABOVE
This ordinary garden door made of wooden slats looks altogether more inviting with the addition of a simple twig wreath, which was made from materials found in the garden.

Trelliswork

Trellis is a great garden material. It can be used as a wall in itself, providing a framework for climbers and ramblers. It can be used as a divider within the garden to lend perspective, and to add height to walls where extra privacy is needed. It can also be used to decorate the walls themselves. The decorative aspect is especially valuable when walls or fences are less than beautiful, or where you would like to add a little extra texture.

■ BELOW
A fabulous Indian metal trellis panel makes an imaginative framework for a special feature. The frame has been painted in verdigris colours, and pale blue urns, planted with *saxifrage*, complete the picture.

The trellis does not have to be ready-made. Old gates, an old window frame without the glass, metal panels or panels made from grape vine stems and other organic materials can all serve the same purpose as ordinary trelliswork. They all have the advantage of looking good even before the climbers have been planted. More traditional trelliswork can be given a head start with a lick of paint, which immediately gives it a more finished and individual appearance.

■ ABOVE
An old wrought-iron gate provides an elegant trellis framework for a miniature climbing rose.

■ RIGHT
Here, painted square trellis has been used as a screen, dividing off one part of the garden. It provides an excellent framework for a climbing rose and clematis. This trellis can also be a pretty solution for a boundary fence.

■ BELOW
Evocative, organic twig trellis panels make a wonderful frame for a montage of climbing roses and additional decorative features such as twiggy stars and metal lanterns.

ADDING COLOUR

Inside the house, once the walls are plastered, you immediately think about decorating them. Outside, people are still a little frightened of colour, preferring to play safe by sticking to the natural tones of stone, brick and wood. In a decorative garden, colour is very important. Not only can the paint you choose suggest mood and ambience, just as it does inside, it can also be used to emphasize the colour scheme of the garden planting.

■ BELOW
Sugar-almond shades differentiate two properties. In the far garden, the pastel pink perfectly matches the climbing rose growing inside the picket fence.

The surfaces you paint may be the house walls, walls of outside buildings such as garages or sheds, or they may be the garden boundary walls. Maybe you have a mixture of fencing and trelliswork, all of slightly different woods and ages, that has resulted in a visual muddle. A coat of weatherproof emulsion (latex) will make all the difference: giving the fixtures all the same decorative finish will produce a much more coherent look for the whole garden.

Or you may have newly erected trelliswork that has a year or more to wait for a verdant covering of creepers. Giving it a coat of paint when you put it up means you will have some attractive colour to look at while the plants grow.

Colour can be used to single out one area of the garden. You can pinpoint the features destined for a particular colour scheme, or you may wish to highlight the planting.

Painted fences and surfaces give year-round colour to the garden and are particularly valuable in winter when many of the plants have died down. This is the ideal time to give fences and gates a fresh coat of paint. Unlike interior decoration, you don't need to spend a lot of time on preparation. There is no need to fill holes or sand down. Just scrub the wood down with warm water to clean it, and allow it to dry thoroughly before applying the paint. If you plan to paint an outdoor house wall, however, you will usually need to apply a primer to the clean and dry wall surface before adding your chosen colour.

■ BELOW LEFT
Colour can be used to transform any of the objects in your garden, and whether the change is permanent or temporary, the effect is the same. Here, a potting shed has been enlivened in an afternoon simply by painting the otherwise plain bins in bright shades of green.

■ BELOW
This window sill edged with brilliant ceramic tiles adds vibrant colour, which is matched in summer by a row of red pelargoniums.

Paint and Wall Options

Nobody would dream of painting a beautiful old stone or brick wall, but if your walls are made of more modern materials they may be less sympathetic to the rest of the garden, or just look dull or grimy. If your fencing is the popular panelled variety, it is likely to arrive coated in a protective preservative, usually a violent shade of rust that you will want to cover up quickly. A coat of paint is the quickest way to bring light and brightness into the shadiest garden, and to add colour that is not seasonal.

There's no need to limit yourself to a single colour when painting a wall or a row of fencing. Paint your wall and cover it with trellis painted in a contrasting colour, or paint the wall in stripes or bold blocks of colour, adding smaller designs using stencils.

And if in a year or two you have changed your mind about your design, or if the planting scheme has changed, just paint it again.

■ OPPOSITE
A decorative edge in stripes of bright Caribbean colours gives life to a plain white wall and door. Masking tape was used to keep the lines straight and, when they were all complete and dry, the leaves were added using a stencil.

■ BELOW LEFT
Three colours of paint have been used to brighten this outdoor setting. Such a bold use of colour, intensified by a vibrant display of plants on the wall and cushions in primary shades, gives the corner a strong Mediterranean feel.

■ BELOW
Don't be put off by thinking white walls look cold and bare in anything but a tropical climate. This brightly painted door adds some positive colour, and is itself offset by the white. The addition of the electric lamp completes the picture of a very smart doorway.

Ideas with Paint

Whether you want to paint your garden wall, or a house wall that faces the garden, there is plenty of inspiration to be had. Experiment not only with colour but with technique.

As well as straight colour, you can create depth by layering the colours. Try trompe l'oeil effects such as marble, stone, slate or moss. Stencil designs on to walls, use potato prints, geometric designs or even simple motifs. The trick is to consider the scale. These effects will have to be seen from much further away than they would if used indoors. Even a 9m/30ft garden is much larger than the average room, so everything has to be exaggerated a little. Paint effects need to be a little less subtle, and motifs generally larger.

■ RIGHT
This sunny yellow wall was given a rough-textured look by trowelling on a ready-mixed medium (joint compound), available from DIY (hardware) stores. Colourwashing in two shades of yellow gives depth and tone.

■ FAR RIGHT
Give new shutters or doors a weatherworn look by applying wax between two layers of different-coloured paint. The colours used here are creamy yellow beneath bright blue.

■ ABOVE
A checkerboard pattern always makes a striking display and is a traditional design in many communities, so it is unlikely to date. This one in tan and cream was inspired by African decoration; the same design in china blue and white would evoke Provence. The design doesn't necessarily have to be neat and even; as here, little irregularities add to its charm. If you trust your eye, paint it freehand, using a fine brush to create the outline of each square and then filling it in with colour. If you would prefer something a little more orderly, cut a large square stencil and position it on the wall. Cover a whole wall if you are feeling adventurous, or simply work the design on window and door reveals and along skirting areas.

■ ABOVE
This cascade of falling leaves was created using a potato print, which can be just as effective outside as in. Choose a simple motif, like this oak leaf, and, using the point of a knife, gently "draw" the outline on to the cut surface of half a large potato. Cut away the potato from around the outline to a depth of about 9mm/⅜in and "draw" in the veins. Give the wall a pale colourwash base. When that has fully dried, dip the potato into a stronger colour of paint, stamp it on a piece of newspaper to remove the excess paint, then stamp on to the wall.

■ ABOVE
Marbling makes the perfect effect for an outside wall, since it works best in oil-based paints that are ideal for outside use. It should be applied to a smooth surface. The veins are applied over a paint base while it is still wet, and splashes of white spirit (turpentine) are added to soften the hard edges.

■ ABOVE
Evocative of the sunny Mediterranean, lemons and limes make wonderful motifs that anyone can manage. Cut a stencil or paint them freehand. Paint the shapes randomly like this or make a trompe d'oeil by painting a simple shelf of plates decorated with lemons.

■ ABOVE
An unprepossessing garden or shed wall gives the impression of having the patina of time when stippled in shades of green to give a mossed effect. First apply a colourwash of mid- to dark green, then roll on a pale green and, finally, stipple on some ochre with the tip of the brush.

■ ABOVE
Naive lizard-like animal motifs are traditional in many cultures. This one, inspired by African art, is not dissimilar to motifs used by Native Americans. Just one lizard in the corner of a sunny wall would transform it from the ordinary to something special.

DECORATIVE GARDEN FIXTURES AND FITTINGS

It is the fixtures and fittings you choose for your garden that help determine your theme. A water feature conveys a tranquil mood, while a brightly-painted play house and a pirate ship built from a tree will make the garden a children's paradise of fairy-tale adventure.

There are a multitude of choices for garden fixtures. Dividers in the form of arches, arbours and pergolas partition your space, with plants trained over and around the structure to soften the impact of the wood or metal materials from which the divider is made. Clever tricks with wood stains and paint will help solve the problem of an unsightly garden shed. The secret is to look at your immovable garden fixtures in a new way, and transform them into features which will contribute an extra architectural dimension to your garden design.

■ ABOVE
Garden paraphernalia has a charm all of its own.

■ OPPOSITE
A collection of pots planted with evergreen plants is the perfect way to decorate a flight of steps throughout the year.

Dividers and Arches

Even the smallest garden can accommodate fixtures such as arches, arbours, pergolas and trellis screens and still have room for a small garden shed or play house. And while the hard landscaping and planted borders will dictate the layout of the garden, it is these vertical elements that greatly affect its structure and overall look.

Vertical structures such as pergolas and garden buildings can be positioned around the garden's perimeter to give shape, while rose arches, walkways and trellis screens can be used as dividers. Anything that divides the garden lends extra perspective because it defines another space, and even in gardens that are fairly limited in size, being able to glimpse beyond into another area creates the illusion of greater space. An arch that forms the entrance to the garden is a particularly successful feature as it governs the visitor's initial impression of the garden, framing the scene beyond and creating interest and atmosphere.

TRELLIS

If you want to screen off part of the garden – to define an eating area, perhaps, or to section off a vegetable garden – the simplest solution is to use trellis, which is wonderfully versatile and comes in a variety of panel shapes and sizes. As well as the basic rectangular panels, there are panels with pointed, convex or concave tops and even with integral "windows", all of which provide plenty of scope for creativity. When it comes to the finishing touches, there is a wide choice of attractive finials in shapes such as globes, acorns, pineapples and obelisks, which can be used as additional decoration.

ARCHES

If you prefer not to screen off a whole area to lend perspective, a rose arch can have the desired effect. Buy a ready-made metal arch or make a simple wooden one using pergola posts. Another option is to use plants, planting young trees either side of a path, and tying them at the top so that they grow into an arch. Remember to make the arch wide enough to get through when it is fully clad with plants, and don't use plants with thorny stems if they are likely to brush against people walking under the arch. The rose 'Zéphirine Drouhin' is an excellent choice as it is thornless.

■ LEFT
Rustic poles fixed horizontally to wooden pillars form a kind of trellis that makes an ideal support for a climbing rose such as 'Felicia', and still works well as a garden divider in winter when the rose is not in bloom.

Climbers for Arches

Akebia quinata (chocolate vine)
Campsis radicans (trumpet vine)
Clematis
Humulus (hop)
Lonicera (honeysuckle)
Rosa (roses)
Vigna caracalla (climbing bean)
Vitis (grape vines)

■ RIGHT
Beautiful walkways can be created by training foliage to grow over metal arches. Here, the light covering of leaves lets in dappled sunlight along the length of the path, providing the perfect setting for a pleasant early evening stroll.

■ RIGHT
A mature rose overhangs the garden wall, providing an elegant backdrop which gives intimacy to the seating area and successfully screens the garden from neighbours.

Walkways, Pergolas and Arbours

As well as serving as a light screen, an arch can mark the beginning of a walkway. If you have enough space in the garden, a walkway has great appeal. There is something peaceful and cloister-like about a walk beneath a leafy tunnel through which natural light filters to the ground. Even in a small garden, a simple, verdant archway offers a sense of romantic adventure – the idea of going somewhere – and it needn't cut into too much garden space.

WALKWAYS

Walkways can be as simple as an elongated archway – probably the best option in a small garden – or a long snaking affair down one side of the garden. They can be made from metal or from wooden poles forming a series of arches. The effect of a walkway can be made even more powerful if punctuated at the end by a focal point in the classical style. In a formal garden, this may all have been planned as part of the landscaping, the walkway leading perhaps to a door or gateway or an exquisite piece of garden statuary. But you can adapt the idea for a more modest setting and still create impact. A specimen plant or a favourite pot or container, beautifully planted up, will provide a satisfying focal point at the end of the walkway, while acquiring a greater sense of importance for itself as it attracts the attention of everyone who strolls there.

PERGOLAS

Pergolas are first cousins to walkways, being covered areas often fixed on to one side of the house. These work well in all sizes of garden, providing an attractive, natural, covered outdoor "room" and serving as a transition area between inside and out. They make delightful shady outdoor eating areas that afford extra privacy from overlooking neighbours.

ARBOURS

Leafy arbours lend architectural form to a garden while taking up very little space. Tucked against a wall, an arbour will create structure in even the smallest garden, offering somewhere shady to sit, relax and read or chat with a friend. At its simplest, an arbour could be formed by training climbing plants up a wall to form an arch over a garden bench, though it is not difficult to make a more permanent structure.

■ ABOVE

This pagoda-topped metal walkway lends an almost oriental feel to the garden. Beautiful old Greek pithoi set in a bed of vibrant euphorbias and hellebores are used to great effect as the focal point at the end.

■ ABOVE

Wonderful cascades of laburnum make a flamboyant golden walkway.

■ RIGHT

The large overhanging fig (*Ficus carica*) and the surrounding rose, clematis and other climbers growing on this house wall have created an intimate setting for the table and chairs, which fulfils all the functions of an arbour even though there is no supporting structure.

■ LEFT

Flanked by greenery and shaded overhead by a roof of honeysuckle, this delightful arbour is set against the fabulous texture of a brick and flint wall. By incorporating the existing structure of the garden, it takes on an authentic "lived-in" feel. The weathered, rustic wooden bench and table are left out throughout the year, offering further structure to this part of the garden.

Trellis Arbour

An arbour is one of the easiest ways to introduce architectural structure to even the smallest of gardens, and it is no more difficult to make one than it is to put up a fence. This arbour is made up of trellis panels, painted with an outdoor stain in a cool, deep colour to tone with the bench. The result is an enchanting, original bower.

1 Gather together the trellis panels and "dry assemble" them to ensure that you are happy with the design. Two of the 1.8m x 60cm/6 x 2ft panels are for the sides and the third is for the top. The two narrow panels and the concave panel form the front and the 1.8m x 90cm/6 x 3ft panel is to be used horizontally at the top of the back. Trim the wooden posts to length: they should measure 1.8m/6ft plus the depth of the metal "shoe" at the top of the post support.

Tools and Materials

lattice (diagonal) trellis panels in the following sizes:

3 panels 1.8m x 60cm/6 x 2ft

2 panels 1.8m x 30cm/6 x 1ft

1 concave panel 1.8m x 46cm/6 x 1½ft

1 panel 1.8m x 90cm/6 x 3ft

6 timber posts 7.5 x 7.5cm/3 x 3in, each 2.1m/7ft long

saw

6 spiked metal post supports, 7.5 x 7.5cm/3 x 3in, each 75cm/2½ft long

mallet

10 x 5cm/2in galvanized nails

hammer

electric drill with No 8 bit and screwdriver attachment

40 x 3cm/1¼in No 10 zinc-coated steel screws

2.5 litre/½ gallon can exterior woodstain

paintbrush

2 Start with the back panel. The posts need to be placed 1.8m/6ft apart. Mark their positions, then, using a mallet, drive in a spiked metal post on each side. Drive a trimmed post into each of the metal "shoes". Using galvanized nails, temporarily fix the top of the trellis to the top of the posts. Using a No 8 bit, drill holes for the screws at intervals down each side of the trellis and screw the panel to the posts.

3 In the same way, position the outside front posts and fix the side panels, then the inside front posts and front panels. Fix the concave panel into the panels either side of it. Finally, fix the roof in position, screwing it into the posts. Paint the arbour with exterior woodstain and leave to dry.

■ RIGHT
Diagonal trellis makes a picturesque arbour for a garden seat even before climbing plants have had time to scramble over it. To soften its lines while it is new, you can provide extra decoration with hanging baskets and plants in containers.

GARDEN STRUCTURES

Any kind of building adds to the framework of the garden and there are few gardens that don't have at least one, be it a garden shed, summer house or play house. They are usually left just as they were when they were put up, but it is never too late to turn them into decorative features in their own right.

A garden shed can be transformed with paint – in pale, pretty stripes like a beach hut, for example – or it can be given a more substantial-looking roof of slates. Climbers can be grown up garden buildings. Play houses can be decorated to give them a fairy-tale appeal. Honeysuckle or clematis can be grown over the roof and hanging baskets hung from the eaves.

Follies were a favourite in the gardens of Victorian homes, built in fanciful styles from Gothic to oriental. It is not difficult to incorporate fun in the form of a folly – a Gothic shed, pagoda or temple. These can be bought ready to put up, or you could scour architectural salvage yards for attractive doors and windows to incorporate in a new design.

■ ABOVE
Architectural salvage, some pillars and posts, plenty of imagination and clever use of paint make an eyecatching latter-day garden folly.

■ LEFT
If you find you can put a dreary garden shed to better use, remove the doors and add seating to build yourself a charming retreat, and to make the most of an existing structure in your garden.

■ OPPOSITE
This delightful gazebo is made from a simple metal frame overgrown with climbers. The bench seating was built around the supporting wooden joist in the centre.

Decorating a Shed

Even the most unpromising garden buildings can be turned into something special. When this one was "inherited" with the garden, it was little more than a concrete block. With the addition of some paint and plaster shapes, available from architectural plaster suppliers, it took on the appearance of a miniature Mediterranean villa.

Tools and Materials

- pencil
- stiff paper
- scissors
- 1cm/½in MDF (medium-density fiberboard)
- jigsaw or fretsaw
- acrylic wood primer
- decorator's and artist's paintbrushes
- emulsion (latex) paint in dark blue
- fine-textured masonry paint in white
- acrylic scumble glaze
- artist's acrylic paint in light blue, red, orange and yellow
- soft cloths
- nails
- hammer
- stiff brush
- palette knife
- exterior tile adhesive
- selection of small, ornamental plaster motifs
- electrical insulation tape
- panel pins (tacks)
- pliers
- natural sponge
- matt exterior polyurethane varnish

1 Draw a Moorish roof motif on a sheet of paper to fit the top of the door. Cut out and place this template on the MDF, drawing around the shape. Cut out using a jigsaw or fretsaw.

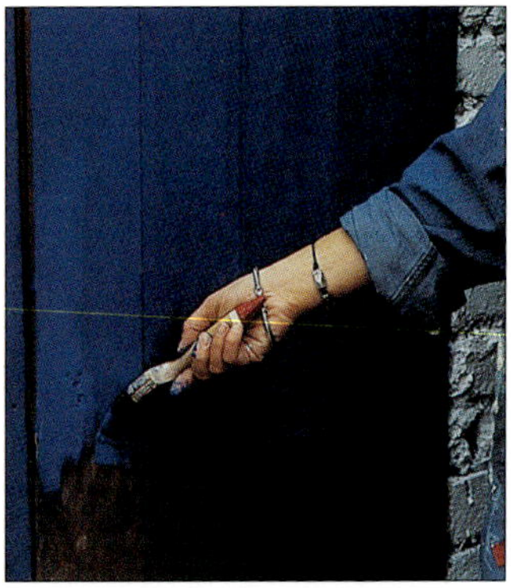

2 Paint both the door and the MDF panel with acrylic wood primer and allow to dry for 1–2 hours. Paint one coat of dark blue emulsion (latex) and allow to dry for 2–3 hours.

3 Mix up a glaze using fine-textured masonry paint and acrylic scumble glaze and add a little water to give the consistency of double (heavy) cream, then tint with light blue artist's acrylic. Paint the door and shaped panel, brushing in the direction of the grain.

4 Quickly wipe off the glaze using a soft cloth to knock back the colour and leave to dry. Nail the MDF panel to the top of the door, and paint the nail heads with the pale blue glaze.

5 Using a stiff brush, scrub the wall surfaces to remove the dirt. Use a palette knife to "butter" the back of each plaster motif with exterior tile adhesive and stick them to the wall. Use electrical insulation tape and panel pins (tacks) tapped into the wall under the shapes to hold the plaster shapes in position overnight while the adhesive dries.

6 Remove the tape and pins with pliers, then paint the wall with one coat of fine-textured masonry paint. Leave to dry for 4–6 hours.

7 Tint three pots of acrylic scumble glaze with artist's acrylic paints – one red, one orange and one yellow – and dilute to the consistency of single cream. Using a damp sponge, wipe the colours randomly on to the wall, blending the edges. Wipe off the excess with a cloth.

8 Using an artist's brush, stipple extra colour into any detailing to add emphasis. Leave the paint to dry for at least 4 hours, then varnish the wall.

■ ABOVE
The dull, cement-rendered walls of this old garden shed have been given a new vibrancy with a mix of hot Mediterranean colours and an assortment of finely detailed plaster ornaments clustered like a colony of exotic crustaceans.

Adding Wall Decorations

Once you are happy with the basic structure and colour of your garden walls, you can start to add more personal touches with the decorations. The most obvious garden decorations are wall-hung pots, sconces, brackets and small items of statuary. But almost any collection could find a home on the garden wall as long as it is weatherproof. Birdcages, birdfeeders, shells, lanterns and willow or wire wreaths can all be suspended on an outside wall. Or you could make a feature of wall-mounted shelves by filling them with pots, bottles and baskets, or with enamel or galvanized ware.

■ RIGHT
An outdoor lantern is a pretty wall decoration both day and night. This one has been decorated with a simple garland of twigs. For a party on a summer evening, it holds a thick church candle tucked into a terracotta pot, and is given a sparkling bow as a finishing touch.

■ OPPOSITE
A group of galvanized containers makes a shapely collection on a cottage wall, their wonderful, soft metal shades blending harmoniously with the garden.

■ BELOW
The elemental colours and textures of seashells make them the perfect foil for plants. A selection of shells have been used here to enhance a ready-made "window" in the garden wall.

Children's Play Fixtures

In family homes, gardens are very much for the children. They need their own outdoor space to play in, and where there isn't enough room to run or kick a ball the best solution is to set aside one area of the garden and build some sort of structure especially for them. They may like a play house, which provides for all-weather play, or they may prefer a climbing frame or a swing. If such structures are well planned, they need not take up too much space.

If you are lucky enough to have a suitable tree in your garden, you may be inspired to build a tree house, which won't take up any space in the garden at all. It is important to build a strong platform, distributing the load across as many branches as possible, and to surround it with a barrier. A temporary house can be made by suspending a tent from the branches above, or you can add walls, a roof and additional features to customize the house. You can also hang a swing from a branch (which should have a diameter of at least 15cm/6in to be strong enough). The best surface to lay under trees used for playing is chipped bark, which looks natural and is hardwearing yet soft enough to land on safely.

SAFETY FIRST

Whether you are buying play equipment for your children or building it yourself, it is important that it is strong, sturdy and steady, that wood is sanded smooth and that nails and screws are safely sunk below the surface. Ready-made equipment should conform to approved safety standards, and, once you have bought the items, everything should be checked and maintained regularly.

■ ABOVE
These steps up to a platform built around a tree lead to a slide. The same idea could be adapted for a tree house.

■ LEFT
Play houses can be decorated to enhance the whole garden. They not only offer a private place for imaginative play in the early years and a den as the children get older, but they also provide storage space for bulkier toys such as free-standing toy kitchens and dolls' houses.

■ RIGHT
A delightful little crooked house, complete with veranda and chimney, is built on stilts with a short stairway leading up to it. The very stuff of nursery stories, many an hour can be whiled away here in imaginative play.

■ BELOW
Climbing frames made from rustic poles blend happily into the garden. Carefully designed, they can be added to as children grow and develop their agility.

■ ABOVE
This well-constructed play house will provide at least five or six years' entertainment for a child. Most children love to have their own small garden plot to cultivate, and it makes good sense to site this just outside the play house. When the children have outgrown the house it can be turned into a potting shed.

■ ABOVE
If there is plenty of space in the garden, a climbing frame can be extended piece by piece to include swings, a slide, a rope ladder and a covered area that could easily double as a play house or look-out post.

■ RIGHT
A large, sturdy tree would be an asset in any garden, but is particularly useful in family gardens because of the potential it offers for children's play fixtures. A simple swing is easily assembled and will provide hours of fun for active children.

■ LEFT
In an average-sized garden a substantial climbing frame may well be the dominant feature, so it should be chosen for its looks as well as for its play value. This well-made wooden frame is nicely in keeping with the style of the garden.

■ ABOVE
A sandpit is one of the easiest pieces of play equipment to construct and then adapt later on. A lid is important to protect the sand from the weather and from cats. This timber decking lid makes an attractive feature in its own right.

■ ABOVE
A tree platform is good fun for older children and is simple to construct in a suitable tree, using sturdy wood off-cuts. Provide access via a rope ladder, which can be rolled up once the children are up.

Customized Play House

You can create an enchanting fairy-tale house that will add interest to the garden, while providing a play area the children will love. Give yourself a head start by buying one off the shelf and customizing it. Play houses usually come pre-treated against rot, which means they already have an excellent base for decoration (but do check this before you buy). This one has been given a slate roof with terracotta baby ridge tiles, shutters and a decorative fascia. The transformation is completed with a couple of coats of paint. This encompasses quite a few skills, so you might prefer to make things simpler for yourself by just painting the house in a range of cheerful colours.

FIXING THE ROOF SLATES

Work out how many slates (composition shingles) you need for each row. If the slates don't fit the width, place as many whole slates in the bottom row as it will take, then cut two equal strips to fill in at each end. Score and snap each slate in half widthways and secure in position by hammering nails through the pre-drilled holes into the roofing felt. The next row of slates will completely cover the first row of half slates. Arrange them so the side of each slate runs down the centre of the slate below. Nail in position. Position the third row so that the slates lie across the width, as for the first row. The bottom of the third row should line up with the top of the first row of half slates. Lay the fourth row like the second row, and so on.

FITTING THE SHUTTERS

Remove the window crossbars. If the shutters are larger than the window openings, cut the openings to fit using a hacksaw. Attach each shutter with a pair of hinges. Re-use the window bars as shutter stops and fit the door magnets in place.

DECORATING

Paint the play house with oil-based paint and allow to dry for at least 4 hours, or overnight, in fine weather. Then finish with a coat of polyurethane varnish.

ADDING THE RIDGE TILES

Mix up the sand and cement according to the manufacturer's instructions. Fill each end of each ridge tile with the mixture and "butter" some along the length of the ridge. Bed the tiles firmly into position and let dry.

ADDING THE FASCIA

Saw the fascia (bargeboard) to length, mitring the ends to match the angle of the roof in the centre. Paint the fascia with an oil-based paint and fix in place by pre-drilling pilot holes then nailing it to the front edge of the roof.

■ RIGHT
To transform a standard wooden play house into a child's dream cottage, add a few pieces of children's furniture to complete the home-sweet-home feel.

■ RIGHT
Plain wooden play houses can be difficult to accomodate visually with the rest of the garden. Painting and decorating the play house in a style sympathetic to the garden will help it fit in more easily.

Tools and Materials

- wooden play house
- mineral-fibre roof slates (composition shingles): enough to cover the roof plus half as much again
- craft knife
- metal straight edge
- 2 x 19mm/¾in nails per slate
- hammer
- 2 pairs louvred shutters to fit the windows (if the exact size is not available, choose a larger size and trim to fit)
- hacksaw
- 8 non-ferrous hinges
- 4 door magnets
- oil-based paint
- paintbrush
- baby ridge tiles to fit the length of the ridge
- ready-mixed sand and cement
- trowel
- decorative fascia (bargeboard) pre-cut from MDF (medium-density fiberboard)
- saw
- electric drill

■ ABOVE
With the roof slates and shutters in position, the play house has been decorated with an oil-based paint.

■ ABOVE
The original window divides have been re-used as shutter stops and door magnets, fixed in place to hold the shutters closed.

Hanging Pictures

Few walls inside the house are complete until the pictures are hung, and there is no reason why pictures should not be hung outside, too, although they will obviously need to be weatherproof. Ceramic tiled panels, mosaics, old enamel advertisements and painted wood panels all make excellent outdoor pictures.

■ RIGHT
A quirky, ceramic mosaic face smiles out from a curtain of ivy.

■ BELOW
A ceramic tile plaque echoes the colours of the painted garden seat and overflowing wisteria.

Wall Mosaic Picture

A wall mosaic in the garden can afford to be quite playful, peering out from its leafy surroundings. This contemplative princess is made up flat on a board and then moved as a whole to be fixed to the wall. The picture uses glass mosaic tiles in vibrant colours, secured to the board with glue, which will not fade when exposed to the elements.

1 Draw the design on craft paper and lay on a board. Make a tracing of the outline and cut out to act as a template when transferring the design to the wall.

2 Cut the tiles for the outline into eighths, using tile nippers, and stick them face down on to the main lines of your drawing using water-soluble glue. Add key features to the face, such as eyes and lips, in contrasting colours.

Tools and Materials

- pencil
- brown craft paper
- board
- tracing paper
- scissors
- vitreous glass mosaic tiles, including pink tiles
- tile nippers
- water-soluble glue
- mirror
- cement-based tile adhesive
- flexible (putty) knife
- sponge
- sandpaper
- soft cloth

3 Cut pink vitreous glass tiles into quarters and glue them face down to fill between the outlines. Cut the mirror into quarters and glue on to the dress and crown. Cut the tiles for the dress and crown into quarters and stick face down between the mirror pieces. When dry, carry the mosaic to the wall on the board. Draw around the template on the wall and fill the area with cement-based adhesive. Press on the mosaic, paper side up, and let dry for 2 hours. Dampen the paper and peel away. Leave to dry overnight. Grout with cement-based adhesive. Clean off any excess cement and let dry. Rub gently with sandpaper and polish with a soft cloth.

■ BELOW
Brilliant glass mosaic with fragments of sparkling mirror will catch the light, and the eye, glinting from a garden wall.

Garden Mosaic Panel

This richly textured panel is composed of tesserae cut from patterned china. Motifs are cut out and used as focal points for the patterns, and some of them are raised to give extra emphasis. The panel is worked on a plywood base to create a more three-dimensional effect on the wall. This means that it can be assembled while lying flat, then hung from a hook like a picture.

Tools and Materials

- pencil
- 2cm/¾in plywood
- jigsaw
- sandpaper
- PVA (white) glue
- paintbrushes
- wood primer
- undercoat
- gloss paint
- mirror plate
- drill and rebate bit
- 2cm/¾in screw
- screwdriver
- ruler, set square or compasses (optional)
- selection of old china
- tile nippers
- tile adhesive
- powdered tile grout
- cement dye
- rubber gloves
- squeegee or flexible (putty) knife
- nailbrush
- soft cloth

1 Draw the outer shape of the panel on a sheet of 2cm/¾in plywood. Cut out around the shape using a jigsaw and sand the edges. Seal the front and edges of the panel with diluted PVA (white) glue. Paint the back with wood primer, undercoat and gloss paint, allowing each coat to dry before applying the next.

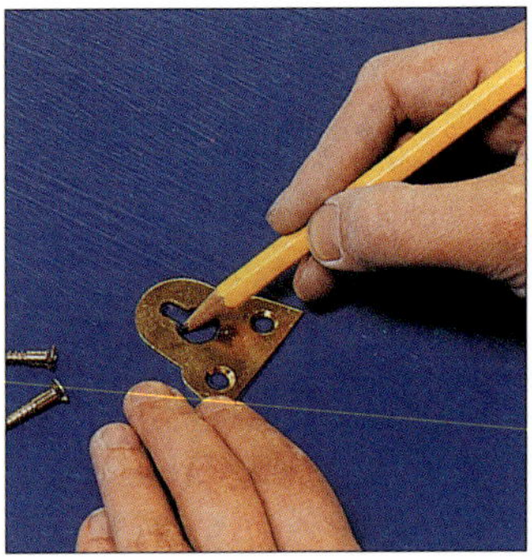

2 Mark the position of the mirror plate on the back of the panel. Drill out the area under the keyhole opening large enough to take a screw head. Screw the mirror plate in position.

3 Draw your design on the sealed top surface. Tools such as a ruler, set square and compasses are helpful if your design has geometric elements.

4 Divide the china into groups by colour and pattern and select motifs for the centrepieces of designs. Cut the china into small squares using the tile nippers. Use smooth edged pieces to edge the panel, pressing the pieces into tile adhesive. Use small, regular tesserae to tile the structural lines of the design.

5 Raise small areas of the mosaic by setting the tesserae on a larger mound of adhesive. Fill in the pattern between the structural lines. Leave to dry for about 24 hours.

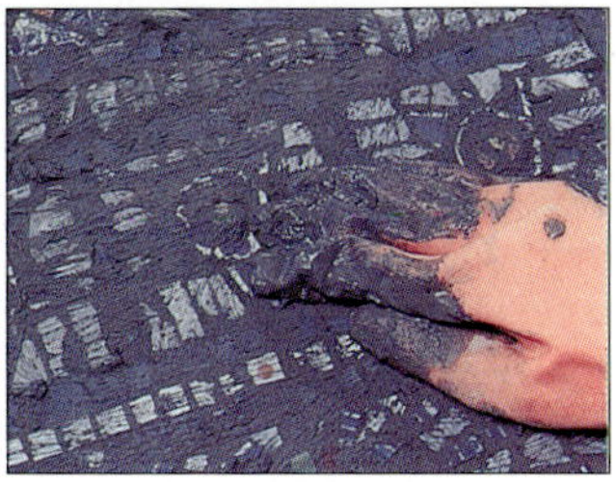

6 Mix powdered grout with water and add cement dye to achieve the colour you want. Wearing rubber gloves, spread the grout over the surface using a squeegee or a flexible (putty) knife and rub into the gaps with your fingers. Allow to dry for a few minutes, then scrub off any excess using a stiff nailbrush. Leave to dry for 24 hours, then polish the mosaic with a soft cloth.

■ ABOVE
This beautiful three-dimensional panel is full of interest, as it is assembled from pieces of patterned china to make a rich pattern of its own.

Stone Effect Wall Mask

It is hard to believe that this wonderful stone-effect wall mask, evocative of medieval times, was created from terracotta-coloured plastic. The slightly pitted quality of the plastic makes it very suitable for painting, which successfully disguises the original material. Once the mask is in position on the wall, nobody would suspect that it is not made from natural stone.

■ RIGHT
A framing of plants around the mask encourages the illusion that it is an old stone feature of the garden wall.

Tools and Materials

- plastic wall mask
- medium-grade sandpaper
- acrylic primer
- decorator's and artist's paintbrushes
- emulsion (latex) paint in stone
- acrylic scumble glaze
- artist's acrylic paints in raw umber, white, yellow ochre and burnt umber
- natural sponge
- matt polyurethane exterior varnish

1 Rub down the wall mask with sandpaper and paint it with acrylic primer. Let it dry for 1–2 hours. Paint with a coat of stone-coloured emulsion (latex) and leave to dry for 2 hours.

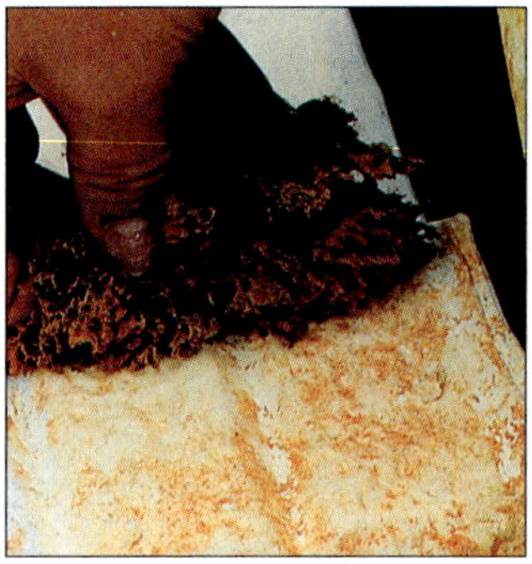

2 Tint some acrylic scumble glaze with a little raw umber and thin with a little water. Sponge on to the mask. Allow to dry for 1–2 hours.

3 Tint some white acrylic paint with a little yellow ochre. Add some scumble glaze and sponge on. Allow to dry for 1–2 hours.

4 Tint some more white acrylic paint with burnt umber and thin as before. Load a large artist's paintbrush and spatter the paint on to the mask with flicking movements. Leave to dry, then varnish the mask.

Water Features

Of all the fixtures in the garden, water features are surely the most entrancing. The gentle sound of water trickling, pattering or gurgling has a wonderfully relaxing effect and the glinting, reflective surface brings a new dimension to the garden. It doesn't have to be a grand affair – there is room for a water feature in even the smallest back yard.

Water features can range from a miniature fountain bubbling up through pebbles to a naturalistic pond that would be at home in a cottage-style garden. In between are formal ponds that can be round, rectangular or even T-shaped. At its simplest, a water feature could be just a garden hosepipe, gently splashing water on to a pile of pebbles below.

Whatever your choice, the water should be kept moving to prevent it from becoming stagnant, and that means organizing a small pump to circulate the water. Submersible pumps can be placed at the bottom of ponds, and some wall masks come already fitted with a pump. You will obviously need to have an electricity supply available where you want to site your water feature, so it is best to plan this before the garden is landscaped or paving laid. An outdoor supply should always be installed by a qualified electrician.

Apart from the electrical side, putting in a pond is not beyond anyone who is handy around the house, especially if you use a pond liner. There is a choice of pre-moulded fibreglass linings and the more easily disguised flexible butyl rubber or plastic sheeting. Once the liner is in place, you can cover its edges with rocks, pebbles and clever planting.

It is best not to site the pond beneath overhanging branches, as autumn leaves will fall directly into it, contaminating the pond as they decay.

■ LEFT
A formal geometric pond with oriental overtones makes a stunning focal point in a small town garden.

If you have small children, opt for a water feature that does not require any depth of water (such as a fountain that drains through pebbles) as a toddler can drown in just a few centimetres of water. Even if you want to plan a larger pool in the long term, you could fill it with pebbles to begin with, letting a fountain splash over these until the children are older and the pebbles can be removed.

■ ABOVE
A delightful miniature pond, filled with water-lilies, has been made in a large glazed earthenware pot, which can be "planted" in the border.

■ ABOVE
This water feature has been planned as part of the garden architecture and is set within a brick-built arch on the wall, which has then been lined with flint pebbles for a rich texture.

■ ABOVE
A well-positioned pond gives visual impact to a garden, and can be used to add interest to a large expanse of lawn.

■ RIGHT
An enchanting little pond, complete with fountain and cherub, mimics designs on a much grander scale.

Shell Fountain

Shells are a natural choice for a water feature. Here, water pours from the mouth of a large snail shell into a series of scallop shells to create a waterfall that flows into a large earthenware pot. The water is pumped back up and through a hole in the back of the snail shell, and the fountain is completed with an edging of more shells and some leafy plants.

■ **OPPOSITE**
Position this small fountain in a shady corner of the garden to add its gentle sound to a restful spot out of the hot summer sun.

Tools and Materials

- damp cloth
- galvanized metal tub
- red oxide paint
- paintbrush
- 5 scallop shells
- old, broken hip tile or similar
- marker pen
- drill
- 5 wall plugs
- hacksaw
- file
- 5 brass screws
- screwdriver
- large snail shell
- round file
- small pump
- fine garden wire
- pliers
- butyl rubber pond liner
- glazed ceramic pot
- sponge
- stones
- scissors
- assorted shells
- potted plants
- fine gravel
- bolt
- small wall planter

1 Rub the galvanized metal tub with a damp cloth to ensure it is free of dirt and grease. Paint the galvanized tub with red oxide paint and leave to dry.

2 Arrange the scallop shells inside the hip tile, with the largest shell at the base, and mark their positions. Drill a hole at each mark, inside the tile, and an extra hole next to the top hole. Fit all except the last hole with wall plugs.

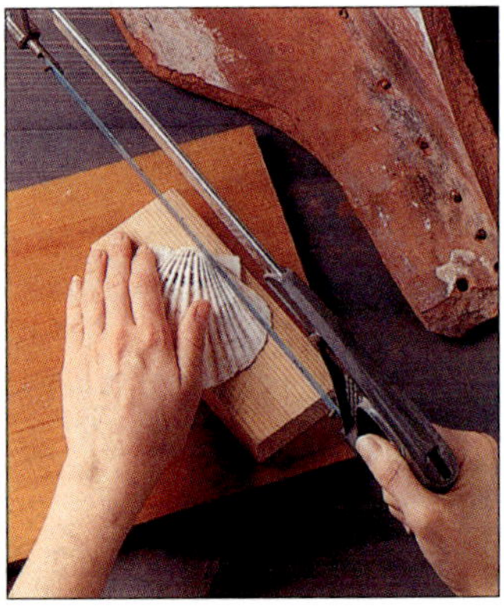

3 Using a hacksaw, trim the bases of the shells to a right-angle to fit inside the tile. File the edges as necessary.

4 Drill a hole in the base of each shell and screw into the hip tile, arranging the shells in order of size.

5 Drill a hole in the back of the large snail shell, taking care not to drill through the rest of the shell. Enlarge the hole with a round file and insert the hose.

6 Attach the snail shell to the top of the hip tile using garden wire. Loop the wire under the top scallop shell and twist the ends together.

7 Line the galvanized tub with a butyl rubber liner and place a ceramic pot inside with the shell fountain behind it. Place the pump out of sight behind the tile, surrounding it with sponge to support it. Fill the tub with stones.

8 Trim the excess pond liner and arrange shells and potted plants around the top of the tub. Sprinkle some fine gravel over the shells. Bolt a small wall planter on to the hip tile through the extra hole drilled at the top, then add a trailing plant.

DECORATIVE STORAGE

Gardeners accumulate an extraordinary amount of practical paraphernalia. Tools, pots and planters, potting compost, raffia, string, seeds and baskets are but a few of the bulky and space-consuming examples. For tools and equipment, a garden shed is the classic solution, though in a smaller garden you may be restricted to a mini-shed or tool store, which might be as small as 30cm/12in deep, tucked into a corner. Sheds can become an attractive part of the garden architecture if painted and decorated sympathetically.

■ OPPOSITE
While storage space is always necessary in the garden, it is often uninspiring to look at. Here, a tall-growing sunflower and splashes of plant colour, teamed with a birdhouse and bird-feeding table, have helped to make a charming feature of this old garden shed.

Putting your goods on show is one option for decorative storage. Garden pots can be very fetching and, displayed on all-weather shelves, can become part of the garden design. This is an excellent solution for very small gardens and patios, all of which still need space for the practicals. Instead of buying ready-made garden shelving, you could build your own from timber and decorate it with exterior-quality paint. Metal shelves old and new can be given a new life using car spray paint or specially manufactured metal paint, which can even be sprayed straight over rust. All shelves should be fixed firmly to the garden wall – avoid using the house wall for this as it could lead to damp problems indoors. Once fitted, use the shelves for displays, to store tools, or for bringing on young seedlings, which can look delightful potted up in ranks of terracotta.

For less attractive, but still essential, garden features such as rubbish bins (trash cans) and fuel stores, disguise is by far the best policy. One of the simplest solutions is to paint the object to blend it in with the surrounding garden. Alternatively, the object can be screened from view using large plants, abundant foliage or trellis. Where space is at a premium, a trellis screen furnished with climbing plants is a more compact option than large shrubs.

■ LEFT
Old French baker's shelves make a practical and attractive garden nursery for growing seedlings.

■ BELOW
Old clay pots make a decorative corner display on a blue-painted plant stand.

■ ABOVE
A thoughtful attempt to beautify an old garden shed has also found a solution to a common gardening problem. Gardening equipment attached to the outside of the shed looks very decorative and helps the gardener find what he is looking for when he needs it.

■ ABOVE
Shelving can be used for purely decorative purposes outside as well as in. Here, a few well-chosen pebbles, arranged on a blue-painted shelf mounted on corbels, make a pretty detail in the garden.

■ ABOVE
Garden sheds typically store a mixed assortment of items, but far from being unsightly, these jumbled collections have an attractive earthy appeal.

DECORATIVE GARDEN FURNITURE

To make your garden a space you can really live in, it must be furnished: choose comfortable-looking pieces that will tempt you to go outside, kick off your shoes and relax, soaking up the sun or cooling off in the shade.

A vast range of garden furniture is available but you can narrow down your options by deciding whether you want your furnishings to be permanent fixtures or moveable feasts. Lightweight garden furniture is inexpensive but often lacks glamour, and makes a good candidate for customized paint treatments, or embellishments with cushions and cloths. Wooden or stone furniture is expensive to buy, but it makes a long-term investment that will add an architectural dimension to your garden all through the year.

Garden furniture performs a practical function, but it is also decorative and can be as quirky as you like. For a really exotic touch, fix a hammock between a couple of trees, or drape an awning around a group of chairs and while away some happy hours in elegant relaxation.

■ ABOVE
The relaxed elegance of this classic garden seat makes it a feature in itself.

■ OPPOSITE
Ornate furniture and an umbrella create a focal point in the garden.

Choosing Garden Furniture

There is an enormous range of furniture available for the garden, from folding metal or canvas chairs, which can be stored in a shed and just brought out when they are needed, to whole suites of hardwood dining furniture. While you may not want your garden to be cluttered with enough chairs to seat a crowd all the time, a few carefully placed permanent fixtures, such as a weatherproof hardwood bench, a metal table and a few chairs on the patio or an inviting wooden bench under an arbour, all play an important role in the garden's structure and make it look especially welcoming and lived-in.

If you fancy a quick coffee break in a brief burst of spring sunshine, you won't want to spend time searching in the shed for a chair to sit on, and a plain wooden bench that lives all year long in the garden is just the place for a breather during a heavy digging session on a cold winter's day.

For furniture that is to be left outside all year, choose durable materials such as painted metal or hardwood (from sustainable sources). Softer woods should be hardened and will need treating with preservative, which will need renewing at least once a year for it to remain effective. Plastic furniture needs little maintenance except for washing, but it has a limited life outdoors and will eventually become brittle and easily breakable.

Other highly decorative materials that are also comfortable include wicker and Lloyd loom, but these are not weatherproof and will need to be stored in a garden shed, garage or conservatory when not in use.

■ RIGHT
This unique piece of furniture, half-chair and half-sculpture, is made from driftwood and fencing stakes, and is perfect for an outdoor setting.

■ RIGHT
Wicker furniture is comfortable, especially if cushions are added to fit the seats. It will look good in any garden setting. Used outside in summer, it will weather to a subtle natural shade, or it can be painted for a brighter look.

■ BELOW
Traditional slatted folding chairs look pretty in the garden and make perfect seating for an al fresco dinner party.

■ RIGHT
Metal furniture is robust enough to need very little maintenance, and can be kept outside throughout the year.

GARDEN CHAIRS

Furnishing the garden gives you somewhere to sit and relax and, at the same time, adds to the architectural element of the garden. Some furniture – a traditional stone seat, for example – is designed to be an almost permanent part of the garden; certainly stone seats are not moved with regularity.

Architecturally, permanent seating provides another step up visually, with its legs equal to balustrades. While such wonderful garden fixtures aren't really within most people's budgets, a similar role is played by old wooden garden benches, which, as they weather to a soft green-tinged grey, take on a permanent air as part of the garden architecture.

Single benches exude a peaceful air, probably because they are not conducive to conversation but are more for sitting and contemplating. Love seats, designed in an S-shape, are far more sociable since the occupants sit facing each other. Groups of chairs around an outdoor table represent social times in the garden, whether you are simply eating outside with the family, taking tea with a friend or having an evening party.

In high summer, there is nothing more enjoyable than lounging around in the garden, and this is when the softer, more reclining types of chair, including canvas deck-chairs and directors' chairs, come into their own. The lounger is the lotus-eater's dream – more day-bed than chair. Wood-slatted steamer chairs were the original loungers, designed for use on long voyages. Their modern equivalents – in wood, metal, or plastic – are fitted with upholstered cushions. Hammocks are another kind of day-bed, and, gently swaying between a pair of trees, they would challenge anyone to stay awake.

■ BELOW
This witty, plastic-covered Louis XIV chair offers indoor elegance outside.

■ ABOVE
Softly weathered wooden furniture fits easily into almost any garden setting.

■ LEFT
This modern wrought-iron furniture is inspired by the French styles of the last century, the elegant lightweight lines of which are now enjoying a revival.

■ RIGHT
Furniture makes its own contribution to the look of the garden and, if it's not being used to sit on, it can make an ideal backdrop for decorative garden "pieces".

■ BELOW
Elaborate cast-iron furniture became a favourite in Victorian times, and its popularity has not waned. Its price, however, means you are more likely to see it as a feature in public parks than in private gardens.

■ RIGHT
What better way to spend a lazy summer's day than reclining in a portable, foldaway chair?

String and Driftwood Chair

You can transform an ordinary chair into something quite special by binding it with jute or garden string and attaching pieces of driftwood collected from the beach. Here, awkward joins are decorated with pieces of flotsam and jetsam, and two "horns" give a dramatic shape to the chair back. Making or changing furniture can be just a matter of using what is at hand. String is hardwearing, cheap, and gives this chair a tactile quality. Other decorative materials include bark, twigs or shells, collected on walks or at the beach.

1 Cut jute or string into manageable lengths and roll these into small balls. Glue the end of a string ball firmly to the top of the chair. You will need to do this each time you start a new ball.

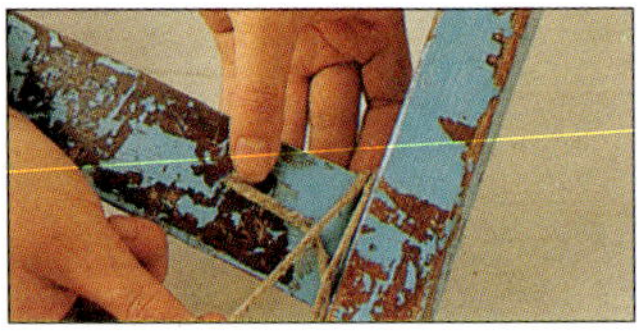

2 Run a thin line of glue along the back of the chair to secure the string. Starting at one end, pull the string taut as you wrap it around the chair.

Tools and Materials

- ball of jute or garden string
- scissors
- glue gun
- chair
- pieces of driftwood

3 Make two criss-cross patterns along the middle of the chair back to decorate. Hold them in place with glue.

4 Glue the driftwood to the top of the chair and secure with string. To finish off, knot and bind the string underneath.

■ RIGHT
Revive an old chair by taking a fresh look at everyday materials.

Sea-weathered Director's Chair

This aging technique instantly transforms furniture from new to old, imbuing the wood with an interesting weathered quality and allowing it to blend perfectly into its outdoor surroundings. Getting away from a pristine paint surface and acquiring an old, worn look makes furniture more comfortable to live with and more relaxing to look at.

Tools and Materials

- director's chair
- scrubbing brush
- bucket
- soapy water
- cloth
- masking tape
- household candle
- emulsion (latex) paint in pale blue and white
- paintbrushes
- sandpaper
- matt acrylic varnish

1 Remove the fabric from the chair and scrub the wood with soapy water. Wipe down with a dry cloth. Let dry.

2 Cover all the metal attachments with masking tape. Rub the wood with a candle, concentrating on the areas that would naturally show wear, such as the edges and corners. Dilute the pale blue emulsion (latex) 3:1 with water and paint over the chair frame. Leave to dry.

3 Rub over the paint with sandpaper to reveal the wood beneath, then rub all over with the candle again. Dilute the white emulsion 3:1 with water and paint the chair frame. Leave to dry.

4 Rub with sandpaper to reveal areas of wood and the blue paint. Seal with matt varnish, let dry and replace the fabric.

■ BELOW
Director's chairs are inexpensive, portable and easy to store – turn yours into furniture that's worth a second look with a simple distressing technique.

Crazy Paving Chair

This old chair, found rejected and battered in a junk shop, has been transformed into an exciting, unusual piece of furniture. It is covered in tesserae cut from a selection of china, and it's important to be aware that a large three-dimensional object like this requires a deceptively large amount of mosaic to cover it, so you would be lucky to find enough china of a single pattern. Here, the problem has been solved by using slightly different designs to cover different sections of the chair.

■ OPPOSITE
Applying mosaic to an old chair turns it into a beguilingly original piece of furniture and a focal point in the garden.

Tools and Materials

- chair
- 2cm/¾in plywood
- paint stripper
- coarse-grade sandpaper
- paintbrush
- PVA (white) glue
- wood glue
- cement-based tile adhesive
- flexible (putty) knife
- pencil or chalk
- large selection of old china
- tile nippers
- powdered tile grout
- rubber gloves
- stiff nailbrush
- soft cloth

1 If the chair has a padded seat, remove it and replace it with a piece of plywood cut to fit the frame. Strip off any paint or varnish and rub down with coarse sandpaper. Paint the whole chair with diluted PVA (white) glue.

2 When the surface is dry, stick the seat in place with wood glue and fill any gaps with cement-based tile adhesive.

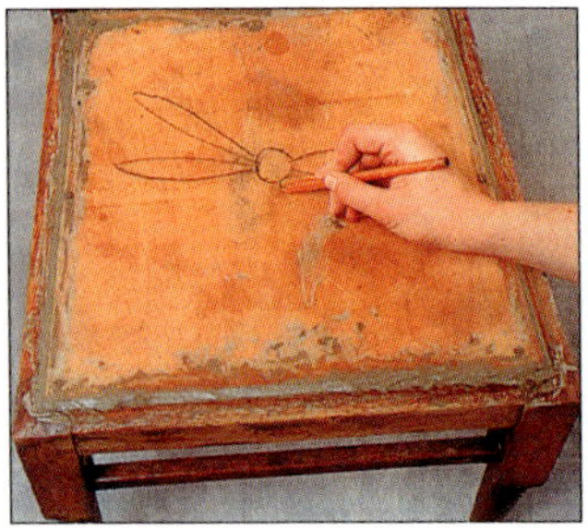

3 Draw a design or motifs on any large flat surfaces of the chair, using simple shapes that are easy to follow such as this flower.

4 Select china with colours and patterns to suit your design. Using tile nippers, cut the china into the appropriate sizes and shapes.

5 Spread cement-based tile adhesive within the areas of your design and press the china tesserae firmly into it.

6 Working on small areas at a time, tile the rest of the chair. Where one section of wood meets another, change the pattern of the china. Cut the china into thin slivers to tile the edges of the chair. Leave to dry for at least 24 hours.

7 Using a flexible (putty) knife, grout the mosaic with the tile adhesive. Wearing rubber gloves, rub the grout over the flat surfaces, cleaning off the excess as you work. Leave to dry.

8 When the grout is completely dry, sand off any excess cement with sandpaper or a stiff nailbrush. Polish with a soft cloth to buff up the china.

A Lick of Paint

Co-ordinating furniture with its surroundings helps to give the garden a harmonious ambience. By painting old furniture, you can also keep the costs down, as you can pick up bargain pieces from junk shops or simply rejuvenate old kitchen chairs that are due for replacement. And you can be sure of perfect toning as paints come in literally hundreds of shades. These chairs were most unprepossessing when they were picked up: the slatted ones were peeling and the Tyrolean-style chair was finished with a tired old varnish.

■ OPPOSITE
Clashing Caribbean colours of pink and tangerine make for a lively look in a brightly coloured garden.

■ BELOW
Taupe and white make an elegant combination for a chair with Italian-style flair. It is an ideal finish for a garden that features a lot of natural wood tones.

■ ABOVE
This Tyrolean-style chair is given a bright, modern finish to team with the painted shed wall behind. It also co-ordinates well with silver-grey foliage and lipstick-pink flowers.

WEATHERING AND DISTRESSING

When looking around antique shops that specialize in old garden furniture, it can be quite shocking to see the prices charged for these items. Simple folding chairs, once used in their thousands in public parks, are now desirable objects with their faded paintwork and weathered wood, and they fetch premium prices. A far less expensive alternative is to buy new hardwood folding chairs and do a bit of instant weathering yourself. Four chairs transformed in this way will cost about the same as one antique chair. The weathered effect is achieved by sanding down the surface, rubbing with wax, then painting and rubbing down again. When the chair is left out in the garden, nature will continue the weathering process, and within a season you will have your own set of heirlooms.

TOOLS AND MATERIALS

folding wooden garden chair
medium-grade sandpaper
household candle
white emulsion (latex) paint
paintbrush
wire (steel) wool

1 Sandpaper the surface of the chair to make a key so that the paint adheres. Rub over the surface randomly with the candle, applying the wax thickly on the edges and corners.

2 Paint the chair with several coats of white emulsion (latex) paint, using random strokes, and leave to dry.

3 When the paint is dry, rub the paintwork with wire (steel) wool to remove the paint from the waxed areas, so that the wood is showing. Wipe the chair with a damp cloth to clean away the dust, and leave to dry.

■ OPPOSITE
Charmingly weathered and worn, this wooden chair looks as if it has been standing in the garden for years.

Garden Tables

A table is at the heart of a whole way of life in the garden. As long as the weather holds, it can take the place of the dining table, the kitchen worktop and the writing desk indoors. Once you have a table in the garden you will use every excuse to use it for breakfast, lunch and dinner – a light lunch, the children's tea, or an intimate supper. Meals outside, when the weather is balmy and the evenings long, are invariably happier and more relaxed, with the air of a picnic.

Choose a table that is substantial but not too huge, solid and not wobbly, and weatherproof so that it becomes a more or less permanent fixture in the garden. You can make your eating area into a garden room, defining the space with a screen of trellis, flower borders, a sheltering arbour, or banks of plants in containers. A pergola overhead will give dappled shade and a sense of privacy.

■ ABOVE
Paint a simple metal tabletop with a shell design then add a wash over the top to give it a weathered look. Varnish the surface to protect it.

■ LEFT
This design has bold lines and strong contrasts that suit the chunky crazy-paving style of the mosaic. It is worked on a plain round wooden table top, screwed to a metal base.

■ RIGHT
Mosaic makes an enduring surface for a garden table, and adds a rich colour accent to the garden as a whole.

■ BELOW
However battered by time and weather, delicate old wrought-iron furniture retains its air of refinement and goes on looking pretty in the garden.

Wooden Garden Table

This sturdy table is ideal for the garden because the wood is already weathered and further aging will make it look even better. You can leave it out all year round without worrying about it, though an occasional coat of clear wood preservative would lengthen its life. The table top here measures 74 x 75cm/ 29 x 30in, but you can adapt the design to the size you require.

■ OPPOSITE
This rustic "occasional" table will happily live in the garden through all weathers, and would be perfect near a favourite garden seat as a place to put down a cup or glass, a book or a shady hat.

Tools and Materials

- 5 weathered planks, 74 x 15cm/ 29 x 6in
- tape measure
- saw
- 1m/39in weathered batten, 5 x 1cm/2 x ½in
- electric drill
- screwdriver
- 4cm/1½in screws
- 4 wooden poles and thick sticks
- hammer
- 7.5cm/3in and 4cm/1½in nails
- pencil
- string

1 Lay the planks side by side. Cut two 48cm/19in lengths of batten, drill holes then screw across the planks about 7.5cm/3in in from either end to make the table top.

2 Saw the four poles into 90cm/36in lengths, for the legs. Cut four sticks 43cm/17in long.

3 Nail a stick a quarter of the way in from each end of each pair of legs, to make two side frames.

4 Lay the table top upside down. Centre the side frames on the battens and draw around the top of each leg.

5 Drill a pilot hole through the centre of each circle.

6 With the table top supported on one side frame, nail through into the legs. Repeat for the other side frame.

7 Cut a thick stick 62cm/25in long. Hold in place and nail it across the two side frames at the back of the table.

8 To stabilize the table, make a cross frame. Cut two lengths of stick 90cm/3ft long and nail each to a front leg and the opposite back leg. Bind with string where the sticks cross in the centre.

Mosaic Garden Table

This striking mosaic table top is made from pieces of broken china pots and chipped decorative tiles, and with clever colour co-ordination and a simple, clear design, it makes the most attractive, weatherproof garden furniture. Although it is resilient to damp, bringing it inside over the winter will give it a longer life.

■ OPPOSITE
Mount the mosaic table top on metal or wooden legs, or simply screw it to an old circular table that is past its prime.

Tools and Materials

- 2.5cm/1in plywood at least 120cm/4ft square
- string
- drawing pin
- pencil
- jigsaw
- wood primer
- paintbrush
- tile nippers
- large selection of broken china
- tile adhesive
- tile grout
- grout colour
- rubber gloves
- washing-up brush
- cloth

PREPARATION
To mark out the circle, tie a piece of string to a drawing pin at one end and push the pin into the centre of the plywood. Tie a pencil to the other end of the string to give you a radius of 60cm/2ft. Draw the circle and cut out using a jigsaw.

1 Draw the design on the plywood circle, adjusting the length of string to draw concentric circles.

2 Prime the table with wood primer and leave to dry.

3 Use tile nippers to cut the broken china into pieces to fit the design and try it out on the table top. Use motifs on the china as focal points in the design.

4 When the design is complete, work across the table top a section at a time, "buttering" each piece of china with adhesive and sticking it in position.

5 Mix the grout with the colour and, wearing rubber gloves, use your fingers to work the grout in between the mosaic pieces. Complete the grouting by scrubbing over the surface using a washing-up brush. Clean off any excess.

Garden Console

This console table was designed for a conventional indoor life, but has been given an outdoor paint treatment for a witty touch in the garden. It makes a useful extra surface for drinks or serving dishes when you are entertaining outside.

Tools and Materials

- console table
- medium-grade sandpaper
- white acrylic wood primer
- medium and fine paintbrushes
- masonry paint
- artist's acrylic paints in terracotta and pink
- fine-textured masonry paint
- acrylic scumble glaze
- cloth
- pencil
- stencil cardboard
- craft knife
- stencil brush
- polyurethane varnish
- varnish brush

1 Prepare the table by sanding all the surfaces thoroughly. Prime with white acrylic wood primer and allow to dry. Tint some masonry paint with terracotta acrylic and use as a base coat. Allow to dry for 4–6 hours.

2 Tint some fine-textured masonry paint with pink acrylic, add scumble glaze and thin with water to the consistency of double cream. Paint on and rub off with a cloth in the direction of the grain. Allow to dry.

3 Draw a leaf shape on a piece of stencil cardboard and cut out. Use terracotta paint to stencil a leaf on each corner of the table. Allow to dry, then varnish.

■ **OPPOSITE**
When the console table is not being used, you can have fun accessorizing it as if it were standing in a room indoors.

■ **RIGHT**
The essence of outdoor style is its simplicity. This garden store cupboard was built from nailed together pieces of driftwood.

Awnings and Umbrellas

Living outside sometimes requires shelter from the wind, or shade from a blistering sun. On a breezy day, a windbreak of some kind will enable you to sit outside even in early spring or autumn. A capacious umbrella or parasol, on the other hand, will allow you to eat outside or simply relax in its shade even in the middle of the day in high summer; and if you want to bask in the sunshine at lunchtime, the food on the table will always benefit from being kept in the shade, out of reach from the glaring sun.

If you have rejected the idea of building a pergola over your patio because it casts too much shade in winter, a more adaptable alternative could be a canvas awning. This will give instant shade on a hot day – and also keep the sun off the house windows, helping to cool the interior – but can be rolled back to the wall on cooler days when you would prefer to sit in the sun.

If you prefer to move in line with the sun, a large portable umbrella with a weighted base can be put up anywhere in the garden.

■ ABOVE
Four chairs, a table and an umbrella instantly make a pleasantly informal seating arrangement – a portable arbour from which to enjoy the garden.

■ ABOVE LEFT
Late summer tasks, such as topping and tailing fruit, become pleasurable pastimes under an awning. Original Edwardian awnings like this consist of a lightweight metal frame that is easily erected before slipping the canvas cover over the top.

■ OPPOSITE
A dead tree provided the inspiration for this elaborate sheltered seating area. The natural awning was constructed from the pruned branches of the tree, while a dovecote on the top means that those sitting beneath the shelter can enjoy the sounds of the visiting birds.

PLANTS IN POTS: THE SOFT FURNISHINGS

Like vases of fresh flowers indoors, plants in containers provide strong accents of shape and colour in the garden, softening the lines of garden structures. They are prima donnas, flaunting their vivid colours while they are in their full glory, then bowing out to be replaced by the next star turn.

Decorative planting is one of the more pleasurable aspects of having an outdoor space. More than anything else, the choice of plants – and the containers they're planted in – will affect the mood of the garden and the finished look. Group containers by colour or create cameo gardens along a theme. Use an eclectic mix of containers or trim and shape shrubs and plants for a witty effect. Window boxes and hanging baskets will add special plant interest, especially if potted with more unusual plant options such as wild strawberries or fresh herbs.

■ ABOVE
Group plants together for a mass of colour and a vibrant display.

■ OPPOSITE
There are no rules when it comes to arranging potted plants, and a witty and original choice of container will add something special.

Decorative Plantings

Once the basic framework of the garden is in place, the fun can start. Indoors, once you had painted the walls and laid the floors, you would be thinking of comfortable furniture, curtains and carpets. Outside, it is the planting that provides the soft furnishing. Without it, the garden would look very rigid and uninviting. Add a few plants, and immediately it takes on a much more comfortable feel. This is the part of gardening that is the most absorbing, even if you start off with no horticultural knowledge. A trip to the garden centre to browse among the seasonal plants becomes a treat.

Putting together the colours and textures to compose beautiful borders is one of the more pleasurable aspects of gardening, and is where your own creativity comes in. But soft furnishing in the context of the decorated garden is not just about borders. Decorative planting is about climbers that clamber curtain-like over arches and soften the outlines of vistas, and the hanging baskets that decorate walls. It is about the low-growing plants that create carpets of colour over what may previously have been uninspiring bare ground, and the plants that grow around and through established trees and shrubs, softening and beautifying their outlines. It is, finally, about feature planting in containers, positioned at focal points in the garden to create interest and impact.

■ OPPOSITE
A floral arbour makes a rich decorative frame for a piece of statuary, creating a theatrical effect. The roses, foxgloves and clematis make perfect stage curtains for this thoughtful stone "player".

■ BELOW
Trellis makes a permanent light screen across part of the garden, curtained in summer by the glossy green foliage and vivid flowers of a climbing rose.

■ ABOVE
The face of a cherub, in reflective mood, peers through the ivy, adding a charming touch to the eaves of a garden shed.

■ LEFT
Statuesque Greek pithoi are used here for architectural interest, rather than for planting. However, they have been softened and beautifully set off by stately euphorbias in vibrant shades of lime green.

Colour Theme Plantings

Create impact in the garden by colour-theming seasonal planting to match the colours of your garden fixtures. This works best with plants in containers, as pots and planters can be chosen or painted to tone with the walls and fences, then planted with flowers in complementary colours. Once the blooms are over, they can be replaced by new plantings for the next season. You don't have to match the colours: using complementary or contrasting colours may be just as effective. In this way, the garden looks fresh and bright all year round, and you have several changes of scene as the seasons pass.

■ BELOW
Fences stained in soft, grey-blue greens set off all manner of greenery, including the foliage of this hebe. The pot has been painted in stripes to link the greens with the pink flowers.

■ RIGHT
The green-blue and purple tones of ornamental cabbage look fabulous in an old galvanized bucket set against the green-blue background of a painted wooden garden fence.

■ ABOVE
Blues and greys make a wonderful combination and even the most basic pieces of garden paraphernalia can be put to good decorative use. This old, blue-painted wheelbarrow, set against a blue wall, creates impact, while making an original container for delicate violas.

■ RIGHT
A yellow poppy and yellow violas look stunning planted in golden pots, set against the warm ochre of a brick wall.

Colour Splash Plantings

Just as you can decorate the inside of your home with colourful flower arrangements, so you can embellish the outside. Use pots of flowering plants to provide a colourful splash in a prominent part of the garden, or to decorate the outdoor living area when entertaining. Create an immediate impact by choosing a colour theme and teaming containers and plants in toning shades. Try painting some terracotta pots to match your favourite flowers. You could also make a tablescape for a special occasion, using a variety of containers and seasonal flowering plants in hot clashing colours or in cool shades of blue, purple and white.

■ BELOW
Create a colour splash for summer parties. Here, hot colours vie and clash in a fabulous, vibrant display. Simple enamel tableware and a wire "coffee pot" make witty containers for strawberry plants, pelargoniums, verbenas in magenta and scarlet, pansies and daisy-like, yellow creeping zinnia.

■ ABOVE
White-painted pots planted with lily-of-the-valley and placed on a stone bracket make an elegant springtime feature.

■ ABOVE RIGHT
Auriculas planted in an old stone urn and overhung with berberis make a rich spring planting in shades of burnished copper. The display is reminiscent of an old sepia photograph.

■ RIGHT
The blue-green leaves of pinks and oxalis perfectly complement the rich verdigris patina on this old French copper builder's bucket, creating a striking feature that can be hung in the garden or near the house. It's a brilliant way to bring colour up to eye-level in spring, when most plants in flower are low-growing.

CREATING CAMEO GARDENS

It is delightful to plan cameo gardens within gardens. They can present a surprise in a small corner, embellish a less-than-full area of the garden or even provide a miniature project for children, who love to be responsible for a garden area of their very own.

Cameo gardens exist solely on the basis of a theme, be it herbs or pansies, miniature vegetables or lavender. After you have chosen your theme, you then need to make up a "sampler", providing a different container for each variety of your themed plants. If you are making the containers themselves the theme, choose watering cans, cooking pots and pans, enamelware or terracotta in different shapes and sizes. Another idea is to design a miniature formal garden, perhaps taking inspiration from a classic style. Choose a piece of miniature statuary as a focal point, then clip some young box plants into a low hedge around your tiny beds and fill with dwarf lavender.

■ BELOW
Serried ranks of watering cans in the soft greys of weathered, galvanized metal make a beautiful feature in themselves. Planted up with hostas and violas, they form a highly original cameo garden.

■ ABOVE
Thyme gardens have a history that goes back through centuries. Their appeal stems from their irresistible aroma combined with the almost endless number of varieties, with leaves that range in shape from round to needle-like, in texture from smooth to woolly, in colour from silver to darkest green. The trick is to choose a selection that will create a rich tapestry. Planting them in small pots keeps the garden to a scale in which the miniature dimensions of the leaves and their various textures can be appreciated.

■ ABOVE
The intense colour provided by this grouping of grape hyacinths makes a striking display for early spring.

■ RIGHT
This terracotta garden is focused around tall long-tom pots planted with hostas, ivies and a clematis left loose so that it trails rather than climbs. Old drain covers and edging tiles add rich details to the picture.

Witty Ways with Everyday Plants

Interesting gardens don't have to depend on a horticulturalist's expert knowledge of plants. Even the most ordinary plants can take on an exotic personality if pruned or planted in an original way. Many garden centres now sell ready-trained or standardized shrubs – you can add your own touch with a witty container, pretty underplanting or an attractive way of tying up the plants. There are no restrictions to the look you can create.

Topiary has come back into fashion, but this time it isn't restricted to large, formal gardens. Box and privet grown in pots can be kept to a manageable size and still be clipped into architectural globes and conical shapes, as can any other plant which holds its shape well as it grows.

■ ABOVE
A standardized hydrangea grown in a pot makes an excellent patio plant. It has the appealing appearance of a miniature tree, and you can enjoy its flamboyant blooms without any worry that it might take over the garden.

■ ABOVE
Small-scale topiary can be arranged, as here, in groups or used as boundary markers, down the edges of paths, between beds or to section off different parts of the garden.

■ ABOVE
As a change from allowing roses to scramble up walls or trellis, this one has been trained around a simple obelisk, the diagonally trailing stems adding greatly to its decorative appeal.

■ ABOVE
A potted chilli pepper plant would add a fun touch to any garden.

■ RIGHT
Fruit trees can be included in even the smallest gardens. Here, a decorative, apple is flanked by ballerina crab apples, which grow in a pole-like fashion.

Plants and Containers

The best way to create impact with seasonal flowers is to contain them in pots or some kind of container: that way you can mass colour in the plantings and group or stack the pots together for an even greater show.

Containers look fabulous in any garden – first, because the vessels themselves, however simple, give architectural form; second, because they allow you to put the plants and colour exactly where you want them. You need a little colour higher up? Plant up a plant stand, hanging basket or wall-pot. You need a little extra colour in a flower bed? Fill a pot with vivid flowers and set it down among the greenery. You can even plant up small pots to nestle on top of the soil in larger pots for a rich, stacked effect.

CLAY POTS AND PLANTERS

There is little to beat the earthy beauty of ordinary clay pots. They blend well with their surroundings and complement virtually every type of plant. Make sure they are frostproof if they are to stay

■ OPPOSITE
For a gloriously rich, banked window display, one window box has been fixed to the front edge of the windowsill, while the other sits on the ledge. The planting scheme of petunias and dianthus in pinks and purples creates a greater impact for being colour co-ordinated, and it is complemented by the huge lilac orbs of the alliums in the foreground.

■ BELOW
White violas in old terracotta pots, white-crusted with age, lend an ethereal air to the white-painted windowsill of a much-used conservatory.

outside when temperatures plummet, otherwise you will find the terracotta flaking off at the rim during the winter months.

The appearance of clay pots depends on where they are made. The typical pots of northern European countries are generally very red in hue, but the colour does soften with age as salts naturally form on the surface. You can hasten this look by scrubbing them with garden lime. Just make up a thick paste by adding a little water to the lime, then brush it on with an old washing-up brush. As the water in the lime dries out, the terracotta will acquire a soft, white bloom. Garden lime is excellent as it is not harmful to the garden (in fact, it is used as a fertilizer), and it won't inhibit the natural mould growth that also enhances the patina of age. Pots can also be aged by rubbing them with natural yogurt then leaving them in a damp, shady place to encourage mould growth, but this takes a little longer.

Clay pots from the sunny Mediterranean look very different to those of northern Europe.

Greek pithoi, for example, traditionally used to store grain and oil, come in many elegant shapes and have a wonderful sandy colour. Some are even frostproof.

ORIGINAL IDEAS

Your choice does not have to be restricted to garden pots. Any type of container will work, as long as drainage holes can be drilled in the base. Try using old beer barrel halves, decorative ceramic pots, old chimney pots, buckets, agricultural baskets such as potato pickers, or traditional garden baskets such as wooden trugs. With a little imagination, shopping baskets, birdcages and lanterns can be transformed into hanging baskets, and old olive oil cans in a row can become original window boxes.

■ BELOW
All kinds of things can be used to add height to planting – particularly useful in spring and early summer when plants are still small. Here, three small hanging baskets have been stacked on top of each other for brilliant high-level planting.

■ ABOVE
Ornate Chinese ceramic pots make a delightful decorative feature when planted with toning flowering plants, such as pelargoniums and petunias, and accessorized with complementary Chinese statuary.

■ RIGHT
Even a couple of ordinary terracotta garden pots hanging on the wall make an interesting decorative detail when they are both planted with a froth of white blooms.

■ RIGHT
Charming cast-iron panels are used here to enclose ordinary plastic pots of plants – a lovely idea that allows you to replace your plants when they are past their prime, and helps to make seasonal changes painless.

Ideas for Window Boxes

Window boxes give a delightful finish to the outside of a building, and can be enjoyed just as much from inside, almost bringing the garden into the room. They can be filled to overflowing with exuberant summer bedding plants, but this need not be their only season of interest. Foliage plants such as hebes and ivies will look wonderful throughout the winter, interplanted with winter-flowering pansies, which burst into luminous colours whenever the weather is kind. If you include some spring-flowering bulbs when planting your window boxes in the autumn, you will be able to watch the fresh new shoots emerging at close quarters, heralding spring and the start of a new gardening year.

Like other containers, a window box can be moved out of the limelight once it is past its prime and replaced with another box containing a fresh planting. Match wooden boxes to your plants season by season, ringing the changes with a lick of emulsion (latex) paint in a colour chosen to complement the plants for maximum impact.

■ BELOW
The soft shapes of violas and petunias perfectly complement this stencilled wooden window box. The scent of the flowers will drift magically indoors when the windows are open.

■ RIGHT
A window box filled with herbs and placed on the kitchen windowsill is both pretty and useful. This arrangement is planted in an old fruit box, colour-washed to tone with the herbs. Borage has been included: its flowers will provide interest later in the season.

■ RIGHT
Create a fragrant herbal window box to sit outside the kitchen window, ready to use when needed. This one has been planted up with golden sage, chamomile, marjoram and wild strawberry in an old agricultural basket. Yellow bidens have been included for extra colour.

Seashore Window Box

As most window boxes are flat-fronted, they are easier to decorate than round pots. Here, the beautiful dark lustre of mussel shells left over from the dinner table lends impact to a co-ordinated planting of lavender and violas. Experiment with different shapes, using some of the shells face up and the others face down for a more varied effect.

Tools and Materials

- mussel shells
- small terracotta window box
- glue gun
- crocks or pebbles
- compost (soil mix)
- trowel
- water-retaining granules
- slow-release fertilizer granules
- 2 lavender plants
- tray of violas
- watering can

1 Arrange the mussel shells on the sides of the window box. When you are satisfied with your design, fix the shells in position using a glue gun. Leave until the glue has dried.

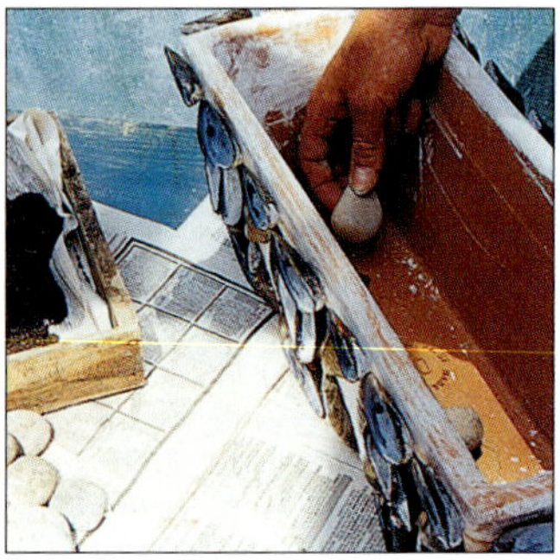

2 Place a layer of crocks or pebbles over the drainage holes inside the window box.

3 Partly fill the box with compost (soil mix), adding water-retaining and fertilizer granules as you go.

4 Plant the lavender at the back of the box. Press extra compost in front of the lavender until it is the right height for the violas. Plant the violas.

5 Top up with compost, firming it gently around the plants, and water generously.

■ **OPPOSITE**
The soft petals and subtle colour gradations of the violas make them the perfect match for the pearly interiors of the shells.

Ideas for Hanging Baskets

When you want colour high up in the garden, whether it is to provide a focal point, frame a view or soften the hard lines of a wall or a building, the easiest way is to plant up a container and hang it up. Ready-made hanging baskets are designed so that as the flowers grow they cascade through the sides and spill over the edge in a joyous show of colour, covering the whole basket.

Unlike stand-alone containers, hanging baskets will need lining inside to stop the soil from being washed out while you are watering. Liners can be home-made from a piece of plastic cut to size, with a layer of moss tucked between the basket and the plastic for a more decorative look. Alternatively, you can use a proprietary liner made from paper pulp or coconut matting. These come in a variety of shapes and sizes to adapt to all varieties of basket.

Whatever type of container you choose, it needs to be filled with a good compost (soil mix). Adding slow-release fertilizer granules and water-retaining granules can also help to promote luscious results.

■ OPPOSITE
A hanging basket successfully raises the height of the garden, and blends the flowers and foliage with garden buildings in a way that planted flowers or stand-alone containers can never do.

■ BELOW
There is no reason why hanging baskets should contain only flowers: the basket on the left contains wild strawberries, while the basket on the right has been planted productively with fresh herbs.

Hanging Gardens

An alternative to a conventional hanging basket is to design your planting so that the basket or container is made part of the display. Ordinary shopping baskets, buckets, agricultural containers, even kitchen equipment such as colanders, pots and pans with drainage holes drilled in the base, can all be used as hanging baskets with character.

If your chosen container is large and might possibly become too heavy when planted to be suspended, a useful trick is to put a layer of broken-up expanded polystyrene (left over from plant trays or the packaging around electrical goods) in the bottom of the container. This is lighter than the equivalent amount of compost (soil mix) and will provide good drainage for the plants.

■ ABOVE
A witty interpretation of a hanging basket, this Indian birdcage makes an ideal receptacle for potted plants. Hung in a mulberry tree, it lends floral interest in early spring before the leaves have burst from their buds.

■ ABOVE
Free-standing, miniature mangers, stacked one over the other, make a vibrant column of colour in a tiny courtyard garden.

■ ABOVE
The most unlikely items can be used as hanging baskets. This pretty metal lantern from the Middle East has been filled with terracotta pots planted with variegated ivies to make a surprising and decorative hanging feature.

Summer Basket

Hanging baskets are summer favourites in even the smallest gardens, bringing a floral splash – and fragrance if you choose appropriate plants – to walls, verandas, patios and even basement areas. Plant them early in the year, once the threat of late frosts has passed, to give the plants time to "get their toes in" and fill out.

Tools and Materials

- hanging basket with chains or rope
- coconut fibre liner
- compost (soil mix)
- trowel
- water-retaining granules
- slow-release fertilizer granules
- 6 variegated ivies
- 2 diascia
- 6 verbenas
- watering can

1 Line the basket with the coconut fibre liner and part-fill with compost (soil mix), adding water-retaining and fertilizer granules as you go, according to the manufacturer's instructions.

2 Knock the ivy plants out of their pots and thread them through the sides of the basket. Place a diascia at either end of the basket. Add the verbenas.

3 Press more compost around each plant and down the sides of the basket so that everything is firmly bedded in. Water generously and hang the basket.

■ BELOW
Verbena and diascia, with their trailing, wiry stems and pretty colouring, make an unrestrained combination that will quickly clothe this basket. The variegated ivy provides a foundation of foliage to offset the colours of the flowers.

Ideas for Containers

Almost any interesting receptacle will make a container for plants; in fact, the more unusual it is, the more impact it will create. Once you begin to see the potential in tins, boxes, baskets and jars, you'll be motivated to create really original plantings. Here are some ideas to get you started.

■ OPPOSITE
In China, glazed pots are frequently used as small ponds in courtyards. This pot contains a water lily, a flowering rush and an aurum lily.

■ LEFT
With a couple of coats of varnish, an old wooden wine case will make an attractive and durable container for a miniature herb garden, which you could keep on the kitchen windowsill or near the back door, ready for use.

■ BELOW LEFT
Plant a kitchen garden in a selection of decorative oil cans, choosing a variety of sizes for a better show. These old cans have been planted with marjoram, nasturtiums, parsley, sage and borage.

■ BELOW
A flowerpot covered in mosaic makes an original container. This pot has been planted with miniature roses to match the flower motif design. A hole drilled into the base allows for drainage.

■ RIGHT
This large, sturdy cooking pot – found in a junk shop for next to nothing – makes a characterful container for plants.

Potted Herb Garden

The use of time-honoured herbal remedies is enjoying renewed popularity as we come to appreciate the healing power of herbs. Here, herbs are planted in terracotta pots embellished with their botanical names and grouped together in a large saucer as a tribute to the apothecaries of old. Marigold, thyme, feverfew, lavender and rosemary have been used here, but you can vary the herbs according to what is available.

Tools and Materials

permanent marker pen

5 x 10cm/4in terracotta pots

selection of herbs: pot marigold (*Calendula*), thyme (*Thymus*), feverfew (*Matricaria*), lavender (*Lavandula*) and rosemary (*Rosmarinus*)

compost (soil mix) (optional)

terracotta saucer 36cm/14in in diameter

clay granules or gravel

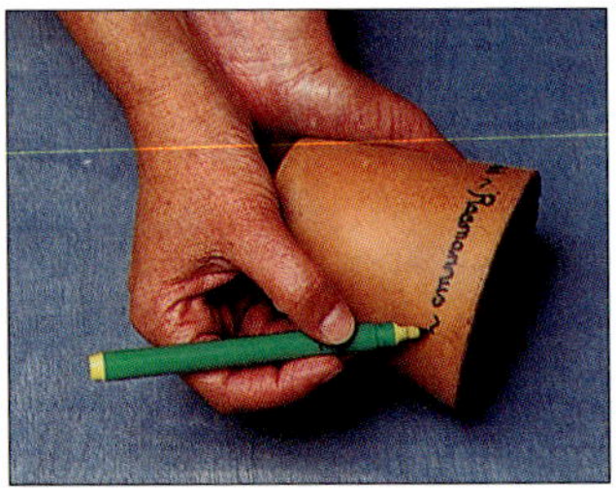

1 Use the marker pen to write the botanical plants' names around the rims of the pots. Plant the herbs with additional compost (soil mix) if necessary.

2 Fill the saucer with clay granules or gravel and arrange the pots on top.

■ BELOW

Thyme, one of the useful herbs in this potted arrangement, can be drunk as a refreshing tisane to aid digestion.

Herbal Remedies

Feverfew: a leaf rolled into a ball of bread can be taken for the symptoms of migraine
Lavender: the essential oil is known to be an effective treatment for minor burns
Pot marigold: a healing and mildly antiseptic herb
Rosemary: use in an infusion for scalp problems; makes an excellent hair rinse
Thyme: drunk as a tisane, purifying and disinfectant

Bouquet Garni Display

The classic bouquet garni consists of parsley, thyme and a bay leaf tied into a posy with string. It is used to impart flavour to stews, soups and sauces. In Provence, rosemary is always added as well. In all but the coldest areas, it is possible to gather these herbs fresh for most of the year. Here, the herbs have been planted in a small, moss-lined wooden crate, which would sit quite happily outdoors, on the kitchen windowsill. Planting containers along a theme in this way makes a delightful compromise between the useful and the decorative. Keep a small stock of the herbs to be dried for use mid-winter.

Tools and Materials

- drill
- wooden crate, 25 x 20 x 15cm/10 x 8 x 6in
- 40cm/16in sisal rope
- permanent marker pen
- paintbrush
- liquid seaweed plant food
- moss
- small bay tree
- thyme
- 2 parsley plants
- compost (soil mix)
- coarse grit

1 To make the handles, drill two holes in each end of the wooden crate. Thread the ends of a 20cm/8in length of rope through each of the holes from the outside and tie a knot in the ends to secure.

2 Use the permanent marker pen to write on each side of the crate. Paint the wood with an equal mixture of liquid seaweed plant food and water, to give it a weathered appearance.

3 Line the crate with moss and plant the herbs in a mixture of three parts compost (soil mix) to one part coarse grit. Tuck more moss around the plants and water thoroughly.

■ BELOW
The ingredients of the traditional bouquet garni will grow happily outside the kitchen window, within easy reach of the cook.

Topiary Herbs

This is one of the most attractive and stylish ways to grow herbs, especially when they are planted in long-tom pots, which complete the sculptural effect. The herbs suitable for this treatment are those with woody stems such as rosemary, lemon verbena, santolina and lavender.

■ OPPOSITE
To display a group of potted herbs to greatest effect, stand them against a plain background so that their shapes are clearly outlined.

Select young plants with a strong, straight central stem, which can be trimmed to create the topiary shape. Once established, provided the herbs are regularly fed and watered and moved into larger pots as they grow, they should reach a good size and live for a number of years. A large plant trained like this would make a perfect centrepiece for a formal herb garden.

Bear in mind that the shape of long-tom pots makes them dry out more quickly than conventional pots, so frequent watering is essential. Prune the herbs every two weeks during the growing season. In colder areas, the plants will need winter protection, so pack them, pots and all, into a large wooden box filled with bark and stand them in a light, frost-free place.

Tools and Materials

- scissors
- young herb plants: rosemary, lavender, santolina or lemon verbena
- long-tom pots
- compost (soil mix)
- coarse grit
- washed gravel

1 Use the scissors to trim any side shoots from the central stem of each plant and to remove the foliage from the bottom half to two-thirds of the stem.

2 Trim the remaining foliage to shape. Transplant the herbs into terracotta pots using a mixture of two parts compost (soil mix) to one part coarse grit. Cover the compost with a layer of gravel. Water and stand in a sheltered, sunny position.

■ ABOVE
When the bloom of your summer roses has passed, cut the stems and stick into florist's foam for a topiary display.

Alpine Shell Garden

Create an alpine garden in a shell-decorated container for an unusual window box or garden decoration. The garden needs to be planted in spring after the frosts; once planted, it will need very little attention, producing masses of little flowers in summer in return for the occasional watering. It will rest in the winter, ready to grow with renewed vigour the following spring.

■ OPPOSITE
Choose alpine plants with small leaves and flowers to suit the miniature scale of this tiny garden-in-a-box.

Tools and Materials

- wooden vegetable box
- lime green emulsion (latex) paint
- paintbrush
- selection of about 8 alpine plants such as sempervivum, sedum and saxifrage
- glue gun
- 12 scallop shells
- large plastic bag
- scissors
- compost (soil mix)
- selection of shells

1 Paint the box with lime green emulsion (latex) paint and let dry. This paint is really meant for indoor use, and will weather down in time to give softer tones. Water the plants thoroughly and allow to drain.

2 Using the glue gun, attach scallop shells all around the sides of the box. Line the box with plastic cut from a large bag, and make drainage holes in it using scissors.

3 Fill the box with a layer of compost (soil mix), then arrange the large shells on top.

4 Remove the plants from their pots and position them in the box. The roots can be wedged under a shell and bedded well into the compost.

5 Water the box thoroughly. Until the plants grow to fill the box, you can add a few more small shells to cover the bare earth, if you like.

Decorating Pots

Transforming an ordinary flower pot into something special really doesn't have to be difficult. There are so many media to choose from that it is an easy matter to find one that suits your decorative style. You may be happy with paint applied in bold geometric patterns or simple motifs. If you are skilled with a paintbrush, you might like to try something a little more figurative. Another easy option is to glue decorations on to your pots – ceramic chips, perhaps, to make a mosaic, or shells arranged in a simple textural pattern.

■ BELOW
This impressive garden urn is decorated with modern faces but has a look that is reminiscent of Byzantine icons. It will add a touch of grandeur to even the dullest corner of the garden or patio.

■ RIGHT
If you break a favourite plate or dish, this is a delightful way to continue to enjoy its colour and pattern. Use ceramic chips in co-ordinated colours and simple patterns to make striking mosaic pots.

■ BELOW
This pot has been given a necklace of weathered glass "beads" dangling on wires from a wire ring fixed under the rim of the pot.

Stencilled Terracotta Pot

Cheap terracotta pots can be made to look stylish and distinctive using simple stencilled designs. Choose paint colours that will enhance your plants and look good within your garden colour-scheme. Terracotta is porous and will absorb a lot of paint, so you may need several coats, depending on the colour you are using.

Tools and Materials

- tape measure
- terracotta pot
- chalk
- ruler
- masking tape
- artist's acrylic paints
- stencil brush
- acetate stencils

1 Measure the circumference of the pot at the top and bottom and divide into equal sections. Join each of these points with a vertical chalk line.

2 Mask off the outlines of the background shapes using masking tape and then paint. Add further coats as necessary and allow to dry.

3 Tape the stencil to the pot and apply several coats of paint. Move the stencil around the rim of the pot and repeat to complete the design.

■ BELOW
Once you have gained some confidence with simple stencils, experiment with freehand designs and other techniques such as sponging, stippling and dragging. Try other types of paint for different effects, such as metallic paints.

Mexican Painted Pots

Rings of folk-art motifs painted over stripes of vibrant colours give simple pots a rich Mexican look. This looks best if you leave some stripes of unpainted terracotta, and the style suits pots with fluted tops especially well. Stacked together and planted up with pelargoniums in hot summer colours, they make a lively garden feature.

Tools and Materials

- terracotta pot with fluted top
- masking tape
- scissors
- white undercoat
- paintbrushes
- gouache poster colours
- semi-gloss polyurethane varnish
- varnish brush

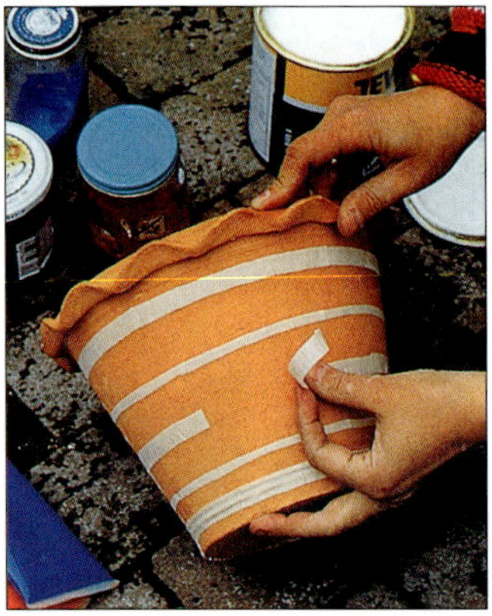

1 Mark the stripes on the pot using masking tape. Cut some lengths into narrower widths to give variations in the finished design. Bear in mind that the areas covered with masking tape will remain natural terracotta.

2 Paint the main body of the pot, below the rim, with white undercoat. When dry, paint in the coloured stripes, changing the colour for each band. Leave to dry.

3 When the paint is completely dry, carefully peel off the masking tape.

4 Using a fine brush and the white undercoat, paint a series of traditional motifs along the stripes. When completely dry, coat with varnish.

■ OPPOSITE The hot colours of these painted pots will hold their own in the sunniest spot on the patio. Fill them with vividly coloured flowering plants or exotic-looking succulents.

Painting a Borage Bucket

There is an old country saying that "a garden without borage is a garden without courage", which refers to the old herbalists' belief that this plant has the ability to lift the spirits. In addition to its medicinal properties – its oil is as potent as that of evening primrose – its pretty, blue, cucumber-scented flowers will gladden the heart when added to a glass of summer punch or used to decorate a salad.

■ OPPOSITE
Beautiful blue borage flowers look great against the silvery grey of a galvanized bucket. Here, they pick up the blue stencilled design on the watering can.

Tools and Materials

- pencil
- stencil cardboard
- craft knife
- cutting mat
- masking tape
- galvanized bucket, 18cm/7in in diameter
- artist's acrylic paints in mid-blue, deep blue and white
- stencil brush
- fine paintbrush
- polyurethane varnish
- varnish brush
- borage plants

1 Draw two or three borage flowers on a piece of stencil cardboard and cut out the outlines with a craft knife to make a stencil. Attach the stencil to the side of the bucket, using masking tape, and paint the flowers in mid-blue in an overlapping random pattern.

2 Using a fine paintbrush, add details to the flowers in deep blue and white. Protect the decoration with a coat of polyurethane varnish and let it dry before adding the borage plants.

■ RIGHT
The borage plant motif can make even the most practical of gardening equipment look charming. Adapt the idea for other pieces, perhaps painting them with other simple flowers such as daisies or pansies.

VERDIGRIS BUCKET

There is something irresistible about the luminous, subtle blue-green tones of verdigris. It is a colour that always complements plants and it is not difficult to reproduce on an ordinary galvanized bucket. Alternatively, you can use the same painting technique, substituting rust-coloured acrylic for aqua, to produce a rusted effect.

TOOLS AND MATERIALS

- medium-grade sandpaper
- galvanized bucket
- metal primer
- paintbrushes
- gold emulsion (latex) paint
- amber shellac
- artist's acrylic paint in white and aqua-green
- natural sponge
- polyurethane varnish
- varnish brush

■ LEFT
The pale, cool aqua tone of verdigris makes a wonderful foil for these delicate and velvety dark violas.

1 Sand the bucket, then prime with metal primer and allow to dry. Paint with gold paint and leave the bucket to dry for at least 2–3 hours.

2 Paint the bucket with amber shellac and let dry. Mix white acrylic with aqua-green to make the verdigris, and thin it to a watery consistency.

3 Sponge the verdigris paint over the shellac and allow to dry for 1–2 hours before applying a coat of varnish.

LEAD CHIMNEY

Lead has been used to make garden containers for centuries, and its chalky blue-grey tones look wonderful with plants. But lead is incredibly heavy and very expensive, so here is a way of faking it, using a plastic chimney and a simple paint effect.

TOOLS AND MATERIALS

- sandpaper
- plastic, terracotta-coloured chimney
- acrylic primer
- paintbrushes
- emulsion (latex) paint in charcoal grey and white
- acrylic scumble glaze
- polyurethane varnish
- varnish brush

■ LEFT
A lead-coloured container looks stunning filled with silvery foliage and pale flowers.

1 Sand the chimney to give a key for the paint. Paint with one coat of acrylic primer and leave to dry for 1–2 hours.

2 Apply a coat of charcoal grey emulsion (latex) and leave to dry for 2–3 hours.

3 Tint some scumble glaze with white emulsion and thin with water. Paint over the chimney randomly using a large artist's paintbrush. Blend the colour by washing over the surface with a wet brush and leave to dry.

4 Add more of the white scumble mixture to parts of the chimney to "age" the surface. Leave to dry, then paint with a coat of polyurethane varnish.

Tin-can Plant Nursery

Seedlings can be decorative in themselves, so pick them out from their seed trays into a collection of tin cans mounted on a wall plaque. They can grow on there, sheltered by the wall and high above any threatening late frosts, until they are ready to be planted out. The plaque itself looks wonderful made from ordinary tinned steel cans, but if you want to add a bit more colour, scour delicatessens for vividly printed cans.

■ OPPOSITE
Printed and plain tin cans take on a new and more interesting appearance when they are massed together on a Mediterranean blue wall panel.

Tools and Materials

- wooden board about 60 x 30cm/24 x 12in
- undercoat
- paintbrush
- blue gloss paint
- variety of empty cans with paper labels removed
- can opener
- tin snips
- pliers
- hammer
- nail
- tacks

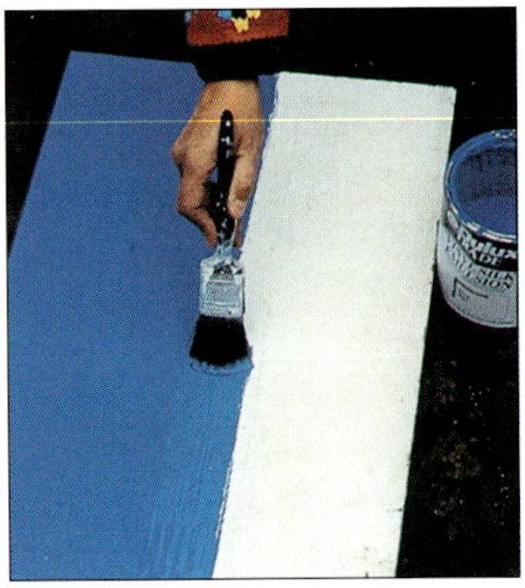

1 Paint the board with a coat of undercoat and one or two coats of gloss paint, allowing each coat to dry before applying the next.

2 Stand the cans open end down and, using the can opener, cut round half of the bottom.

3 Using tin snips, cut open the side of the can to make two equal flaps.

4 Open out the sides with pliers and snip a V-shape into each one. Bend up the can bottom in line with the sides. Pierce the bottom of each can by hammering a nail through it.

5 Arrange all the cans on the board, then tack them in place, hammering a tack through each point of the side flaps.

Dea
Dea
Dea
White Tower
ΟΜΟΣΠΟΝΔΙΑΣ
OMOSPONDIAS
THESSALONIKI
GREECE - GRIECHENLAND

Moss and Netting Urn

This rustic urn is created from nothing more remarkable than chicken wire and moss: a collection of these elegant containers would make wonderful garden decorations for a special occasion, flanking steps or ranged along a balustrade. Even without the moss filling, the wire shape makes a quirky sculpture in itself. When the urns are not in use, they will keep their colour longer if they are kept in a dark place, as moss fades quite quickly in daylight.

Tools and Materials

wire cutters
chicken wire
moss
florist's wire
20cm/8in plastic pot

1 Cut a 1.5m/1½yd length of chicken wire. Fold it in half so that the raw edges meet and pack a layer of moss between the layers of wire.

2 Fold the chicken wire and moss "sandwich" in half lengthways and join the edges securely together with lengths of florist's wire.

3 Slip the plastic pot into the top end of the tube (the end with no rough edges) and form the lip of the urn by folding the chicken wire outwards from the rim of the pot.

4 Leaving the pot in place, firmly squeeze the chicken wire with both hands just below the pot to make the stem of the urn.

5 Make the base by folding the rough edges in and squeezing and squashing the wire into the desired shape. Stand the urn up periodically while you do this to check that it is level.

■ RIGHT
Whether the moss is fresh or has been allowed to dry out, the container has a pleasingly textural quality.

Earthy Painted Pots

Liquid seaweed plant food is a wonderful rich brown colour and can be diluted and painted on to terracotta pots to encourage the growth of moss and give the appearance of age. Undiluted, the colour is very deep and looks beautiful as a decoration for terracotta. You can either preserve this rich colour with a coat of varnish or you could leave the pots unsealed: most of the coating will be worn away by the weather if the pots are left outside, leaving soft faded patterns, like traces of ancient frescoes.

Tools and Materials

- masking tape
- terracotta pots
- liquid seaweed plant food
- paintbrushes
- matt polyurethane varnish
- varnish brush

1 Use masking tape to protect the areas of the pot that you want to remain unpainted. Brush liquid seaweed plant food on to the unmasked areas and leave to dry completely.

2 Peel off the masking tape and seal the whole pot with a coat of matt varnish, if you wish to retain the rich brown colour.

■ ABOVE
Beautiful pots in rich natural hues of terracotta and earthy dark brown hold a winter arrangement of twigs and cones.

Garden Decorations and Accessories

Now comes the icing on the cake and the finishing touch: when your garden is looking a picture and you really want to draw attention to its design and its planting, add some well-judged artefacts to draw the eye or raise a smile for a truly decorated garden.

Decorating your outdoor room is enormous fun. Allow yourself to be idiosyncratic in your choice of embellishments. An antique metal birdcage may seem incongruous to the garden landscape but, if festooned with flowers, it can become a wonderfully original feature. Mobiles and wind chimes look delightful and produce gentle chimes to soothe the ear, while a customized birdhouse will attract bird life to your garden and help to support the birds through the winter months. If you're looking to add romance to your garden, hang a few decorative hearts here and there.

■ ABOVE
Galvanized metal artefacts work best dotted casually about the garden.

■ OPPOSITE
Whether it is fruit, vegetables or seedlings you want to protect, make a scarecrow to double as an amusing garden sculpture. This dapper chap with a colander face wears a denim jacket and a sporty panama hat.

GARDEN SCULPTURE

The classic garden decoration is sculpture: for centuries, stone statues, busts and fountains have graced formal gardens, providing focal points or charming surprises in secluded spots. Classic figures are still popular as reproductions, along with baroque-style cherubs and the little imps known as *putti*.

■ RIGHT
An exquisite male torso, turned modestly towards the wall, contributes art and structure at a secluded side of the garden.

Original stone statues, aged by lichens, natural salts and the passage of time, obscuring detail and combining to create an authentic patina, are exquisite but prohibitively expensive. Economic alternatives are available, however: accelerate the aging process on modern stone copies by coating them with live yogurt and keeping them in damp, shady places.

MODERN VALUES

Beautiful as the traditional forms of sculpture are, contemporary alternatives may be more relevant to your garden and far more personal to you. Metal and wire sculpture is fashionable nowadays and works very well outside, as does willow, woven into dynamic figures. Mosaic, too, can be a lovely medium for sculpture as it quickly transforms all sorts of unpromising bits of paraphernalia. Plants themselves can become sculpture in the form of topiary, where small-leaved evergreens are clipped into spirals, cones, orbs or animals. It is a slow process as the shrubs take time to grow, but some garden centres sell them already started, so all you have to do is keep them trimmed to shape.

■ ABOVE
Metal and water combine in a fascinating, dynamic sculpture that is a cross between a birdbath and a water feature.

■ LEFT
Even a rusty old chair frame can become sculpture. This one, flanked on two sides by neatly trimmed trees, is given throne-like importance.

■ LEFT
Old galvanized baths and bowls have been light-heartedly decorated with mosaic cut from broken china, plus a couple of old teacups and some ginger-jar tops.

■ ABOVE
Classical Roman and Greek statues make elegant focal points, set at the end of vistas.

■ LEFT
Tradtional sculpture, such as this stone urn, gives an austere sense of formality to the garden design, and would add something of a regal touch to a large sweeping garden.

■ RIGHT
Positioned down the length of the garden, pots and containers can create a visual feast that is less formal than traditional garden sculpture.

■ RIGHT
Topiary is making a comeback, and clever trimming will help to keep its effect strictly contemporary.

OUTDOOR DECORATIONS

Sculpture is the classic outdoor art form, but if you don't have money to spend on garden decorations or if the space in your garden is limited, then there are plenty of alternatives. You can use anything that adds structure and form to the garden.

Large plant pots and boxes are decorative as well as functional. The traditional example is the classic urn, but you don't even have to go that far. Ordinary pots, painted or carefully arranged in groups, can make a statement, as can novel containers. Think of some unusual hanging baskets, such as colanders, baskets or buckets, or gather potted plants into a spectacular container, such as an old wheelbarrow, to make a display. You can add more purely decorative ideas, such as whirligigs, wind chimes, driftwood or pebble collections. Or you can fashion your own decorations – motifs such as hearts or stars made from twigs and branches, wire or raffia.

■ OPPOSITE
An old wicker mannequin teamed with a miniature wirework version makes an amusing and unexpected decoration.

■ ABOVE
A collection of limpet shell rings hung on strong threads makes an attractive, joyous wind chime.

■ ABOVE
This inexpensive, painted bamboo birdcage, filled with potted pinks, makes a charming ornament.

■ LEFT
Even simple galvanized shapes take on decorative appeal: all they need is a couple of coats of paint.

Decorative Mosaic Spheres

Mosaic spheres inspired by millefiori African beadwork would make unusual garden decorations. Based on wooden or polystyrene balls, they can be decorated with broken china, glass mosaic tiles or fragments of mirror. If you use a polystyrene foundation, the spheres will be quite light and could be hung in a tree.

■ BELOW
Mosaic stars dotted amongst the foliage can add an element of surprise to a blooming hedge of roses.

Tools and Materials

- polystyrene or wooden spheres
- PVA (white) glue
- paintbrush
- pencil
- selection of old china
- mirror
- tile nippers
- rubber gloves
- waterproof tile adhesive
- powdered waterproof tile grout
- vinyl matt emulsion (latex) or acrylic paint
- nailbrush
- soft cloth

1 Seal the polystyrene or wooden spheres with diluted PVA (white) glue. Leave to dry.

2 Using a pencil, draw a simple design on a sphere. A combination of circular shapes works well, but experiment with other geometric shapes and abstract designs.

3 Cut the china and mirror into different sized pieces using tile nippers. Stick the pieces to the sphere using waterproof tile adhesive. Leave overnight to dry.

■ RIGHT
Position the spheres to suggest bowls mid-game for a fun and very modern ornamental display.

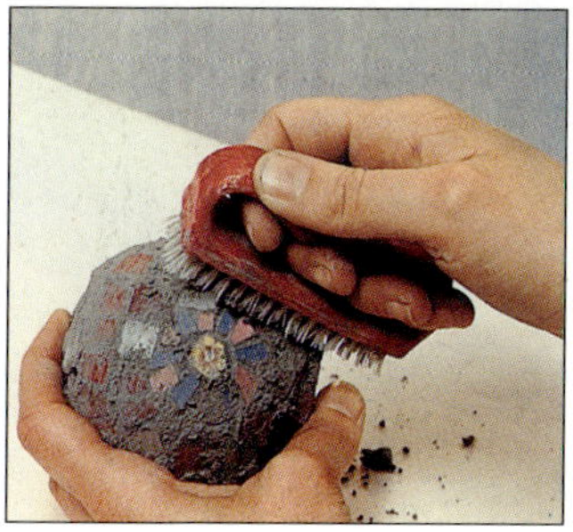

4 Mix powdered grout with water and use a little vinyl matt emulsion (latex) or acrylic paint to colour it. Wearing rubber gloves, rub the grout into the surface of the sphere, filling all the cracks between the tesserae.

5 Leave for a few minutes until the surface has dried, then brush off excess grout using a stiff nailbrush.

6 Leave to dry overnight, then polish with a soft dry cloth.

OUTDOOR FRAMES

There's no reason why garden walls should not be decorated with pictures, just as you would the walls of a room, whether they are merely glimpsed through a curtain of foliage and flowers or provide the focus of interest on an unclothed wall.

Stone, metal or tiled plaques can be fixed to the walls, but pictures in frames also have a place. The frames themselves should be weatherproof, so the most appropriate material to use is wood that has already been aged and hardened by the weather. You could recycle lengths of timber from old fencing or garden furniture, or collect some beautiful, bleached driftwood from the beach. To fill the frames, put together collages of natural subjects that will be perfectly in keeping with the garden: an arrangement of leaves or soft downy feathers; shells collected on holiday, or a mosaic decoration made from broken pieces of patterned china or shop-bought tesserae. As an alternative, you could frame an old mirror and hang it cleverly from an accommodating branch or prop it in a niche in a wall, to visually expand the space, giving the impression of another garden beyond the wall.

■ BELOW
The muted, weathered tones and contorted shapes of driftwood just beg to be used. Here, a shabby old mirror frame has been transformed using the curved edge of an old garden table for the top and various pieces of driftwood to make a wonderful organic decoration, quite in keeping with its surroundings.

■ ABOVE
This green and twiggy frame will give your outdoor room a log cabin touch. Artificial grass, available from modelmaker's suppliers, was glued to a piece of hardboard before the twigs were added in a lattice design.

■ LEFT
Neatly tailored male pheasant feathers look wonderful in ordered lines. The soft grey tones of this frame, made of wood recycled from an old barn door, are echoed in the down on the feathers.

■ RIGHT
Cover the outside edge of a mirror with a rich collection of shells and coral, glued in position, for an outdoor frame with an inimitable touch of seashore style.

■ RIGHT
This recycled picture frame celebrates the beauty of weathered timber. The wonderful texture and colour mean that the frame is easily enhanced with pebbles, string and seaweed to make a naturally organic picture.

China Tiles

If you want to use mosaic as a garden decoration but are daunted by a large-scale project, you could try making some of these small one-off tiles. Try out simple patterns, using a selection of broken china, and think of the tiles as sketches or experiments before embarking on more complex mosaics.

■ OPPOSITE
These mosaic tiles could be displayed singly or in groups, stuck on a garden wall or used to decorate a table.

Tools and Materials

- plain white tiles
- PVA (white) glue
- paintbrush
- pencil
- selection of old china
- tile nippers
- tile adhesive
- acrylic paint or cement dye
- powdered waterproof tile grout
- rubber gloves
- nailbrush
- soft cloth

1 Prime the back of a plain tile with diluted PVA (white) glue and leave to dry. Draw a simple design on the back of the tile using a pencil.

2 Cut a selection of china into small pieces that will fit into your design, using tile nippers. Arrange the tesserae in groups according to colour and shape.

3 Dip the tesserae into tile adhesive and press them, one by one, on to the tile, using the drawing as a guide. When the tile is completely covered, leave it to dry overnight.

4 Mix acrylic paint or cement dye with powdered waterproof tile grout. Add a little water and mix to a dough-like consistency. Wearing rubber gloves, rub the grout into the surface of the mosaic, making sure that all the gaps are filled. Leave to dry for about ten minutes.

5 Scrub the surface of the tile with a stiff nailbrush to remove all the excess grout, then leave the tile to dry for 24 hours. Polish the surface with a soft dry cloth.

Mosaic Clock

This clockface is decorated with mosaic made from hand-painted Mexican tiles. While the painting on the tiles is very free, and they have been cut into uneven shapes, the resulting tesserae are used to construct a precise geometric design that draws attention to the positions of the hands, making it easy to read the time. The base of the clock is made from two pieces of wood, with a hole cut into the thick piece at the back to accommodate the clock mechanism and batteries. The clock can live outdoors, but position it in a sheltered place, where it will receive the maximum amount of protection from the weather.

Tools and Materials

- 4mm/⅙in plywood
- 2cm/¾in chipboard
- compasses
- marker pen or pencil
- ruler
- jigsaw
- drill and bits
- clock movement and hands
- PVA (white) glue
- paintbrush
- strong wood glue
- 4 clamps or heavy weights
- tile nippers
- selection of plain and patterned tiles
- cement-based tile adhesive
- shells
- flexible (putty) knife
- rubber gloves
- sponge
- sandpaper
- soft cloth

1 Draw a 40cm/16in circle on both the plywood and the chipboard, and cut out with the jigsaw . Drill a hole through the centre of the chipboard circle large enough to take the jigsaw blade. Saw a hole to accommodate the clock mechanism and batteries. Drill a hole through the centre of the plywood circle for the spindle. Prime both pieces with diluted PVA (white) glue and let dry.

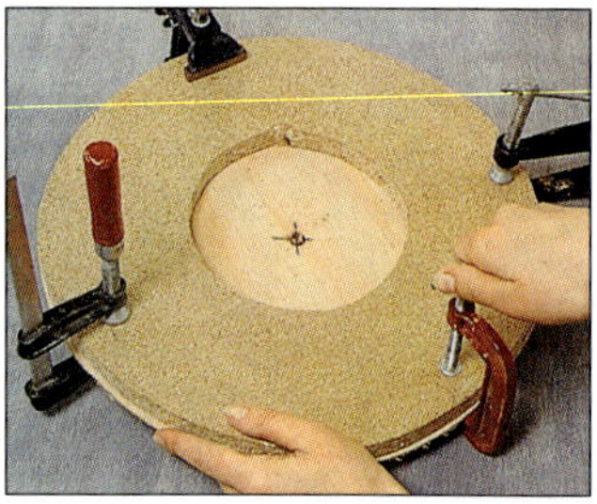

2 Stick the plywood and chipboard circles together using strong wood glue. Clamp the pieces together or leave under heavy weights overnight to dry.

3 Draw a circle in the centre of the plywood circle with a radius of the length of the minute hand. Using a marker pen or pencil, divide the face into quarters and use these as the basis for your design.

4 Using tile nippers, cut the patterned tiles into small irregular shapes. This design uses tiles in three different patterns, to differentiate the areas of the clockface. Stick the tiles on with cement-based tile adhesive, making sure they lie flat.

5 Cut plain tiles into small rectangular shapes for the rim of the clock. Tile the border, marking the positions of the quarter hours. When attaching the shells, make sure they are positioned so that they will not obstruct the movement of the clock hands.

6 Use a flexible (putty) knife to smooth tile adhesive around the rim of the clock. Wearing rubber gloves, work the adhesive over the clockface, making sure all the gaps are filled. Wipe clean with a sponge and leave to dry for approximately 24 hours.

7 Sand off any excess cement and polish with a soft dry cloth.

8 Attach the clock, fitting the movement and batteries into the hole at the back. Insert the spindle through the central hole and fit the hands.

■ RIGHT

Simple groups of pretty shells have been used to mark the quarter hours on this clockface.

Birdhouses

Birds are the most welcome of garden visitors. They are fascinating to watch, delightful to listen to, and earn their keep by eating garden pests such as snails and aphids. Nowadays, as the natural habitats of many species diminish, even quite small gardens can provide an important proportion of their territories, and they won't need much encouragement.

■ OPPOSITE
A charming, scaled-down dovecote makes a tiny folly for a miniature garden in a trough or window box.

Encourage birds to visit your garden regularly with birdhouses, bird-feeding tables and baths. Seedheads left standing in the winter border and shrubs that bear berries such as cotoneaster and daphne ensure a winter food supply. Remember that if you feed garden birds in winter you must do so regularly, as they will come to depend on you.

Even better than garden visitors are permanent residents: bird-houses are rewarding to watch when occupied and will become garden features all year round.

Birds can be encouraged to make nests even in the most urban of areas, and if you provide a suitable nesting box they will both feed and breed in your garden. A bird's own choice of nesting place would be a sheltered spot, so take care to place your birdhouse away from possible disturbances, up a wall or tree trunk, and facing away from prevailing wind and rain.

■ ABOVE RIGHT
A whole row of basic birdhouses, painted in bright, contrasting colours looks like a row of smart beach huts.

■ RIGHT
A New England-style clapboard house for upwardly mobile birds: mount the house on a stout post and site it out of reach of overhanging trees if cats frequent the garden.

Customized Nesting Box

Ready-made nesting boxes are available in every shape and size, but a simple box can be transformed with a lick of paint and a few decorative touches. This house is painted in Shaker style and finished with a finial cut from scrap timber and an apple twig for a perch. To ensure that a nesting box gives you maximum pleasure, position it so that you will be able to see it from a window when you are indoors as well as when you are out in the garden.

Tools and Materials

- nesting box
- vinyl matt emulsion (latex) paint in 2 colours
- paintbrush
- marker pen
- decorative finial
- PVA (white) glue
- drill
- apple twig

1 Paint the box with emulsion (latex) paint in the first colour and leave to dry. Draw the door shape and the heart motifs using a marker pen.

2 Fill in the design and paint the finial with the second colour of emulsion paint and leave to dry completely.

3 Glue the finial in place at the front of the roof ridge using PVA (white) glue. Drill a hole to fit the apple twig beneath the entrance hole. Apply glue to the twig and push it into position.

■ **OPPOSITE**
Hang this pretty nesting box where the birds will be safe from predators; they will be happier if there is some overhanging foliage to give them a little shelter and privacy.

■ **LEFT**
If your birds would prefer a more metropolitan dwelling, paint a ready-made nesting box blue-grey and roof it with copper foil. The door surround is also made from copper foil – bend this back on itself, not into the hole, so that there are no sharp edges around the entrance to the box.

Hanging Bird-feeding Table

If you put out food and fresh water regularly, your garden will soon become a haven for wild birds. The birds quickly get to know and will pass the word around to make your bird-feeding table a popular stopping-off point.

There is immense pleasure to be gained from watching the different species that come to feed daily. This bird-feeding table is made from rough timber, with a lip around the edge to stop nuts and seeds rolling off.

Tools and Materials

- 2 lengths of rough timber, 25 x 12.5 x 1cm/10 x 5½ x ½in
- 2 battens 25 x 2.5 x 2.5cm/ 10 x 1 x 1in
- nails
- hammer
- 4 battens 28 x 5 x 1cm/ 11 x 2 x ½in
- wood preservative
- small decorator's paintbrush
- pencil
- ruler
- 4 brass hooks
- scissors
- 2m/6½ft sisal string

1 To make the base of the table, lay the two lengths of rough timber side by side and place the 25cm/10in battens across the wood, one at each end. Nail the battens securely in place.

2 Nail the four 28cm/11in battens around the edges of the base, allowing a lip of at least 2.5cm/1in. Paint all the surfaces of the table with wood preservative and leave to dry.

3 Use a pencil and ruler to mark a point in each corner of the table. Screw in a brass hook on each of the points.

4 Cut the sisal string into four equal lengths and tie a small loop in one end of each piece. Attach each loop to a hook, then gather up the strings above the table and tie in a loop for hanging.

■ OPPOSITE
String is tied to a hook in each corner so that the table can be hung in a tree, out of reach of predators.

■ LEFT
Specialist bird seed suppliers can provide information about which types of seed will attract which particular species of bird.

Copper Birdbath

You will have endless pleasure watching the birds preening and cleaning in this beautiful, yet eminently practical, beaten copper birdbath. Maintain a constant supply of fresh drinking water all year round to ensure the health and happiness of the birds in your locality.

1 Using a chinagraph pencil and a piece of looped string, mark a 45cm/18in circle on the copper sheet.

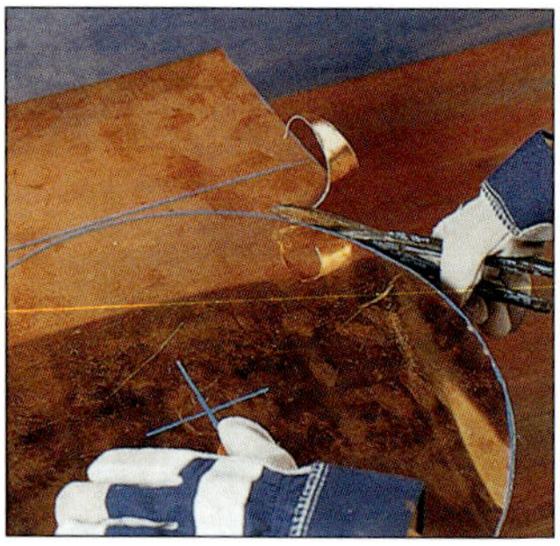

2 Wearing protective gloves, cut out the circle with a pair of tin snips. Smooth the sharp edge using a file.

Tools and Materials

- chinagraph pencil
- string
- 9mm/⅜in 20 SWG copper sheet
- protective gloves
- tin snips
- file
- blanket
- hammer
- 4m/13ft medium copper wire
- bench vice
- strong hook
- slow-speed electric drill
- 3mm/⅛in bit

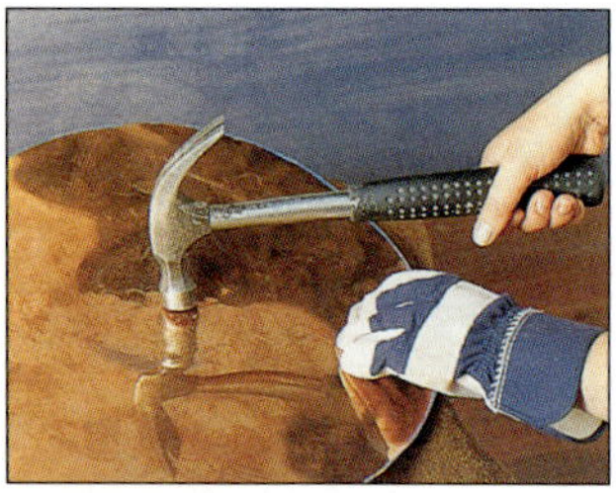

3 Lay the copper circle on a blanket and lightly hammer it from the centre. Spread the dips out to the rim. Repeat, starting in the centre each time, until you have the required shape. To make the perch, loop 1m/39in copper wire and hold the ends in a vice. Fasten a hook into the chuck of a drill. Put the hook through the loop and run the drill to twist the wire. Drill three holes, equally spaced, around the rim of the bath. Divide the remaining wire into three equal lengths and knot one end of each. Thread through the holes from beneath the bath. Slip the twisted wire over two straight wires to form a perch, and bend the tops of the wires together into a loop for hanging.

■ ABOVE
This elegant birdbath, with spare, modern lines, features a wire perch suspended over the water for the birds to stand on as they drink.

Gazebo Feeder

Constructed from a small glass lantern and some recycled tin cans, this little bird-feeder will hang like a jewel amongst the foliage of a tree.

Tools and Materials

- glass lantern
- tape measure
- thin glass
- chinagraph pencil
- try-square
- glass cutter
- ruler
- protective gloves
- shiny tin can, washed and dried
- tin snips
- flux and soldering iron
- solder
- try-square
- fine wire mesh

1 This lantern required extra glass to be installed. If this is the case with yours, measure the areas required and reduce all measurements by 6mm/¼in to allow for the metal border. Using a chinagraph pencil, mark the measurements on the glass, then cut out by running a glass cutter in a single pass along a ruler. Wearing protective gloves, tap along the line to break the glass. Cut 9mm/⅜in strips of metal from a tin can using tin snips.

2 Wrap a strip of metal around each edge of each glass panel. Trim, then smear soldering flux on to the mating surfaces of each corner. Solder the corner joints of each panel. Heat a joint with a soldering iron and apply the solder. Remove the iron to allow the solder to cool and set.

3 Measure the openings for the hoppers and fold sections of the tin can to suit, using a try-square or ruler to keep the fold lines straight. Solder the meeting points of each hopper. Cut out a platform from fine wire mesh and solder the platform, the panels and the hoppers in place on the framework.

■ BELOW
This sophisticated bird-feeder makes a delightful detail in a quiet garden corner.

Functional Decorations

The very paraphernalia of gardening can be decorative. An old garden fork, its handle polished with use, a galvanized watering can, turned soft grey with time, or a wheelbarrow, pitted with wear, all have attractive forms that can give structure to the garden. Somehow, the balance and symmetry that good tools must possess in order to work efficiently usually also result in shapes that are easy on the eye. They have reassuring associations, too: they evoke a sense of outdoor life and remind us that people are nearby. So let them loiter around the garden; leave them where they were last used, and they will reward you with their spontaneous decorative appeal.

■ OPPOSITE
An old watering can, its curves reminiscent of a vintage car, provides a simple structural note left at the edge of a pathway.

■ BELOW
Sundials may not be moveable decorations, but their original *raison d'être* reminds us that these are not fripperies. They were clearly more necessary in centuries gone by than they are today, but they still exude a functional quality that is both honest and pleasing.

■ LEFT
Even old garden tools make decorative garden ornaments, left just where they were last used.

TWIGWAM

Plant supports are functional, but that doesn't mean they can't be decorative too. This one, made from branches pruned from garden trees interwoven with willow, makes a charming structural detail in a flower bed. Alternatively, it can be used to support clematis or any other climber for a wonderful, free-standing, outdoor floral display.

TOOLS AND MATERIALS

- 3 unbranched poles, about 90cm/3ft long
- string or strands of willow
- 3 unbranched poles, about 30cm/12in long
- plenty of fine, freshly cut willow branches

1 Stand up the three taller poles to form a "wigwam" and tie them together at the top with string or willow.

2 Stand the three shorter poles between the longer ones and tie them in the same way. Start to weave the willow branches in and out of the poles, working upwards from the bottom.

3 Once enough of the wigwam has been woven to keep the shorter poles securely in position, untie them. Continue weaving until the shorter poles are almost covered.

■ RIGHT
This woven willow support would look pretty entwined with sweet peas or nasturtiums, to give instant height in a summer border.

Chicken Wire Cloche

This quirky chicken wire cloche can be used to protect plants from slugs and birds or can be simply "planted" into the flowerbed as a charming and original miniature obelisk.

Tools and Materials

- wire cutters
- fine-mesh chicken wire
- pliers
- medium-gauge garden wire

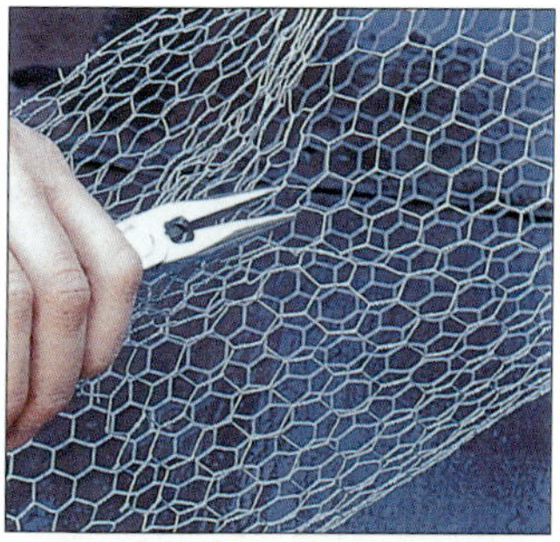

1 Using wire cutters, cut a piece of chicken wire about 50 x 50cm/20 x 20in. Roll it to form a tube, making sure the twisted sides of each lozenge shape run vertically. Join the tube by twisting the cut ends of the wire securely in place around each other.

2 Use the pliers to squeeze the wire into shape. At the top, squeeze each lozenge shape as tightly as it will go. Continue to pinch the wires together down the tube, squeezing each hole less and less until you reach the fullest part of the shape.

3 At the bottom of the cloche, make a "skirt" by narrowing the shape again, then letting it fan out gracefully. Wind garden wire tightly around the top to finish the cloche.

■ RIGHT
With a bit of original thought, you can turn an everyday material like chicken wire into an amusing miniature folly for the garden.

PRETTY EFFECTS IN PRACTICAL AREAS

Vegetable patches need not be the Cinderellas of the garden. There is something beautifully voluptuous about burgeoning fruits and first-class vegetables, and the structures they need to climb up can be very appealing. Make a virtue of your vegetable garden, whether you grow your produce in a separate part of the garden, or mix fruits and vegetables in amongst the plants in the flowerbeds.

■ OPPOSITE
Keeping track of plant labels can be practically impossible once the plants are growing and overflowing their original sites, so turn them into a decoration in themselves. Make a noticeboard from a piece of plywood, giving it a decorative motif at the top, such as these tulips. Paint it in bright colours, screw in some hooks and use it to keep an attractive garden record of what you have planted.

■ ABOVE
A row of pea sticks has a special appeal, because the twiggy branches refuse to be regimented in the vegetable garden, and have the appearance of a wild hedgerow up which the peas are scrambling. However, they are extremely practical, as the tangled twigs offer plenty of support.

■ ABOVE
Soldier-like bamboo canes take on an even more regimental appearance when the plants have their labels tied uniformly along the line.

ALPINE
IBERIS
'Little Gem'

Chicken Box Plant Stand

It is fun, especially in spring when the plants are low, to hoist a few flowers on high. And here is a witty way to achieve that: make a decorative wooden chicken nesting on a box, raise it on a stake and fill the box with pots of seasonal flowers.

■ OPPOSITE
Use this bright wooden chicken to bring a splash of instant colour to any part of the garden that needs perking up for a week or two as the seasons change.

Tools and Materials

- pencil
- paper
- tape measure
- scissors
- MDF (medium density fiberboard), 60 x 60cm/2 x 2ft
- jigsaw
- 25mm/1in plywood, at least 75 x 45cm/30 x 18in
- 6 screws
- screwdriver
- undercoat
- paintbrushes
- enamel paint in red, orange, white, blue, black and green
- 7.5 x 5cm/3 x 2in post, about 120cm/4ft long

1 Draw the chicken shape on paper, with a box back for it to stand on measuring 17 x 9cm/6½ x 3½in. Cut out the template and transfer the design to the MDF. Cut out using a jigsaw. Cut three pieces of plywood 17 x 9cm/6½ x 3½in and one piece 17 x 5cm/6½ x 2in.

2 Screw the two larger plywood panels to the chicken, one on either side. Screw the narrower panel between them, 3cm/1in from the bottom edge of the side panels, to make the base. Screw the final plywood panel onto the front.

3 Paint both sides of the chicken and the box with a layer of undercoat and allow to dry.

4 Sketch the chicken's features on both sides of the chicken shape and paint with enamel paints. Paint the box green. Allow to dry overnight.

5 Screw the post to the back of the box to allow it to stand upright.

WIND CHIMES

A walk on the beach or in the woods to gather weathered driftwood and twigs, and a forage in the potting shed, will provide you with all the materials you need to make these rustic wind chimes. The bells are made from miniature terracotta pots with metal vine-eyes as clappers. Provided the pots have no cracks, the wind chimes will sound like distant cow-bells, adding the extra dimension of gentle sounds to the sensual delights of your garden.

TOOLS AND MATERIALS

- wire cutters
- galvanized wire
- drill and bit
- 3 corks
- 4 weathered twigs of different sizes, the largest 30cm/12in long
- 2 metal vine-eyes
- 2 miniature terracotta pots

1 Cut one 50cm/20in and two 30cm/12in lengths of wire. Drill a hole through the centre of each cork. Make a hanging loop at one end of the longer piece of wire. Just beneath the loop, twist the wire around the centre of the longest twig and thread on a cork.

2 Add the next twig, either twisting the wire around it as before, or drilling a hole and threading it on. Add a second cork, followed by the third twig and the third cork. Make a hook in the end of the remaining wire, trimming it if necessary. Drill a hole through one end of the final twig and hook it on to the wire.

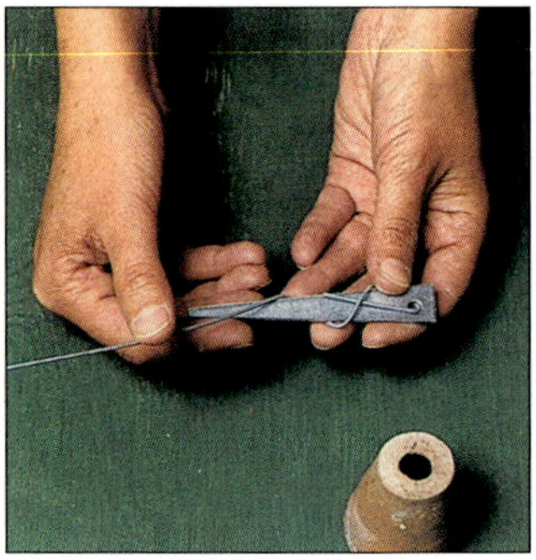

3 Thread a vine-eye on to each of the shorter lengths of wire and bend over 2.5cm/1in of the wire so that it lies flat against the vine-eye. Wrap the long end of the wire around the vine-eye in a spiral. Thread each vine-eye through the drainage hole in one of the terracotta pots, so that the wide end of the vine-eye becomes the clapper and the narrow end protrudes from the pot

4 Hang up the wind chimes and attach the bells, making sure that the wind chimes balance. Twist the wires protruding from the bells securely around the twig.

■ OPPOSITE
Wind chimes made with natural materials found in the garden blend effortlessly into its decorative scheme.

■ RIGHT
The charm of this alternative wind chime lies in its simplicity. Sand dollars provide the form, while the cockle shells strung onto raffia provide the music.

Seaworn Shell Mobile

Spend a day on the beach hunting among the rocks and pebbles and you are bound to come across plenty of materials for this delicate mobile. Limpet shells worn by the sea and sand often develop central holes, which makes them perfect for stringing. The stone-effect beads used here come in a range of smooth shapes and natural colours. Real pebbles that have weathered holes in them could also be used, but they might be too heavy to allow the mobile to move in the breeze.

1 Drill a hole through both ends of two pieces of driftwood, each about 36cm/14in long. Cut two 56cm/22in lengths of string and knot a bead 3cm/1in from the end of each. Thread one end of each piece of string through the hole in the driftwood for the top of the frame, and secure with a knot. Thread the other end through the hole in the bottom piece of wood. Thread a small, drilled cockle shell on to the end of each piece of string and secure with a knot.

2 To make the limpet wind chime, drill six holes, about 2cm/¾in apart, along a small piece of driftwood. Cut six 38cm/15in lengths of rough string. Thread and tie the limpet shells on to the strings and thread through the holes in the driftwood. Secure with knots and cut off any excess string.

Tools and Materials

- assorted pieces of driftwood
- drill
- scissors
- rough string
- assorted stone-effect beads
- 2 cockle shells
- weathered limpet shells
- natural raffia
- large winkle (periwinkle) shell
- 5 conch shells
- epoxy resin glue
- sticky tape

3 For the tailed winkle (periwinkle) shell, cut some short lengths of raffia and glue four or five into the mouth of each conch shell, using epoxy resin glue. Leave to dry. Drill a hole in the top of the large winkle shell.

4 Make a plait with three long strands of raffia, bind one end with tape and thread it through the hole in the winkle shell. Tie a knot in the end of the plait and pull it inside the shell. Tie beads and small pieces of driftwood on to the plait.

5 Gather together the conch shells and glue the ends of their raffia tails inside the mouth of the winkle shell, so that the shells hang down like a tail.

6 To assemble the mobile, drill two holes in the top of the frame. Thread the raffia plait through one of the holes and knot at the top. Tie a doubled length of string to each end of the top of the wind chime. Tie both strings around a large, round bead, then thread the ends through the second hole in the top of the frame and secure with a knot.

■ ABOVE
Hang the shell mobile where it will catch the breeze and its gentle tinkling will remind you of days at the seaside.

Mosaic Hearts

Most gardens are a source of treasure, however modest it might be. As you turn the soil, you are almost bound to uncover broken and weathered pieces of china and glass: save them to make decorative small mosaics. There is a real sense of satisfaction to be gained from turning a previous gardener's discarded rubbish into something attractive.

■ OPPOSITE
Pieces of weathered green glass set in tile cement are used to make these pretty hearts, moulded in biscuit (cookie) cutters. Hang the hearts on a wall or fence, or you could set them within a rock garden.

1 Use your fingers to coat the inside of the biscuit (cookie) cutter with a layer of petroleum jelly so that removing the finished mosaic heart will be easier. Wear rubber gloves if you prefer.

2 Cut a short length of garden wire and bend it into a loop. Position the loop at the top of the heart with the end of the wire under the edge of the mould and bent up inside it.

3 Place the mould on the sheet of cardboard to protect your work surface, and half fill it with the tile cement. Smooth the surface of the cement, using your fingers.

Tools and Materials

- heart-shaped biscuit (cookie) cutter
- petroleum jelly
- rubber gloves (optional)
- green garden wire
- scissors
- thick cardboard
- ready-mixed tile cement
- weathered pieces of glass

4 Press the pieces of glass on to the surface of the cement. Leave the mosaic to dry for at least 24 hours.

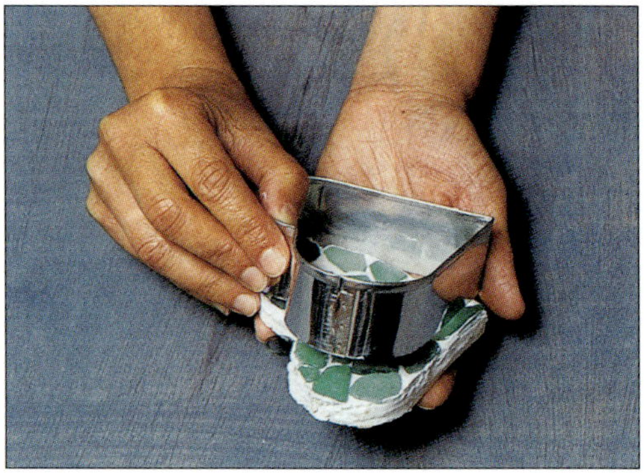

5 When the cement feels solid to the touch, gently remove the mosaic from the mould. Leave the mosaic to dry completely before taking it outside.

HEARTS IN THE GARDEN

Hearts hold universal appeal, and there is no reason why they shouldn't find a home in the garden. You will be surprised by what you can make from the most rudimentary weather-proof materials. Garden wire, chicken wire, twigs and raffia are all ideal. The beauty of the heart shape is that it is very easy to achieve. Just start with a circle of wire and bend it into a dip at one side and a point at the other. Twigs can be coaxed into curves to make the two halves of a heart, then bound together at the top and bottom.

■ ABOVE
A simple chicken wire heart decorated and suspended with paper string makes a pretty decoration for a shed door or the bare side of a wall in a sheltered spot.

■ ABOVE
This heart-shaped wreath carries a seasonal message. The twig framework is wound with variegated ivy and red berries, with a Christmas rose to finish.

■ ABOVE
A heart made from garden wire is knotted all around with sturdy bundles of natural raffia dyed green and ochre.

■ LEFT
Few things can be more romantic than a lavender heart. Make this with fresh lavender bound on to a wire frame, then let it dry naturally.

Wire Heart

This delightful filigree heart is not difficult to make from ordinary garden wire, and it is certainly robust enough to withstand a winter outside. It is composed of small hearts bent into shape with pliers, then wired together in a beautiful overall design. Make one to hang in a tree, or make several in different sizes, so that they take on a sculptural quality. This one, flanked on all sides by neatly trimmed trees, is given throne-like importance.

Tools and Materials

- wire cutters
- medium-gauge garden wire
- pliers
- florist's or fuse wire
- raffia for hanging

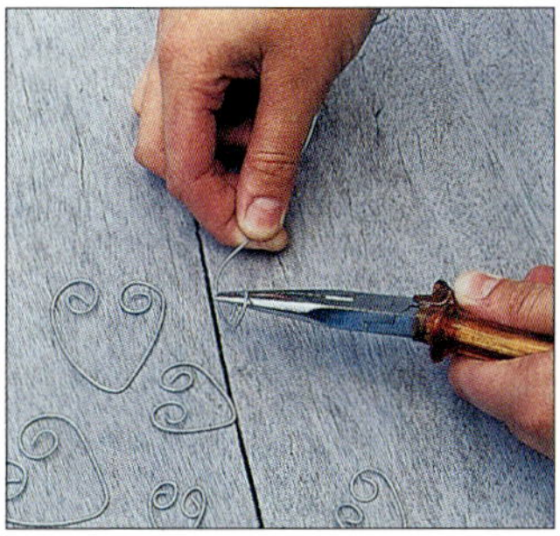

1 Make several small heart shapes in various sizes by cutting short pieces of wire, bending them in half and curling the ends with pliers.

2 To make the large heart shape, cut a length of wire, bend it in half for the bottom of the heart and make a loop in each end. Cut a shorter length and form a loop at each end for the top. Link the looped ends to complete the outline. Lay the small hearts inside the frame as you make them, until they fill the shape.

■ BELOW
This fanciful little heart makes an unexpected garden detail – all the prettier because it is a surprise that so delicate a decoration should be made with ordinary garden wire.

3 Using florist's or fuse wire, bind the small hearts to the large heart and to each other where they touch, until the whole ensemble is stable. Make a hanger from raffia.

House Number Plaque

A mosaic number plaque will add a distinctive touch to your front entrance, hanging beside the door frame, or fixed to the garden gate. The tesserae for this design are cut from brightly coloured ceramic tiles, with fragments of mirror to enliven the background. As this mosaic is going to have to face all weathers, it's a good idea to paint the grouted areas with a transparent water sealant, but if you do this, clean any sealant from the surface of the tiles before it dries.

Tools and Materials

- 1cm/½in chipboard
- jigsaw
- pencil
- tape measure
- marker pen
- PVA (white) glue
- paintbrushes
- tile nippers
- selection of old china
- mirror fragments
- waterproof tile adhesive
- flexible (putty) knife
- damp cloth
- black weatherproof tile grout
- sponge
- exterior paint
- clip, for hanging
- soft cloth
- clear glass cleaner

1 Cut a piece of chipboard to size for the plaque. Draw the house number on the board, making each stroke at least 1.5cm/⅝in wide. Mark the positions for the mirror pieces.

2 Paint the chipboard all over, including the edges, with a coat of diluted PVA (white) glue. Leave to dry thoroughly.

3 Cut the china and mirror into small pieces using tile nippers. Tile the number first, sticking on the pieces using waterproof tile adhesive. Fill in the background, cutting and applying small pieces of mirror, randomly spaced. Wipe off any excess adhesive with a damp cloth and leave the plaque to dry for 24 hours.

4 Cover the surface with black weatherproof tile grout, making sure all the gaps are filled. Spread the grout along the edges of the plaque, and let dry for 10 minutes. Wipe off excess grout with a sponge and leave to dry for 24 hours. Paint the back of the plaque with exterior paint and fix a clip for hanging. Polish the surface of the mosaic with a soft cloth and clear glass cleaner.

■ OPPOSITE
Mosaic is hard-wearing and weatherproof. Use strongly contrasting colours for the number so that it can be read from a distance.

ENJOYING YOUR GARDEN ROOM

To get the most pleasure from your garden, you need to make it a comfortable space to live in. The place where you want to spend your leisure time should be somewhere that combines all the best aspects of your garden: it will be well secluded, yet will have plenty to look at, perhaps with fragrant plants and a water feature.

Once you have created the perfect spot you will want to share it with others from time to time. Outdoor parties can be great fun, whether the event is a simple lunch, a birthday tea or a romantic dinner for two. Lighting will help to create atmosphere, and offers lots of choices, from magical fairy lights to scented oil lamps or insect-repellent candles.

Theme your party table by decking it out in dusky ocean blues or vivid Mediterranean colours. As a final flourish, make an arrangement of sweet-smelling flowers or decorative garden produce for that just-right table centrepiece.

■ ABOVE
Once you have decorated your outdoor space, it's just a question of lighting the lamps and living in it. Warm summer evenings have never been so enjoyable.

■ OPPOSITE
The charm of a beautifully thought-out garden room is hard to resist.

Creating a Comfortable Space

If you set up a comfortable living area in the garden, you are much more likely to use it. With table and chairs standing ready, it is so much easier to bring the coffee and rolls out for breakfast al fresco. When an area is set aside for the children to play in, they will much more readily spend time outside. The priority is to earmark a sheltered living area with a cosy, room-like feel. If it is not next to the house, it will need to be screened by hedges or trellis to lend a sense of intimacy. You don't need a large space – just think how cramped some restaurants can be, yet once seated you feel comfortable.

■ OPPOSITE
Instead of lighting the table with candles for dinner on summer evenings, you could use oil lamps instead, scenting the lamp oil with a few drops of lavender essential oil to create a romantic and aromatic atmosphere.

Once the living area is established, try to incorporate something that stimulates each of the senses. Place a handsome specimen plant within view of the seating area or position the chairs to look on to a pleasant vista. Nature will offer plenty to please your ear: summer birdsong, the hum of bees and the whisper of trees and shrubs gently stirred by a breeze can be enhanced by the music of wind chimes, and a water feature can offer the relaxing sound of trickling water.

For fragrance, site plants with richly perfumed blooms near the seating area. Old-fashioned roses and honeysuckle are hard to beat, or try aromatic lavender and rosemary. Many flowers exude most scent at night: summer jasmine and tobacco plants (nicotiana) are two favourites. For touch, you can plant a contrast of textures, from feathery love-in-a-mist and ferns to luxuriant succulents. Finally, taste can be stimulated by nearby aromatic herbs or fragrant fruits such as strawberries and blackberries.

■ ABOVE
Lunch taken outside in the summer can be a memorable occasion. Attractive garden furniture and a pretty wild flower arrangement create a restful ambience, while fresh fruits and salads look wonderful set out on colourful china.

■ ABOVE
Throw a blue-checked cloth over the garden table, add some seasonal potted plants, and you have the perfect setting for drinks outside on a sunny day, even in early spring.

Animal Friends

Even in the densest urban areas, the outdoors is not devoid of wildlife. Countless wild creatures consider our gardens to be their home. Many of them we very much welcome, and we delight in watching their activities. And wild creatures can often be very useful as they help to maintain the ecological balance, eating unwanted guests such as greenfly and other pests.

Most wild garden visitors like to be self-catering and will not hesitate to organize their own homes, though with a little encouragement, such as the provision of a shallow dish of fresh water, they will appreciatively settle on your plot. Some plants attract beneficial insects such as butterflies and bees. The most obvious ones are the more highly scented species such as buddleia (known for this reason as the butterfly bush), lavender and honeysuckle. Birds can be encouraged by birdtables in the winter and birdbaths in the summer. Toads, which are consummate devourers of flies, like to set up house in cool, damp places – in flower pots laid on their sides in a leafy, damp private place, perhaps, or under a pile of stones. Once in residence, they usually stay and will make themselves useful, gradually working their way through the insect population almost as fast as it grows.

■ ABOVE
Butterflies can be attracted into the garden by planting their favourite nectar-rich flowering plants, such as buddleia and this exquisite pink autumn-flowering sedum.

■ LEFT
A birdbath is not only essential for garden birds, but can also become a piece of sculpture. This mosaic bowl nestles in a bed of marigolds and wallflowers.

■ ABOVE
A simply-made bird-feeding table will help encourage birds to visit.

■ RIGHT
Stir nuts and seeds into lard and mould the mixture into balls on lengths of string to provide a winter treat for the birds in your garden.

■ BELOW
String a selection of nuts on to a length of twine and hang it in an area of the garden, where you will be able to watch who is feeding and when.

LIGHTING EFFECTS

Enjoying the garden after nightfall is dependent on garden lighting, and in most domestic gardens, that is sadly lacking. If you are having your garden landscaped, you might like to consider having electricity cables laid and bringing in an expert to work out a plan. This would usually include general lighting, plus perhaps some spotlighting for focal points such as a favourite piece of statuary. But even if you don't want to go to that expense, there is a lot you can do.

■ OPPOSITE
Garden lighting adds its own special atmosphere – whether the event is an elaborate outdoor party or an evening of quiet seclusion.

Outdoor lighting will not achieve the same level of illumination as indoors, although this is rarely a problem: part of the appeal of being outside at night is the moody, shadowy lighting and being able to appreciate the moon and stars.

The easiest solution for general outdoor lighting is to fix a powerful halogen light to the outside of the house. Since the living areas of the garden are usually near the house, this should be ample. Another easy idea is to have an electrician fit an all-weather socket to the outside of the house. It is always useful to have access to electricity outdoors, but particularly if you wish to plug in both light and sound for fabulous evening entertainment. For special occasions you may like to hire all-weather strings of lights to hang in the trees. Plain white bulbs are particularly effective.

As well as the practical effects, such as showing changes of level or the edges of path, lighting also allows the best features of the garden to be highlighted while leaving others hidden, and brings the garden to life in a different and very special way.

■ ABOVE
This well-placed spotlight illuminates the textured edging of the stone urn, and makes a beautiful nightime display of the white petunias and lavandula 'Hidcote Pink'.

■ ABOVE
A lantern can be suspended from the same bracket as a hanging basket, where its soft light will enhance the flowers magically after sunset.

Candle Power

Candles must surely be the most romantic outdoor lighting. The light they cast is natural and flattering, holding the same fascination as any flame in the darkness, evoking ancient campfires and casting a magic circle of protective light around the table. They are also very practical for use in the garden as, unlike electric light, they are completely portable.

The ordinary candles you use on the dining table can simply be taken outside, candelabra and all, for a candle-lit dinner. If the night is at all breezy, use lanterns or some other holders which will protect the flames from the elements. Choose lanterns that will take substantially sized candles, otherwise you will be forever jumping up and down to light replacements. Also, check that the metalwork is robust, as some imported aluminium lanterns simply collapse once a candle flame melts the solder holding them together.

As well as lanterns, you could try Victorian night-lights, tumbler-like glass containers that hang on wires, huge glass hanging lanterns and candles in garden pots or galvanized buckets which – once they burn down below the rim – are protected from the wind. Candles that are specially designed to cope with the elements are garden flares, which produce a huge flame and can burn for up to three hours. The light they emit is surprisingly bright, which makes them ideal for general lighting or for lighting pathways.

You need to bear in mind when using outdoor candles and flares that the wind does blow the flame, so it is always important to position them well away from any foliage or furniture.

■ ABOVE
Lanterns provide perfect candle-light for the garden, as they protect the flame from the wind.

■ ABOVE
Garden flares produce a considerable amount of light. Many are also scented to help discourage insects.

■ RIGHT
Victorian night-lights hung on wires create a romantic glow in the trees.

■ ABOVE
This candle display cleverly emphasizes the beauty of garden paraphernalia: candles in vegetable shapes share the shelves with terracotta pots.

■ ABOVE
Adding candles needn't make for a fussy display. This simple supper table is casually dotted with groups of candles in soft pastel shades, complementing the colours of both the tableware and the potted plants, and pulling the different elements together to make a very natural-looking arrangement.

■ RIGHT
A large glass hanging lantern makes enchanting lighting for a special evening in the garden. Lotus-like flower candles float in water above a bed of shells in the glass lantern, looking like an exotic lily pond. Burning scented candles or fragranced essential oils would add to the effect.

Gilded Pots

Ordinary terracotta pots, gilded and filled with candle wax, make beautiful, sparkling garden lights. Use pots in a range of sizes and group them on tables, patios, walls and outdoor shelves for a magical effect in the soft evening light.

■ OPPOSITE
Fabulous golden pots glitter in the candle flames for a simple supper or an evening party in the garden.

Tools and Materials

- assorted terracotta pots
- self-hardening clay
- red oxide primer
- paintbrushes
- water-based gold size
- Dutch metal leaf in gold
- soft cloth or soft-bristled brush
- amber shellac
- artist's acrylic paint in white and aqua
- scissors
- wick
- wooden skewers
- candle wax
- double boiler

1 Plug the drainage hole of each pot with a little clay and leave to set. Prime the pots with red oxide primer and leave for 3–4 hours to dry

2 Apply a coat of water-based gold size and allow to dry for about 30 minutes, or until the size is transparent and tacky.

3 To apply the Dutch metal leaf, lift the sheets carefully and lay them on the size, gently smoothing each one with a cloth or soft-bristled brush. Brush off any excess leaf and polish gently with a soft cloth.

4 Apply a coat of amber shellac to seal the metal leaf and leave for at least 30 minutes until completely dry.

5 To age the pots, tint a little white acrylic with aqua and thin with water. Brush on the paint and rub off with a cloth. Leave to dry. Suspend a length of wick in each pot by tying it to a skewer laid across the top and check that it reaches the bottom. Melt the wax in a double boiler and pour it into the pot. Leave to set overnight.

Citronella Candles

The pleasure of a summer evening in the garden, sitting around the table for a relaxing al fresco meal, can be quickly ruined by the presence of biting insects intent on their own feast. Candles scented with essential oils that have insect-repellent properties will serve a dual purpose: providing soft light and seeing off the enemy. Citronella oil is most commonly used as an insect repellent and is agreed to be the most effective, but if you dislike the scent you could use lavender, peppermint or a mixture of geranium and eucalyptus instead. On evenings when insects are particularly troublesome, add a few drops of the oil to an oil burner near the table, to encourage the insects to leave before you sit down to eat; these candles will then continue to act as a deterrent.

Tools and Materials

- 2 7.5cm/3in terracotta pots
- self-hardening clay
- 175g/6oz paraffin wax
- 50g/2oz natural beeswax
- heatproof bowl
- saucepan of simmering water or double boiler
- wooden spoon
- scissors
- wick
- 2 wooden skewers
- citronella essential oil

1 Plug the hole in the base of each of the terracotta pots with self-hardening clay and leave to set. Melt the paraffin wax and beeswax gently together in a heatproof bowl set over a saucepan of simmering water or in a double boiler over an electric ring or hotplate. Cut two 15cm/6in lengths of wick and dip into the wax. Leave for a several minutes to harden. Return the bowl frequently to the saucepan to prevent the wax from setting.

2 Rest the skewers across the pots. Position each wick to hang centrally in the pot and fold the end of the wick over the skewer. Add the essential oil to the wax and stir well to mix.

3 Pour the wax into the pots to just below the rim, tapping the sides of the pot to release any air bubbles. Reserve the remaining wax. As the candles cool, a dip will form around each wick. Remelt the wax and fill this dip with the remaining wax. Trim the wicks.

■ OPPOSITE
Candles in terracotta pots make pretty lights for evening parties outdoors, and these lemon-scented candles have the added benefit of keeping insects at bay.

IRON LANTERN

Give a new aluminium lantern the more appealing appearance of aged iron. Even the simplest shapes and brashest finishes become infinitely more pleasing when given the well-worn look of a lantern of yore.

TOOLS AND MATERIALS

- masking tape
- metal lantern
- medium-grade sandpaper
- white metal primer
- paintbrushes
- silver paint
- small natural sponge
- emulsion (latex) paint in black
- artist's acrylic paint in red oxide
- water spray
- satin polyurethane varnish
- varnish brush

1 Stick masking tape over all the glass of the lantern. Sand the metal to provide a key. Paint all the metal parts of the lantern with a coat of metal primer. Allow to dry for 2–3 hours, then paint on a silver base coat.

2 Dip the natural sponge into black emulsion (latex) and dab on to the lantern. Allow to dry for 1–2 hours.

3 Mix red oxide acrylic paint with a little water and, using an artist's paintbrush, drip this down the lantern to resemble rust. Spray with a water spray. Allow to dry for 1–2 hours. Varnish, leave to dry, then remove the tape.

■ BELOW

Subtle and darkly interesting, this lantern gains an antique quality once it has been painted.

Glass Jar Night-light

When lit with a small candle, this stained-glass night-light throws patches of coloured light on to the surrounding foliage. One jar is used as the base and another is broken into small fragments that are painted with glass paints. The fragments are then stuck on to the base jar and the gaps grouted. If your jars are not the same size, use the smaller one as the base.

Tools and Materials

- 2 glass jars
- old dish towel
- goggles
- protective gloves
- hammer
- scrap paper
- newspaper
- reusable adhesive
- glass paints
- paintbrushes
- solvent-free, rapid setting epoxy resin glue
- white cellulose filler
- grout spreader
- scourer
- sandpaper
- acrylic paint

1 Wrap a jar in a dish towel. Wearing goggles and gloves, and covering your hair, smash the jar with a hammer. Place the pieces to be used as tesserae on scrap paper with the sharp edges facing downwards to avoid cutting yourself. Wrap the unused glass in newspaper and dispose of it carefully.

2 Use reusable adhesive to pick up the broken pieces of glass and turn them over so that the sharp edges face upwards. Paint the concave surface of each fragment with glass paint in different colours. Leave to dry. Glue the painted fragments to the base jar using solvent-free epoxy resin glue. Leave until completely dry.

3 Spread cellulose filler over the surface, smoothing it into the top and bottom edges of the jar, and wiping off any excess. Let dry. If any cracks appear as it dries, smooth over more filler. When dry, clean off excess filler with a scourer and water, and sandpaper. Paint over the filler with acrylic paint.

■ RIGHT
This delightful lantern gives a subtle glow in the garden at night, looking like a miniature stained-glass window.

ENTERTAINING OUTSIDE

What a joy it is, when all is said and done, to invite friends over and relax together in the garden. It is the wonderful casualness of al fresco eating that is so appealing. The food can be simple: fresh salads, vegetables and fruits, perhaps home-grown. Meat or fish can be grilled or barbecued with fresh herbs, the aroma complementing the scent of the herbs growing in the beds. Add some bread and a couple of bottles of wine and you have all the ingredients necessary for a memorable occasion.

■ RIGHT
Use your own fresh garden herbs in pretty and delicious summer drinks when entertaining in the garden. Freeze snippets of herbs and edible flowers into ice cubes as a finishing touch.

Decorating the outdoor table is wonderfully effortless. All you need for a stunning evening party is a table centrepiece of fresh seasonal flowers or potted plants from the garden, and a collection of candles to softly light the scene.

■ RIGHT
Teatime, when the heat of the day is subsiding, is a wonderful time to get together in the garden, even if it's just for a cup of tea and a chat.

■ BELOW
With the gentle sounds of the garden and the heady perfume of flowers in the hot afternoon sun, an informal gathering will become a memorable occasion.

Decorating Tables with a Theme

Out in the garden as well as indoors, a thoughtfully decorated table will charm your guests, stimulating conversation and appetite, and making your dinner party a visual as well as an edible feast. Let your surroundings dictate the styling of your table: in place of crisp white damask and silver, let the colour and naturalness of the garden setting spill on to the table, with simple pots of flowers picked from the borders, organic materials like wood, raffia and shells, and rustic dishes in earthy browns and creams, or bright sunny glazes.

■ ABOVE
Blue and white are classic colours for china, reminiscent of old Chinese designs and traditional English patterns. Blues on blues make a wonderful mix, looking especially beautiful under the blue sky of a summer's day. You can keep to lavender blues, lean towards greener denim blues or mix them all together: blend at least three shades to achieve a pleasing overall effect. White and blue look fresh and clean together, and this combination is readily available in both table linen and china. Dried lavender is the ideal material for an everlasting table decoration in this setting, or make a simple arrangement of newly-picked fresh flowers in white.

■ ABOVE

The neutral tones and beguiling forms found on the beach provide wonderful inspiration for table decorations. The silvery greys and soft beiges of pebbles, driftwood and old galvanized metal, teamed with the coral pinks of shells and sea-washed terracotta, create a winning combination. Simplicity is the key: a bowl of mussel shells set beside a jar of wild flowers are enough to suggest the subtle tones of a seashore table setting. Even a naturally-sculptured piece of driftwood by itself would make a wonderfully elegant centrepiece.

■ BELOW
Evoking hot summer days in Greece, Portugal or Provence, this sun-filled Mediterranean style is simple, rustic and colourful. The typical palette is chalky blue and turquoise set against sun-baked terracotta and white. Paint is a favourite medium in the Mediterranean, and everything is given a lick of colour: woodwork, furniture, tableware; even old cans can be turned into decorative containers. Here, old plates and bowls have been painted and decorated with simple but striking designs and napkins boldly embroidered. Vibrantly coloured flowers add the finishing touch before the guests are seated, the wine starts to flow and the hors d'oevres arrive.

■ RIGHT
Much of the joy of entertaining outdoors is the impromptu feel of the occasion: you can make a beautiful table by simply gathering together whatever is in season and allowing that to govern your colour scheme. Marigolds, iris leaves and tree ivy were the starting point for this elaborate setting.

■ RIGHT
Arranging a table on a theme is very easily achieved: decide the theme, then gather together crockery and table linen which will tie in with your chosen style. The synchronization of colours alone can be enough to suggest a harmonious arrangement.

Table Decorations

Outdoor table centres are the very easiest to put together because they are at their most successful when they complement their surroundings. So plunder the garden and then combine the ingredients with flair. You may cut a few flowers, add foliage or even fruit and vegetables; or you may simply gather together some of the smaller plants in pots from around the garden. The concentration on a table of what grows in naturally looser arrangements throughout the garden serves to focus the overall look.

■ **ABOVE**
Ivy plants in sundae-glass shaped galvanized containers, accessorized with a couple of canes pastel-painted to look like straws, make a witty cocktail table centrepiece.

■ **LEFT**
In summer, potted strawberry plants are easily transformed when they are held in a wire container and accessorized with a few ripe fruits.

■ **RIGHT**
In a wire basket woven with natural raffia, pots of verbena are gathered together and surrounded with tiny pots of variegated ivy. The resulting arrangement is casually beautiful, perfectly in accord with its setting.

■ **BELOW**
Ornamental cabbages make an unusual table centrepiece, very appropriate to the garden table. The cabbages are complemented by individual leaves decorating the napkins.

■ LEFT
The sun-drenched colours of the Mediterranean pervade this vibrant dried flower arrangement in a raffia-tied terracotta pot, perfectly partnered by a vivid Provençal cotton tablecloth.

■ ABOVE
Decorate the table with a romantic herbal dish, which you can fill with strawberries or other soft fruits. Simply set a bowl in the centre of a florist's foam ring lavishly filled with flowers and herbs. Enchanting daisy-like chamomile flowers have been set in an aromatic base of rosemary and oregano to make an arrangement reminiscent of a summer meadow.

■ LEFT
The ruffled charm of this sage arrangement makes a deliciously aromatic, softly coloured table centre, co-ordinated with rosemary napkin ties.

■ RIGHT
Wild-looking flowers make the prettiest table garlands for summer celebration meals. Garlands do use a lot of material, so if you don't have enough suitable flowers in the garden, look in the florist's for cultivated versions of those that grow wild. This garland is a combination of frothy white dill, green bupleurum and purple knapweed.

■ ABOVE
This herbal ring of mint, flat-leaf parsley and fennel flowers makes a sophisticated green frame for summer fruit, but if you prefer something a little more showy you could add some daisy flowers, such as feverfew, which would look charming.

■ RIGHT
This simple herbal tussie mussie is made from chive flowers, rosemary and comfrey, but the idea could be adapted so that any seasonal flowers can be used. The sweet-smelling herbs will scent the table throughout the meal.

STAY-PUT TABLECLOTH

Tablecloths on the garden table look pretty and fresh, but can quickly act like a sail if the slightest breeze starts up. Lunch ceases to be fun when the corner of the cloth is whipped up on to the table, dropping into the beetroot salad or knocking over a couple of glasses of wine. A weighted cloth is the solution to this inevitable problem of outdoor eating. Just slip some circular metal curtain weights into the corners of the cloth: they will keep it firmly in place, and can be quickly removed before laundering the tablecloth.

TOOLS AND MATERIALS

- 2m/2yds fabric, 1.5m/1½yds wide
- scissors
- iron
- tape measure
- sewing machine
- matching sewing thread
- 15cm/6in heavy-duty self-adhesive Velcro
- 4 circular metal curtain weights
- satin polyurethane varnish

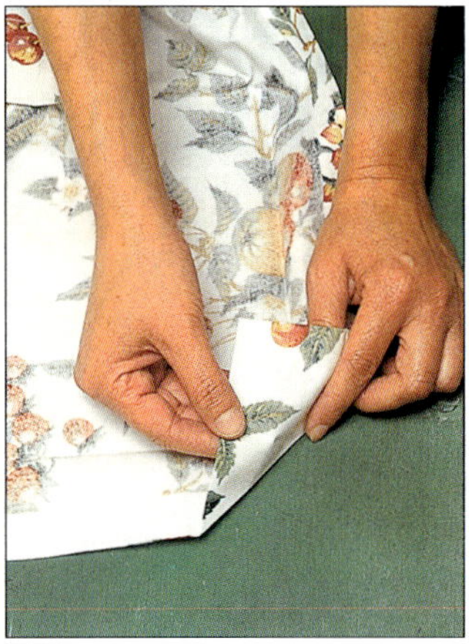

1 Fold the fabric diagonally across itself to make a right-angled triangle. Cut across the width, along the edge of the triangle, to make a square. (Make napkins from any extra fabric.)

2 Open out the fabric and fold in and press a 2.5cm/1in hem along all four edges. Fold in the corners of the cloth to make triangles 8cm/3¼in high, and press in place.

3 Fold over a 6cm/2½in around all edges and press to form a mitre at each corner. Stitch all around the cloth 5mm/¼in from the edge and again 5mm/¼in inside the edge of the hem.

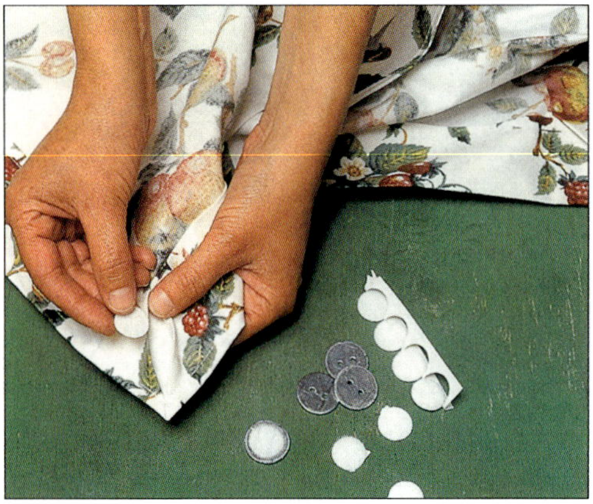

4 Remove the backing paper from a piece of Velcro, insert into one of the corner folds and stick in place. Attach the opposite piece of Velcro to one of the curtain weights. Repeat in the other three corners. When you are using the cloth, slip the weights into position and the Velcro will hold them in place.

■ OPPOSITE A weighted tablecloth can make all the difference to the success of a meal eaten outdoors.

Organdie Cloth

The lightness of exquisitely detailed guinea fowl feathers perfectly complements the delicate fabric of this tablecloth and, tucked into little tulle pockets, they are easy to remove for washing. Buy plenty of feathers as you need to be able to select at least 24 of a similar size. Bunches of extra feathers, secured by organdie ties, make charming details at the corners.

■ RIGHT
Delightful spotted guinea fowl feathers lend natural detail to a delicate organdie tablecloth, which would be perfect to set on the table for afternoon tea.

Tools and Materials

- 110 x 120cm/43in x 4ft white cotton organdie
- scissors
- needle
- white sewing thread
- 100 x 10cm/39 x 4in white tulle
- pins
- white stranded embroidery thread
- 24 guinea fowl feathers

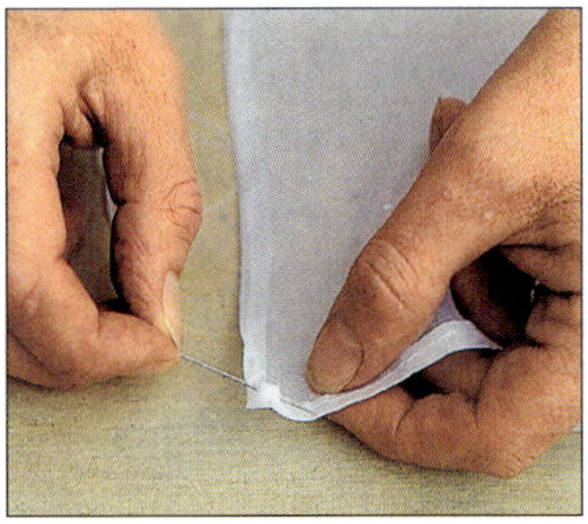

1 Trim the organdie to make a 110cm/43in square. Turn in and stitch a double hem around all four sides. Cut the tulle into 12 rectangles about 7.5 x 5cm/3 x 2in.

2 Pin the pockets on to the cloth: arrange four in a diagonal line from corner to corner, and a parallel row of three on either side, and one near the remaining corners. Stitch each pocket around three sides, leaving one short side open.

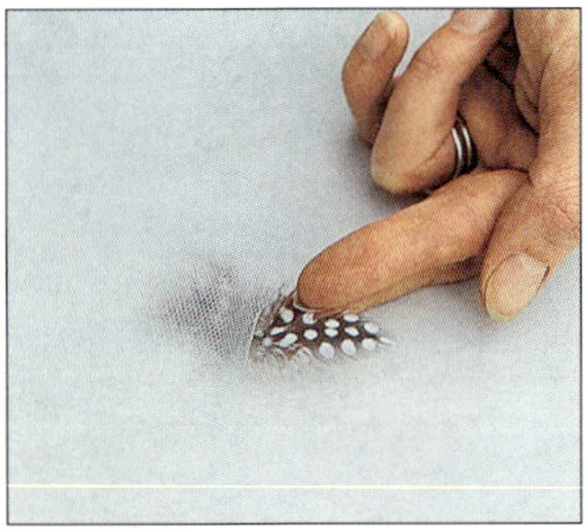

3 Select 12 similar-sized guinea fowl feathers, and slip one into each pocket, quill end first. For each corner of the tablecloth, cut a strip of organdie about 22 x 2.5cm/8¾ x 1in.

4 Fold the organdie strips in half lengthways, turn in the sides and ends and slipstitch all around to make a tie. Make a bunch of three feathers and stitch them to the middle of the tie. Tie the organdie in a knot around the feathers. Stitch (or tie, if you want to remove the feathers for washing) each feather trim to the tablecloth corners.

Cushions

You have arranged your favourite garden chair in the perfect place, or slung your hammock between two trees. You have a good book, a convenient table for your coffee and sunglasses. There is just one thing missing from this garden idyll: a blissful abundance of cushions, for your head, your back and your feet, so that you can drift away in perfect relaxation.

You could, of course, just pick up a cushion from inside the house and take it with you whenever you sit out, but it really is much nicer to have a separate collection of cushions for outdoor use only.

Even with the best intentions in the world, whatever you take outside will make contact with grass cuttings and fallen leaves, and these will conspire to limit the relaxation you are looking for.

■ ABOVE
The luscious corded and cutwork embroidered cushions lining this hammock make it irresistibly alluring.

■ ABOVE
A small linen cushion with a filling of dried lavender exudes its fabulous fragrance when warmed by the sun.

■ LEFT
Rest a weary head on a relaxing mixture of chamomile and lavender. Sewn inside the stuffing of a gingham cushion, the dried herbs will calm you down at the end of a hectic day.

■ RIGHT
Hang small cushions filled with herbs over the back of a chair to bestow a delicious waft of scent when you sit down.

■ RIGHT
Hops are too pretty to hide, so if you want to take advantage of the relaxing qualities of their scent, use them to fill a cushion of fine muslin or gauze trimmed with lace rosettes.

Twiggy Tray

A tray of twigs is very easy to make and surprisingly robust – all for the cost of a few strands of raffia. This tray is made from young willow shoots, but any twigs will do as long as they're fairly straight and of a similar thickness. The end result is a tray that is wonderfully organic – perfect for outdoor apéritif drinks or a light lunch.

Tools and Materials

raffia

about 60 young willow (or similar) shoots, 45cm/18in long

secateurs (pruners)

1 For the base of the tray, fold one strand of raffia in half and place the end of one willow stick in the loop. Now bring the lower piece of raffia up and the upper piece down, enclosing the stick, and place the next stick between the two lengths of raffia.

2 Bring the lower piece up and the upper piece down again to enclose the next stick, and position the third stick. You will find that you soon develop a twisting rhythm. Continue until you have woven in 44 sticks. Weave in three more lines of raffia about 9cm/3½in apart down the length of the sticks and one near the other end, to create a firm, flat mat for the base.

3 Cut eight sticks to fit the short sides of the tray base. Make the first side of the tray by laying down four full-length sticks at right angles to four of the shorter sticks. Tie the middle of a strand of raffia around one of the long sticks. Place one of the short sticks at right angles on top of this and tie that in. Continue until all eight sticks are used up, then tie firmly to secure.

4 Create the other three corners in the same way until you have made up a rectangular frame that will become the sides of the tray.

5 Place the frame over the base. Feed the raffia into the side of the base at the end of one of the lines of weaving. As before, work the two ends of raffia up the side and down again, tying them together at the bottom. Repeat wherever the frame meets the ends of the woven raffia on the base, and at two equally spaced intervals along the short sides.

6 To attach the short sides, fold a piece of raffia in half and feed one end from underneath the base between two sticks, over the lowest frame stick and back between the sticks to meet the other end of the raffia. Tie underneath. Then bring one end up between the next two sticks, over the bottom frame stick, and down again. Tie the two ends together again tightly. Continue in this way until the width of the frame is tied to the base at one end. Repeat at the other end to complete the tray.

■ ABOVE
Choose straight, even-sized young shoots for a neat result.

■ RIGHT
In an outdoor setting, an organic tray blends with the garden, and looks particularly charming.

Decorative Gardener's Accessories

In the decorative garden, there's no reason why the tools and other accoutrements used by the gardener should not be just as beautiful to look at as everything else. Gardening is always a pleasure, but it can be enhanced even further if the equipment you use has its own visual appeal. Good, well-looked-after garden tools, with handles polished with use and age, have a beauty and integrity of their own. Decorative details will beautify the rest of your gardening paraphernalia too, so that you really enjoy every task in the garden.

■ ABOVE
Decorate a ready-made apron with flower pot pockets and brass rings, to hold all your gardening essentials.

■ ABOVE
If you have fruit to pick, make the job a real pleasure by gathering it in an elegant slatted basket. This one is stencilled with images of apples and pears and given an aged look with a coat of tinted varnish.

■ ABOVE
Find your boots easily among the pile at the back door by personalizing them with charming painted designs. Just use enamel paints and take your inspiration from the garden.

■ ABOVE
You could paint an alternative design on the other boot.

■ ABOVE
Hand tools with plain handles are easy to lose sight of in the summer border. Bright yellow paint and eye-catching insect stickers sealed with varnish make them hard to miss.

■ ABOVE
Small hand tools like trowels and forks are needed daily in the garden, so choose shapes that are comfortable to hold and a pleasure to use.

■ ABOVE
The traditional trug is a piece of garden equipment that has endured for many years and is still appreciated for its practicality, durability and fine design. Woodstains will not spoil its elegance, but they can give it individuality and provide a colour accent in the garden.

■ ABOVE
The potting shed tends to attract lots of bits and pieces, and this pretty rack will help to take care of them. Make a simple frame from lengths of garden wire and wrap a piece of chicken wire around it, binding it firmly to the frame with wire.

■ LEFT
Small storage drawers are handy for keeping fiddly accessories such as plant labels and rings. Label each drawer with an example of its contents so that you know exactly where they are.

■ ABOVE
Hessian bags are useful for storing bulbs that you have lifted after flowering, as they allow the bulbs to breathe. A picture of the contents, cut from the original bulb packaging, makes the bags look good in the potting shed.

■ ABOVE
If you collect your own seeds, store them prettily in home-made paper seed packets decorated with colour photocopies of your own photographs of the flowers. This is a lovely way to give surplus seed to fellow gardeners. Write details of the plant and instructions for cultivation on the back of the packet.

■ LEFT
A wooden box with a well-fitting lid is ideal for storing half-used packets of seeds that will still be viable next season. Decoupage, using old engravings of fruit and vegetables, makes an attractive and appropriate decoration for the lid.

SUPPLIERS

UNITED KINGDOM

Avant Garden
77 Ledbury Road
London W11 2AG
Tel: (0171) 229 4408
Wirework topiary frames, candle holders, wall sconces, candle baskets, terracotta pots

Brett Specialized Aggregates
Fordwich Road
Sturry
Kent CT2 0BW
Tel: (01227) 712 876
Paving supplies

Clifton Little Venice
3 Warwick Place
London W9 2PS
Tel: (0171) 289 7894
Wirework and ironwork, topiary shapes, jardinieres and wall masks

Drummonds of Bramley
Horsham Road
Bramley
Guildford
Surrey GU5 0LA
Tel: (01483) 898 766
Architectural salvage

Finnigans Hammerite
Hunting Specialized Products
Prudhoe
Northumberland
NE42 6LP
Tel: (01661) 830 000
Specialized single-coat metal paint, both spray-on and brush-on

Indian Ocean Trading Company
155–163 Balham Hill
London SW12
Tel: (0181) 675 4808
Wooden furniture and benches, deck-chairs, steamers and garden umbrellas

Keim Mineral Paints Ltd.
Muckley Cross
Morville
Nr Bridgnorth
Shropshire WV16 4RR
Tel: (01746) 714 543

Marshalls Mono
Southowram
Halifax
HX3 9SY
Tel: (01422) 366666
Natural clay pavings and concrete block paving

Paint Magic (Jocasta Innes)
79 Shepperton Road
London N1 3DF
Tel: (0171) 354 9696
Decorative paint finishes that can be teamed with varnish for light outdoor use

Rusco Marketing
Little Faringdon Mill
Lechlade
Gloucester GL7 3QQ
Tel: (01367) 252 754
Wooden and metal garden furniture, umbrellas and hammocks

UNITED STATES

Exterior masonry paints, gloss paints, stains, varnishes, as well as concrete, granite and concrete stone pavings can be found in general hardware stores and home-improvement centres.

Alsto's Handy Helpers
P.O. Box 1267
Galesburg
IL 661401
Tel: (800) 447 0048
Cedar patio furniture and swings, metal lawn chairs, gliders

Ballard Designs
1670 DeFoor Avenue NW
Atlanta
GA
30318 7528
Tel: (404) 351 5099
Cast architectural ornaments, metal and glass chairs, benches and tables

Bamboo Fencer
31 Germania Street
Jamaica Plain
MA
02130
Tel: (800) 775 8641
Bamboo fencing

Bufftech
2525 Walden Avenue
Buffalo
NY 14225
Tel: (800) 333 0579
Vinyl fencing

Crescent Bronze Powder Company
3400 N. Avondale Avenue
Chicago
IL 60618
Tel: (312) 529 2441
Metallic pigment paints and lacquer

Discount Pond Supplies
P.O. Box 423371H
Kissimmee
FL 34742-3371
Fax (407) 932 4019
Water garden supplies

Gardener's Eden
100 North Point Street
San Francisco
CA
94133
Tel: (800) 822 9600
Garden ornaments, metal, twig and wicker garden furniture

Hens & Feathers & Company
10 Balligomingo Road
Gulph Mills
PA 19428
Tel: (800) 282 1910
Urns, planters, fountains and statuary made from banded marble resin in hand-finished patinas

CANADA

Avant Gardener
2235 West 4th Avenue
Vancouver
BC V6K 1N9
Tel: (604) 736 0404

Creative Wood Products
88 Shoemaker Street
Unit 1
Kitchener
Ontario
N2E G4
Quality Cedar furniture

Cruikshanks Mail Order
Tel: 1 800 665 5605
Gardening supplies and accessories

Mason's Masonry Supply
6291 Netherhart Road
Mississauga
Ontario L5T 1A2
Paving Supplies

AUSTRALIA

Amber Tiles
Tel: 132 241 for NSW stores
Tiles, slate, pavers, terracotta

Chris Cross
1575 Burke Road
Kew
Vic 3103
Tel: (03) 859 2666
Unusual landscape material

Cotswold Garden Furniture Pty Ltd.
42 Hotham Parade
Artarmon
NSW 2064
Tel: (02) 9906 3686
Imported teak furniture

Elegant World Pty Ltd.
73-75 Market Street
Condell Park
NSW 2200
Tel: (02) 708 5079
Pots, planters, fountains, birdbaths, statues, columns, balustrading, steps, paving, architectural monuments

The Lattice Factory
121 Church Street, Ryde
NSW 2112
Tel: (02) 809 7665
Pergolas, fences, planter boxes - all made to measure

Whitehouse Gardens
388 Springvale Road
Forest Hill
Vic 3131
Tel: (03) 877 1430
Statues, ponds, birdbaths, pots

INDEX

Acknowledgments

The author and publisher are grateful to acknowledge the work of Robert Crawford Clarke, who has kindly extrapolated the plans for the gardens. These plans do not necessarily reflect the original designer's plan. Where known, the garden designers have been acknowledged below.

t = top, b = bottom, l = left, r = right, m = middle

A-Z Botanical Collection Ltd: p69tr Sylvia O'Toole; p79tl Mike Vardy; p149t; p178 James Braidwood; p179t Adrian Thomas (design by Wendy Bundy); p233t A. Stenning; p245t Adrian Thomas.
Pat Brindley: p38t; p55t; p121; p179b.
Jonathan Buckley: p13 (photographed at The Priest House, West Hoathly, England); p85t; p118; p33b; p146; p174; p217; p232; p271; p284bl; p310t; b, p311, p326, p329.
John Freeman p405t, b,429

The Garden Picture Library: p12 Gil Hanly (Ethidge Gardens, Timaru, Canterbury, New Zealand, Nan and Wynne Raymond; p23 Gil Hanly (Penny Zino Garden, Flaxmere, Hawarden, New Zealand); p34 Henk Dijkman; p36 J. S. Sira; p37t Ron Sutherland (Michelle Osborne Design); p37b Ron Sutherland (Smyth Garden, Jersey, Anthony Paul Design); p38b Ron Sutherland (Paul Bangay Design); p39t Ron Sutherland (Chelsea Flower Show, London, Hiroshi Nanamori Design); p43b Jerry Pavia;); p43m David Askham; p43bl Steven Wooster (Sticky Wicket, Dorset; p49 Ron Sutherland (Murray Collis Design, Australia); p51t J. S. Sira; p51t, l Ron Sutherland (Paul Bangay Design); p59l Ron Sutherland (Anthony Paul Design); p62 J. S. Sira (Chelsea Flower Show, London); p63Brigitte Thomas; p64t Jerry Pavia; p64b Ron Sutherland; p61 Henk Dijkman; p66 Steven Wooster; p67t Marijke Heuff; p67b Ron Sutherland (John Zerning Balcony); p68bl Friedrich Strauss; p72b Ron Sutherland (Anthony Paul Design); p77tl Ron Sutherland (Eco Design, Melbourne, Australia); p81t Ron Sutherland (Anthony Paul Design); p81t Brigitte Thomas; p90 J. S. Sira (design by Japanse Garden Company, Chelsea Flower Show, London 1991); p92 Ron Sutherland (Paul Flinton Design, Australia); p93t Lamontagne; p93b Alan Mitchell; p94 Ron Sutherland (Anthony Paul Design); p95t Ron Sutherland; p95b Ron Sutherland (Anthony Paul Design); p100b Ron Sutherland (Paul Flemming Design, Australia); p105t Lamontagne; p103t Ron Sutherland; p109l Ron Sutherland (Paul Flemming Design, Australia); p111t Ron Sutherland (Hiroshi Nanamori Design); p113b Ron Sutherland (Anthony Paul Design); p119 Brigitte Thomas (Preen Manor, Shropshire; p200 Ron Sutherland (Anthony Paul Design); p121t John Glover; p122 Ron Sutherland; p123t Ron Sutherland (Anthony Paul Design); p123b Steven Wooster (Duane Paul Design Team, Chelsea Flower Show); p135 Jerry Pavia; p139 Brian Carter (Van Hage Design); p143 Steven Wooster (Mailstone Landscaping); p151b John Neubauer (Solomon Garden, Washington); p156b Steven Wooster (Julie Toll Design, John Chamber's Garden, Chelsea Flower Show, 1990); p157t Mayer/Le Scanff (Jardin de Campagne, France); p167t Steven Wooster (Gordon Collet Design); p176b Ron Sutherland (Paul Flemming Design, Melbourne, Australia); p177 Gil Hanley(Bruce Cornish Garden, Auckland); p191bl John Glover; p199t Marianne Majerus (John Brooks Design, BBC Garden); p202 J. S. Sira (Action for Blind People, Chelsea Flower Show, 1991); p204 Steven Wooster (designer H. Weijers); p205t Marie O'Hara; p207 Brian Carter (design by Geoff and Faith Whitten, Chelsea Flower Show, London 1989); p221 Ron Sutherland (Michael Balston Design); p223b Ron Sutherland (Rick Eckersley Design); p225 Ron Sutherland (Godfrey Amy's Garden, Jersey, Anthony Paul Design); p227t David Askham; p359b; p381tr; p474bl; p475.
Michelle Garrett: p262tr; p292; p319r; p325; p327; p355; p368; p369; p408; p409; p410; p411; p415; p418; p419; p424; p425; p444; p445; p446; p447; p458; p459; p462; p463; p473; p480; p481; p483; p484; p491; p498; p502; p503; p504; p505; p506; p507.
Marie O'Hara: p332b; p340; p341; p390; p403.
Robert Harding Picture Library: p72t Ian Baldwin Pool; p193t James Merrell; p195b BBC Enterprises/Redwood Publishing (design by David Sanford); p197t BBC Enterprises/Redwood Publishing (design by Jean Bishop).
Harry Smith Horticultural Collection: p30; p147; p148.
Houses & Interiors: p169t; p205b.
Tim Imrie: p267; p272; p275; p293; p345; p346; p347; p364; p365 p372; p406; p414; p434; p435; p438; p439; p440; p441; p466; p467.
Andrew Lawson Photographic: p175.
Simon McBride: p265; p320l; p337b; p391tr; p393bl.
Peter McHoy: p13 (David Sanford); p27; p29; p35; p40; p41; p42; p43t; p44; p45; p46; p47; p55bl, br; p57 (design by Kathleen McHoy) p57b; p60; p61; p69tr, bl; p70; p71; p72t; p73b; p.74; p75; p75; p87t; p88tr; p88br; p89; p91; p96; p97; p98; p99; p100t; p.101; p102; p103; p111b; p115; p116; p117l, mb, r; p124; p125; p126; p127; p128; p129; p130; p130b (design by Alpine Garden Society); p131; p137 (design by Natural and Oriental Water Gardens); p141; p144m, bl; p145m; p145tr; p145br; p149b; p150; p151t; p152; p153; p154; p155; p157b; p158t; p159b; p161t; p163t; p165b (design by Jean Bishop); p171t; p172; p173; p176t; p180b; p181b; p182; p183; p184l; p185b; p186l, bl; p200t, c, b; p201; p203; p206; p209; p210t b; p211t, b; p212t,b; p213b; p219t; p223tl. tr; p228t, br, bl; p229; p231; p232; p231b; p234; p235t, b; p236t, b; p237t,c, b; p238t, b; p239; p240; p241; p242t, b; p243; p247t; p249 (design by Christopher Costin); p249; p253tr, c, b; p256; p259, p258 p259; p260; p289.
David Parmiter: p442; p443; p448; p449; p473t, bl.
Spike Powell: p287; p293; p304; p305; p320; p358; p359tl, tr, p362; p363; p372r; p373t; p378b; p437t.
Derek St Romaine: p253l; p255t.
Adrian Taylor: p323tl, tr.
Juliet Wade: p474r.
Peter Williams: p302; p303; p374; p375; p436br; p437t; p460; p461; p504tr.
Polly Wreford :p357; p361tr; p373b; p399t, b, p402l, r, p485; p486; p487; p488; p489; p492t,c,b; p493br; p499b.

The publishers would like to thank the following artists for contributing the projects featured in this book: Helen Baird, Stephanie Donaldson, Mijke Gesthuizen, Andrew Gillmore, Karin Hossack, Gilly Love, Mary Maguire, Cleo Mussi, Andrew Newton-Cox, Jenny Norton, Liz Wagstaff, Wendy Wilbraham and Peter Williams.